P9-DNE-587

Praise for
*Strategic Project Management
Made Simple*

"Terry's books guide your thinking about any reasonably complex goal you're trying to achieve. I've seen very few things in this space that make sense past the paper they're written on. This is a remarkable exception."
—David Allen, author, *Getting Things Done*

"We used this method to organize and execute an awards campaign that earned numerous nominations and awards, including an Oscar®."
—Don Levy, Senior Vice President, Sony Pictures Digital

"Terry has created a powerful and actionable methodology for change. Our team at eBay got immersed in it, loved it, and have taken it to heart. I'm definitely adding this valuable tool to my management tool belt!"
— Arnold Goldberg, Senior Director,
Systems Engineering, eBay

"The benefits of planning with your approach are crystal clear."
—Adam Gilmore, Space Station Mechanisms Lead, NASA

"Your system is simple and practical for use in work and in life. I use this with my work team to improve productivity, and to plan my career and family future."
—Wanchai Sri-Isaraporn, General Manager,
Toyota Motor Thailand Co., Ltd.

"Pound for pound, Terry is the world's best strategic project consultant."
— Joseph Sunio, Project Manager, Boeing

"Terry is a master at the Systems Thinking Approach® to Strategic Management and only a master can do what he has done here. I highly recommend this book to all leaders and project teams as an essential part of your working knowledge."
—Stephen Haines, Founder,
Haines Center for Strategic Management

"Terry is one of the best project practitioners I know. His methods are fresh, powerful, and effective. You are wise to read this book if you want to avoid the pitfalls that doom many critical projects."
— George Morrisey, Author, *Morrisey on Planning* series

"Learn from a master as Terry offers practical hands-on tools for tackling the tough issues that keep good leaders awake at night. Terry takes you from the surreal to the real world of strategic thinking and planning."
— James Whalen, Vice President, DirecTV, Inc.

"Most projects get off track because the rails have been improperly laid. Terry's insightful book provides practical ways to ensure that your rails are properly aligned."
—Gordon Peters, Founding Chairman, CEO,
Institute for Management Studies

"Your framework is very effective for linking corporate goals to business unit targets and individual outcomes."
—Patchara Thanattrai, Vice President, Human Resources,
The Stock Exchange of Thailand

"Terry provides a clear and compelling methodology for creating enterprise-wide strategies that integrate all of our sub-departments. This is a must read book for any leader who wants to revitalize their organization."
—Dale Hough, Chief of Reengineering,
Los Angeles County Assessor's Office

"As an engineer, I'm reluctant to get all weepy about management processes, but your model is a logical and demonstrably effective tool for organizing and executing complex strategies."
—David Sanders, Engineer, TRW

"Hits the nail on the head with fresh approaches to design and implement projects that achieve their goals."
—Philippe Goetschel, Director (Retired),
Microsoft Corporation

"Anyone charged with project responsibility will benefit from reading this book. These easy-to-follow steps to turn strategy into action will really make a positive difference."
—Jeffrey M. Chase, PhD, Chairman,
National Traffic Safety Institute

"Lots of management tools sound good in theory, but are hard to apply. Terry provides a practical planning breakthrough that has helped our team to start faster, think smarter and get more done."
—Lynn Ballard, IT Security Manager,
Beckman Coulter

"This book provides concise, simple, and highly effective tools to turn problems into action plans. No project is too complex when broken down using Terry's four strategic questions and the Logical Framework tool."
—Anne Wu, Lean Six Sigma Black Belt, 3M Unitek

"You changed how I do my planning and this has significantly increased my ability to reach my goals."
—Laurie Triplett, Environmental Physicist,
Los Alamos National Laboratory

"*Strategic Project Management Made Simple* demystifies the art of converting a fuzzy problem into an action plan. Definitely 'simple' without being 'simplistic.'"
—Noel Ellis, Chief Process Engineer, Raytheon

"We use your breakthrough methods to nail down our business strategies and to avoid the preventable pitfalls of execution."
—Wolfgang Royer, General Manager Customer Service Central Europe, Middle East & Africa, Sony Ericsson Mobile Communications AB

"These are effective management tools that can translate strategic plans into projects that deliver."
—Elaine Khoo, Manager, Design Singapore Council

"These tools will not only benefit you, but will benefit your whole team."
—Kumar Talinki, Senior Software Engineer,
Symantec Corporation

"Makes it much easier to visualize complex and large projects. This helps you to effectively communicate and present your ideas to the whole team."
—Keith Bonnici, Program Manager, Tekes, Finnish Funding Agency for Technology & Innovation

"I put your creative and flexible system to work and got results right away. Thanks for the insights."
—Gary G. Lo, Regional Finance & Information Management Director, Johnson & Johnson Vision Care, Asia Pacific Division

"If a road map's worth is measured not solely by your arrival, but also the confidence by which you travel, then this is a priceless map to organizational success. Using this has unleashed motivation and generated company-wide optimism that surpassed our expectations. This is one road map you should not travel without."
—David Skinner, President, Holiday Group

"Terry brings his dynamic presentation style to an innovative project planning book that makes a traditionally boring but critical subject come alive."
—Donald S. Remer, PhD, PE, Oliver C. Field Professor of Engineering, Harvey Mudd College

"Logical, systematic, and quick tools for making better decisions in business and life."
—Dr. Boonmark Sirinaovakul, Associate Professor, Assistant President, Rangsit University, Thailand

"This approach gave our planners, managers and analysts the tools and insight to successfully redirect a major process reengineering effort taking place in a rapidly changing IT landscape."
—Michael J. Greenhalgh, Supervisor, Sacramento Municipal Utility District

"Strategic management can be a very dry subject. However, true masters can turn this dry topic into a most enlightening and highly usable management tool. Terry is one such rare master. You would be wise to read his book and even wiser to attend his course."
—Regent B.H. Khor, Senior Marketing Officer, JTC Corporation, Government of Singapore

"Your Strategic Project Management tools are powerful resources all responsible managers should have in their arsenal."
—David Lam, IT Director, Stephen S. Wise School

STRATEGIC PROJECT MANAGEMENT MADE SIMPLE

PRACTICAL TOOLS FOR LEADERS AND TEAMS

TERRY SCHMIDT

WILEY

John Wiley & Sons, Inc.

Copyright © 2009 by Terry Schmidt. All rights reserved.

Published by John Wiley & Sons, Inc., Hoboken, New Jersey.
Published simultaneously in Canada.

No part of this publication may be reproduced, stored in a retrieval system, or transmitted
in any form or by any means, electronic, mechanical, photocopying, recording, scanning, or
otherwise, except as permitted under Section 107 or 108 of the 1976 United States Copyright
Act, without either the prior written permission of the Publisher, or authorization through
payment of the appropriate per-copy fee to the Copyright Clearance Center, Inc., 222
Rosewood Drive, Danvers, MA 01923, (978) 750-8400, fax (978) 646-8600, or on the web
at www.copyright.com. Requests to the Publisher for permission should be addressed to the
Permissions Department, John Wiley & Sons, Inc., 111 River Street, Hoboken, NJ 07030,
(201) 748-6011, fax (201) 748-6008, or online at http://www.wiley.com/go/permissions.

Limit of Liability/Disclaimer of Warranty: While the publisher and author have used their
best efforts in preparing this book, they make no representations or warranties with respect to
the accuracy or completeness of the contents of this book and specifically disclaim any implied
warranties of merchantability or fitness for a particular purpose. No warranty may be created
or extended by sales representatives or written sales materials. The advice and strategies
contained herein may not be suitable for your situation. You should consult with a professional
where appropriate. Neither the publisher nor author shall be liable for any loss of profit or
any other commercial damages, including but not limited to special, incidental, consequential,
or other damages.

For general information on our other products and services or for technical support, please
contact our Customer Care Department within the United States at (800) 762-2974, outside
the United States at (317) 572-3993 or fax (317) 572-4002.

Wiley also publishes its books in a variety of electronic formats. Some content that appears in
print may not be available in electronic books. For more information about Wiley products,
visit our web site at www.wiley.com.

Library of Congress Cataloging-in-Publication Data:

Schmidt, Terry.
    Strategic project management made simple : practical tools for leaders and teams /
Terry Schmidt.
      p. cm.
    Includes index.
    ISBN 978-0-470-41158-2 (cloth); ISBN 978-0-470-44292-0 (ebk);
    ISBN 978-0-470-44293-7 (ebk); ISBN 978-0-470-44319-4 (ebk)
      1. Project management. 2. Strategic planning. I. Title.
HD69.P75S363 2009
658.4'012—dc22

                                            2008036135

Printed in the United States of America

10 9 8 7

To Mom, who taught me to think;
to Dad, who inspired me to take action;
and to my Sweetheart as well.

Contents

PART THREE:
Putting The Concepts Into Action

Acknowledgments

Many people along my career journey have helped to make this book possible. Thank you to Leon Rosenberg, Molly Hageboeck, and Larry Posner, the leadership team at Practical Concepts Incorporated (PCI), an international development consulting firm where these concepts originally blossomed. Long conversations with PCI colleagues Merlyn Kettering, Marcus Ingle, Larry Cooley, and Moses Thompson deepened my understanding of strategic concepts.

When UCLA Extension invited me to teach in their esteemed Technical Management Program two decades ago, I adapted these concepts to business and technology environments. UCLA's Dr. Bill Goodin, Dr. Frank Burris, and Joon Lee have provided ongoing support.

Harvard Business School Professor Joe Bower's strategy courses added immensely to my knowledge base, as did the later work of classmate Michael Porter. Janice Laureen, Stan Rosen, and colleagues from the Association for Strategic Planning also enriched my insights.

The Institute for Management Studies (IMS) has been extremely supportive. Thanks to Gordon, Jon, and Lisa Peters, Steve Daniel, and Cecile Morgan for providing my books to all their corporate members. Thanks also to all the chairpersons of the European and North American IMS regions who hosted my seminars.

John Assaraf, Alan Weiss, Bill Gower, and Dr. Keith Russell provided encouraging words just when I needed them most. Dr. Hendrie Weisinger inspired new ideas in his unique way.

Steve Haines and colleagues at the Haines Centre for Strategic Management have provided a stimulating forum for linking these tools to business excellence. Thanks to colleagues Stephen Lin, Jim McKinley, Valerie MacLeod, Gail Aller-Stead, Alan Bandt, Chander Mohan, Frank and Alison Foster, Geri and Eric Dennison, Barbara Collins, Nigel Wyse, Henry Kwok, Gary Nelson, and others.

My editorial team provided bench strength when I needed it. Kerry Dean Hooper helped breathe life into dull paragraphs. Shari Fowler used her magic to create smoother flow in the early edition. Leanna Blackmon went the extra mile and pulled all-nighters to meet the final deadline. Mike Kent made the graphics sparkle.

This manuscript would still be piles of meandering mush without Somrutai Binhason ("Maiky") and Benjawan Binsumsee ("Wa") who deciphered my scribbles and typed an endless stream of messy revisions without complaint. I couldn't have done it without them and the rest of my team, especially Missy Adams, Sastrawut Panaree, and Sinee Angel.

A crackerjack review team put great energy into critiquing early drafts. Thank you Pugdee Manaves, David Giramma, Pamm St. John, Rob Farrington, Deanna Deeds, Brian Cracchiola, Walter Grassl, Jamie Truong, Naomi Becker, Benjamin Grover, Robert Martinez, Eugene Garrilov, Gerald Turner, and Dean Sanderpoint.

My outstanding literary agent Jeff Herman found the ideal publisher for this project. It was a privilege working with the enthusiastic team of John Wiley & Sons pros—Shannon Vargo, Deborah Schindlar, and Christine Kim. Marketing expert John Kremer coached me on how to make this book a winner.

The thousands of men and women who attended my seminars over the years challenged me to make my concepts simpler and easier to apply in their business and daily lives.

My deepest appreciation goes to the many clients I have been privileged to serve. By rolling up our sleeves and solving real problems together, we proved that these concepts make a difference where it really matters. You provided the classroom for lifelong learning and the projects we tackled were fabulous teachers.

And to all the others who I can't recall at the moment but should also mention—my thanks.

Writing a book can be a long and lonely process. My three superdogs—Bingo the pound-hound, Mushka the shy ShitZu, and Chico the lion-hearted Maltese—snuggled under my desk to keep me company during many nights of writing, rewriting, polishing, and (finally) finishing.

This book was a labor of love that would not have been completed without the incredible encouragement and support of my entire team. Thanks to you all!

Introduction

My mother deserves the credit for inspiring my career path with her early words of wisdom, which encouraged me to think often. I can still remember the important lessons she gave me as a kid, which came during frequent scoldings—usually well deserved. She'd wave her index finger and sternly say, "If you think you can get away with that, mister, you've got another think coming!" Decades later, I'm grateful for all those extra thinks, because they taught me to become a strategic thinker.

Many different experiences during my 35-year career have contributed to my passion for strategic thinking, project management, and organizational excellence. These started in high school and continued beyond getting my MBA from Harvard, after which I worked in a program planning role in the Office of the Secretary of Transportation in Washington, D.C. I then switched careers to become an international development consultant, where I learned and taught a planning approach based on systems thinking that came to be a foundation for my life's work.

After starting my own consulting company, my client base shifted to corporations, government agencies, and research institutions. These clients were very different from my previous clients in developing countries, but they faced similar issues—organizing across boundaries, sorting out complexity, and managing change. Surprisingly, I found that the same strategic management tools that worked well in developing countries were also suited for handling the complex tangle of issues my new clients faced.

I've had the privilege of helping clients in corporate and governmental settings to get started on ambitious projects, which ranged from setting up education systems in Bangladesh to helping American scientists design surveillance systems for detecting nuclear tests by rogue nations. They've included programs to strengthen security in financial institutions, grow new enterprises to the next level, consolidate IT systems after mergers, improve the ways correctional institutions handle prisoners, and streamline service delivery in governmental agencies.

These projects have taken place in high- and low-tech environments, in Fortune 500 companies, small firms, state and federal government agencies, research laboratories, and academic institutions in 34 different countries. Along the way, I've learned some valuable ways to approach any project—small or large, simple or complex—and make it succeed.

This book completes a decade-long writing effort and contributes to my life mission: To share the very best strategic management practices with motivated men and women who aspire to make a positive difference in all dimensions of their work and their lives.

Why I Wrote This Book

The reasons why I wrote this book come from my experience as a strategic management consultant who approaches projects from a different angle than most. I believe these same reasons are why you should read this book.

The world has dramatically changed over the past 30 years and continues to do so. Today, everything happens at a lightning-fast pace. Every activity is more demanding and competitive than it's ever been. Today we all face challenges more complex those that confronted us in decades past. As the pace picks up, we are asked to do more, and we must do it well.

Far too many educated, experienced, and talented people fail to accomplish what they want for lack of the right tools to think, plan, and act effectively. Their approach to problems may be incomplete or scattered, their action plans lack the potency required to get the results they are truly capable of accomplishing. The frustrating gap that remains affects both their personal and organizational success.

The system you will be reading about in this book offers truly useful strategic thinking, planning, and action tools tuned to the tempo of the times. They will give you the edge you need to achieve the results you want in today's new world.

This book offers practical solution approaches for leaders and teams of all types facing issues of all types and sizes. Leaders— including CEOs, senior executives, program managers, and others involved in strategy and projects—will find fresh insights for communicating strategic intent to those who execute such critical activities.

Project teams and managers—as well as wild-eyed visionaries, dreamers, and entrepreneurs—can use this step-by-step, flexible approach to plan and execute change initiatives more rapidly and effectively than by using any other method.

This book can benefit anyone with Goals, whether they are personal or professional. And it doesn't require that you have an engineering-type mind.

Like it or not, being well-educated, competent, and hard working is not enough to lead to professional success, career advancement, and personal satisfaction in today's world. Expertise in your own professional area is *necessary*, but not *sufficient*. Being good at what you do is a must, but by itself, it's not enough.

By mastering the new discipline of Strategic Project Management, you will maximize your ability to execute the new ideas your organization needs, as well as advance your own career, whether you are already a certified project pro, a beginner, or somewhere in between.

Getting the Most from This Book

Strategic Project Management Made Simple offers a vital thinking process that is usually missing in project management and strategic planning. These proven concepts will help you consider what you need to think about before you turn to traditional project management tools. Applying these ideas will increase your team's ability to:

- Convert any problem, idea, or opportunity into clear Objectives and action plans that can be smoothly implemented.
- Sharpen the logic of your strategy so that it's aligned both within the project and with the larger organizational Strategies, Goals, and Vision.

- Communicate strategy concisely to build shared understanding, support, and accountability among champions, stakeholders, and project teams.
- Uncover and deal in advance with the probable pitfalls that can derail your efforts.
- Organize cross-functional and other task forces into committed and effective teams that are clear about who needs to do what, when, and how.
- Improve working relationships, reduce conflict, and encounter fewer persons who are obstacles on the path to success.
- Increase performance, productivity, and profits—saving time, money, and frustration.

The bottom line is that the techniques and tools you'll learn in *Strategic Project Management Made Simple* will equip you to do the upfront critical thinking that will give you and your team the end results you need—you can plan on it!

Three Logical Parts

Part One of this book explores the principles that make Strategic Project Management so effective. Chapter 1 describes what makes this approach unique and points out mistakes to avoid. Chapter 2 introduces the Four Critical Strategic Questions, If-Then thinking, and the art of formulating hypotheses. Chapter 3 unveils what may be the World's Best-Kept Management Secret: The Logical Framework. Chapter 4 describes how any business unit, intact team, program or project team can leverage these ideas to improve their effectiveness.

Building on that foundation, the four chapters of Part Two offer step-by-step instructions on how to design executable projects by answering the Four Critical Strategic Questions. Chapter 5 covers the fine points of defining and aligning Objectives, and Chapter 6 tackles Measurement issues. Chapter 7 demonstrates how to reduce problems in advance by managing Assumptions; and Chapter 8 covers the nitty-gritty of work planning. At the end of each of these four chapters, you'll find application steps that will help you build a strategic project plan.

Part Three pulls it all together in three chapters. Chapter 9 explores the human dynamics of projects. Chapter 10 discusses the art of action-learning and execution. Chapter 11 describes a dozen ways to implement these ideas and provides tips for getting started.

Each chapter includes client and project examples, along with a Key Points Review at the end of each. The Appendix contains a wealth of resource information, including checklists, a glossary of terms and usages, a variety of client best-practice examples, references to published articles, and other helpful resources to deepen your knowledge.

Along the way, you'll also learn how some of my clients have put these tools into action. While all the examples and case studies are real, some have been edited for confidentiality, abbreviated to fit the space, or modified to highlight key learning points. For readers who want more in-depth knowledge, you'll find downloadable versions of the abbreviated case studies and other examples at *www.ManagementPro.com*.

You can also subscribe to my complimentary report, *Take It From Terry*™, which includes diverse strategic management articles and case studies on a whole range of topics, both professional and personal.

At the risk of annoying English purists worldwide, certain words in this book are always capitalized, even in mid-sentence. These are strategic management terms that have been given precise definitions in the book and are therefore capitalized to emphasize their explicit use.

The best way to master the materials in this book is to read it at least twice. The first time, simply aim to understand how the concepts fit together. On your second time through, follow the tips at the end of each chapter and apply them to your own issues. These ideas are meaty, so I encourage you to underline key sentences and scribble in the margins to make this book your own.

While the tools presented here are powerful, there is a catch: You may have to reinvent how you think. You'll have to expand your mental models so that you see your environment in new and different ways; and you must be willing to embrace the mindset of both a strategic planner and a project manager. Ideally, reading this book will be a stimulating way to enjoy and learn because we all have "another think coming"!

Strategic Project Management Made Simple empowers you to think bigger, plan smarter, move faster, and accomplish ambitious Objectives more consistently. People who can do so are a rare breed—and you are about to become one!

Part One

Are You Strategic?

The question "Are you strategic?" is simple. And so is being strategic—if you have the right concepts and tools and know how to use them. The terms *strategic* and *strategy* have multiple meanings. What I mean by being strategic is to consistently think, plan, act, and assess in a way that best achieves your desired results.

These first four chapters examine the power of Strategic Project Management, which is a blend of tools, concepts and techniques that combine to give you the edge.

- *Chapter 1* explores what Strategic Project Management is and how it will benefit you.
- *Chapter 2* introduces the Four Critical Strategic Questions for building the backbone of great projects. You will learn how to creatively use If-Then logic to develop sound plans.
- *Chapter 3* invites you to join my workshop and explore a practical systems thinking tool for developing project plans that are powerfully linked to the big picture.
- *Chapter 4* explains how to align your project Objectives with strategic Goals. You'll also learn how to do quick and clean strategic planning that brings value at any level.

These concepts can be applied in both personal and professional arenas. By the time you reach the end of this book, you'll understand how to be much more effective in all aspects of your work and life.

1

Thinking Outside
the Bar Chart

Knowing is not enough, we must apply.
Willing is not enough, we must do.

—Johann Wolfgang von Goethe

My introduction to formal project management came in college when I built what must be the world's biggest bar (Gantt) chart. This back-bending project deserves a footnote in project management history, if not a mention in *The Guinness Book of World Records*.

As an aerospace engineering sophomore at the University of Washington in Seattle, I took a part-time job that Boeing advertised as a "hands-on project management role" setting up the tracking system for the very first Boeing 747. This was during an era when project scheduling software was still in its infancy. Sounded exciting!

The true meaning of "hands-on" became clear on my first day when they handed me a big box of quarter-inch thick black tape and instructed me to install parallel grid lines on a mile-long white Formica wall in a tunnel under Boeing's manufacturing facility in Everett, Washington. I'm not exaggerating when I say it was a mile long.

The Everett Boeing plant is one of the world's largest buildings—you could fit all of Disneyland inside the building.

The top parallel line had to be seven feet high, so I stood on tiptoes to reach high and spread my roll of tape out horizontally across a mile. Then, I'd drop down eight inches and tape another mile-long strip. The bottom few rows required that I crawl, and for the very bottom row I sat on my rump and scooted along the cold concrete floor. So far, I didn't exactly love project management work.

Much to the relief of my aching back, it was finally time to paste in the vertical grid lines, spaced a foot apart—one for each day counting down to aircraft roll-out. When I finished, the Boeing engineers began to populate the cells of my jumbo-sized grid with blocks of text, identifying tasks on the critical path that would integrate all of the things that had to be done to get this ground-breaking aircraft launched into the air.

I would arrive at work each afternoon after calculus class and head downstairs for my project management mission deep in the tunnel.

Being in that tunnel, my perspective was severely limited, until one day a production engineer walked me around the plant for a close-up look at the maiden Boeing 747. I reached out my hand to touch this wondrous piece of technology that was slowly coming together on the assembly line. The concentric ribbing of the partially finished fuselage looked like the skeleton of a giant dinosaur.

The engineer spoke with pride about how the 747 would revolutionize air travel and fulfill Boeing's strategic vision of being the world leader in commercial aircraft.

When I understood the lofty vision, it was as if a light bulb switched on in my head. I was inspired. What I learned that day after emerging from the tunnel was that the real action was "thinking outside the bar chart" and out of the metaphorical tunnels, which is where projects start and where smart thinking can most leverage your results.

Project management has certainly benefited from technological advancements. These days software seamlessly handles the tedious task-management chores I used to do the old-fashioned way, by hand. Yet I am a big critic of project management as it is conventionally interpreted and practiced. Traditional project management focuses on task-level details and loses sight of the benefits projects aim to deliver. Thus I teach and practice my own more strategic version because the conventional approaches perpetuate tunnel vision at a time when we need to see the big picture.

So, regardless of the scope of your project or the size of your dreams, this book is designed to give you hands-on as well as minds-on tools to stay focused on the vision while creating executable plans that work.

Tackling the Big Hairy Issues

My clients are my best teachers. I've been fortunate to consult with interesting men and women all around the world facing every kind of issue you can imagine. All of them have been accomplished professionals doing important and challenging work.

I'd like you to meet some of my favorites. Their situations may appear very different, but from a broader perspective, there are some common overarching themes. Can you spot them?

- A satellite television provider needs more sophisticated ways to combat identity theft and fraud.
- An innovative, family-owned company that manufactures sophisticated, portable optical-electric equipment must ramp up to handle explosive growth.
- A pioneering web-based timeshare resale company chooses to reinvent itself to handle fierce new competition.
- A county assessor's office needs to upgrade legacy computer systems and prepare for top leadership transition.
- A nuclear scientist must organize technical experts from several national research laboratories to recover and dispose of radioactive materials that could be diverted to make dirty bombs.
- The director of a social service agency caring for mentally and physically handicapped residents must solve the root cause of mysterious injuries to the residents.
- A Middle Eastern sheik needs to win the peace after winning the war against foreign-financed insurgents.

What's common? Each organization faced a unique situation involving multiple players and tricky issues. Success required managing difficult political and organizational variables in addition to technical and cost factors. In most cases, the optimum path to the Goal was not apparent from the start; so a solution had to be thoughtfully created and skillfully implemented.

Their projects involved one or more of these dynamics:

- **Hard to measure.** Can't easily kick the tires to track progress.
- **High stakes.** Important to the organization.
- **Complex.** Can't always see a clear solution path at the start; must learn by doing.
- **Consequential.** Success brings benefits; failure brings pain.
- **Ad hoc team.** May require new players coming together as a team.
- **Time pressure.** You need to move fast.
- **Multiple stakeholders.** Involves and impacts many parties.
- **Risky.** You can't control all the variables that the solution requires.
- **Visible.** People who count are watching and keeping score.

To be successful, all needed a Strategic Project Management approach, not the tactical task/schedule focus that dominates traditional project management. They needed an approach like that of this book in order to deliver the results they sought; and they succeeded by following the sound methodology you are reading about now.

Sound Familiar?

My presumption is that your work includes one or more of the dynamics listed above. How many of them sound familiar? If your own endeavors involve planning or executing important projects of one type or another, and if any of the dynamics listed above rings true for you, this book will benefit you immensely.

Based on hundreds of successful consulting projects conducted around the world, I've sharpened a planning process that addresses the tough issues, opportunities, and problems on your plate. The process you are about to discover will give you the insights you've always needed and sensed were missing from other approaches you've tried.

Along the way, I'll make things as simple as possible without becoming simplistic. As Oliver Wendell Holmes Jr., the great American jurist and scholar, once wrote, "I would not give a fig for the simplicity on this side of complexity, but I would give my life for the simplicity on the far side of complexity."

The methodology is not complicated or abstract, though applying it takes some effort. But once you get the hang of it, the bright ideas in *Strategic Project Management Made Simple* will illuminate your dark project tunnels so you and your team can move confidently along clear paths to reach valued Goals.

Mastering Strategic Project Management

Today, we all deal with projects in one way or another, whether as sponsors, team members, project managers, or stakeholders. Your job title may not include *Project Manager*, but nevertheless managing projects is a given in any form of professional work.

Like it or not, being educated, competent, and hard working is not enough to ensure professional success, career advancement, and personal satisfaction in today's world. Expertise in your own professional area is *necessary*, but not *sufficient*.

Today, every knowledge worker must be multi-skilled and quick to adapt new technologies as they emerge. Mastery of your own specialty is no longer enough because the most critical work requires collaboration across different technical disciplines, organizational elements, and stakeholder interests. Project management skills are valuable, but to triumph in today's competitive arena, you must also be *strategic*, with a skill set and mind-set to handle the challenges of an increasingly complex world.

By project management skills, I don't mean just knowing how to build better bar charts and the like. While important, these project management tools aren't enough unless they are front-loaded with some sort of strategic thinking process to help you design and develop the *right* projects.

Taking Off the Blinders

There's a centuries-old story about six blind men from Hindustan who were tasked with determining what an elephant looked like by feeling different parts of the elephant's body. This is an apt metaphor for the challenges that organizations face in linking projects with strategic intent.

The tasks were divided up and each blind man was assigned a different part of the elephant's body to explore. Each did his job and reported back to the project manager.

The blind man who felt the giant animal's legs said, "The elephant is like a pillar." The one who felt the creature's tail observed, "The elephant is like a rope." The blind man assigned to feel the trunk concluded, "The elephant is like a tree branch." The man told to explore the elephant's giant ear determined, "The elephant is like a great hand fan." The one who felt the elephant's belly inferred, "The elephant is like a great ceiling wall." And finally, the blind man who felt the beast's tusks reported, "The elephant is like a hard, solid pipe."

These ancient project team members were all well-meaning and did their jobs according to their instructions, but none was able to comprehend the whole elephant because it was bigger than the scope of just one person's perspective.

Well-meaning organizations today often do the same thing on large projects–they think in terms of separate parts, not cohesive wholes. Each person perceives just one part and no one understands the logical whole. It's a wonder that any project succeeds!

But it's not usually the fault of project managers and team members. The seeds of confusion and ambiguity may get planted during the organization's strategic planning process, or take root during a clumsy hand-off of the strategic intent from those who envisioned the project to those who carry it out. Other blinders come from using wrong tools and/or working from a piecemeal rather than a Systems Thinking Approach®. Obviously, with blinders on, it's easy to get blindsided.

Your own organization, project, or elephant is more than just a collection of parts. Each part is an element of a larger system whose individual parts must work together smoothly to accomplish a higher Goal. Understanding and achieving that higher Goal requires tools that remove the blinders from our minds' eye. Such tools provide robust enough insight for team members to comprehend the nature of the beasts they are trying to manage and how their piece fits within the large context.

Start Smart

According to *Fortune* magazine, nearly 70 percent of all strategies fail. That's a startling statistic, but even more surprising is that most of these strategic plans were basically sound. The problem was that they couldn't be executed.

I've devoted my career to teaching individuals and organizations how to become part of the 30 percent who succeed more consistently. The most valuable planning lesson I preach is elegantly summed up by NASA's Rule #15.*

A review of most failed project problems indicates that the disasters were well-planned to happen from the start. The seeds of problems are laid down early. Initial planning is the most vital part of a project.

—NASA Rule #15

This simple lesson is also the most obvious—especially in hindsight, when projects go awry.

NASA Rule #15 has been put into economic terms by Dr. Donald S. Remer, President of the Claremont Consulting Group and the Oliver C. Field Professor of Engineering Economics at Harvey Mudd College. Dr. Remer has examined and/or worked with hundreds of projects across a broad spectrum of industries and government organizations for more than 30 years. His research confirms the need to get it right early because the cost of correcting errors later increases dramatically.

Remer's Rule of 10 states that it costs approximately 10 times more to fix the problem at each later stage of the project. For example, if it costs $10,000 to fix a problem during the planning stage, it will cost $100,000 to fix it at the design stage, and $1,000,000 to fix it during the construction stage. Several published studies have confirmed that Remer's Rule applies to all kinds of projects.

For example, a NASA study of software development projects concerning the relative cost of repair showed that it costs 10 times more to fix a defect during the coding phase than during the design phase and 100 times more to fix a defect during the testing phase than during the design phase.

The lesson is clear: Invest sufficient planning time and effort early because the cost savings are huge. But this tends to go against the cultural grain of most professionals in the United States because

---

*Taken from a list of One Hundred Rules for NASA Project Managers, first compiled by Jerry Madden, Associate Director of the Flight Projects Directorate at NASA's Goddard Space Flight Center.

we like to jump in and get started on the fun stuff and get moving. By contrast, the Japanese spend much more time planning, and routinely beat the U.S. automobile companies to a finished product by more than a year.

Isn't it ironic that those people who claim they don't have enough time to plan always have enough the time to start over when their shoddy initial planning drives their project over a cliff?

This approach equips you to do the initial planning right, with the right tools, at the right time. These tools work if you put them to work.

Lessons Learned Along the Way

The insights in this book reflect lessons learned during a career and life path that blended multiple experiences and exposed me to very different ways of thinking.

My passion for projects and technology all began in ninth grade, when I built a small rocket and "launched guppies into inner space," as *Rocket News* later described it. The national press buzz that followed my sending a pregnant guppy and her slim companion a thousand feet in the air inspired me to become a rocket scientist. It's amazing how one pivotal experience can launch an entire career.

In high school, I was too small to play football and too shy to date girls. So I played chess. Chess is a marvelous way to learn business strategy because it encourages "down-board thinking" and mental flexibility. Chess forces you to carefully examine the future implications of current moves and to explore "what if" scenarios before each decision—vital in project work. Chess has one clear Objective—capture the King. One must also pay attention to the shifting competitive environment of the game board, and make informed Assumptions about what is likely to unfold.

Between summers while studying aerospace engineering at the University of Washington, an internship with NASA's Marshall Space Flight Center's found me devouring all the program management books in their library. The highlight of my summer was a two-hour, one-on-one meeting with my hero, Dr. Wernher von Braun, the visionary rocket scientist who led the U.S. lunar landing program. Dr. von Braun seemed both intrigued and amused by my rocket-fish experiments.

After getting an MBA at Harvard, I accepted a program management position in the Office of the Secretary of Transportation in Washington D.C., where we coordinated program planning for federal transportation agencies.

Then I radically switched careers to become an international development consultant. At a Washington D.C. management consulting company, I learned a process tool for managing complex projects that was originally created to help the U.S. Foreign Aid program be accountable to Congress. For several years I taught strategic management and coached project teams in countries such as Bangladesh, Belize, Thailand, Trinidad, Indonesia, Ivory Coast, Senegal, and the Sultanate of Oman.

More recently, I've introduced these strategic management concepts to the private sector through consulting and executive education programs. These concepts are attracting raving fans because of the impressive results they produce when applied. Readers of this book who take these ideas for a spin will get where they want to go faster and enjoy the ride.

Why I Am a Critic

While I'm a project management expert who teaches the subject all around the world, I'm also a big critic of most traditional project management tools and approaches. In my opinion, the official set of project management competencies—known as PMBOK (*Project Management Book of Knowledge*)—doesn't include the right mix of skills today's knowledge workers require, and mostly addresses projects after they are underway.

It's a fact that most people involved with projects are not engineers and don't need to learn hundreds of pages of equations and analytic tools. Only the small percent of "hard-core" project managers need this in-depth technical knowledge. But we can all use the common sense concepts in this book (which includes only one equation and very little discussion of—you guessed it—bar charts).

I am also critical of strategic planning because, as typically practiced, it's a ritualistic exercise and a huge waste of time. With some notable exceptions, most strategic plans aren't worth the paper they are printed on. I recently served on the Association for Strategic Planning's national task force to establish certification standards for the profession. I have observed that the majority of strategic plans are vague, full of jargon, and lack the right "hooks" to be actionable. No wonder they are viewed so cynically by employees and suffer from the dreaded SPOTS syndrome—meaning "Strategic Plan on Top Shelf," where plans usually gather dust. And, no wonder the strategic success rate is only 30 percent.

Both of these disciplines are vital; and when done well, distinguish exceptional individuals as well as organizations. But they are usually separate practices and processes. This book aims to combine the best ideas from Strategic Planning and Project Management into *Strategic Project Management* in a very simple and flexible way.

Why Read This Book?

If you are new to project management, or are an "accidental project manager" who is suddenly assigned project responsibility without having formal training, the concepts and tools in this book will give you a solid organizing framework. If you are a seasoned pro, or PMI certified Project Management Professional (PMP), this book offers you the missing conceptual nuggets that distinguish visionary project managers from the rest of the crowd. Team leaders will discover a fresh way to pull together cross-functional teams. Individual contributors will learn how to be more effective on their piece of the project pie.

Executives, project sponsors and champions will find a methodology to concisely communicate their strategic intent to those responsible for delivery. Whatever role you play, using this state-of-the-art approach will multiply what you can accomplish by changing how you think, plan, and act.

Seeing Projects in a New Light

While projects have been around since the Pharaohs built the pyramids, today's projects deserve a fresh definition. The common definition of a project—an organized set of activities to achieve specific Objectives, on time and within budget—remains valid, but projects are much more than this definition implies. Missing from this definition is the need to impact the problem and fulfill strategic intent. A modern definition is that *projects are engines of change,* flexible organizing frameworks for executing strategic initiatives, vehicles of collaboration that unite people and resources in order to reach important organizational goals.

The famous Kevin Costner line from the movie *Field of Dreams* says, "If we build it, they will come." Good project managers can get it built on time and within budget, but that doesn't guarantee "they will come" or ensure reaching the even higher Objective that motivates the project. (We'll return to this example in Chapter 2.)

The projects we face are not easy to pull off. These are not our parents' projects with clear goals and simple structures in stable environments. Many require managing the intangibles of information, behaviors, and processes. Very few projects today follow a straight path, with direct solutions that are obvious from the beginning. Most travel curved paths, demanding frequent mid-course correction. Typically, we must draw our own maps while advancing toward the destination in an ongoing cycle of learning and discovery. You'll get optimum results from a thinking-planning-action-review process that regards plans as living documents that easily adjust based on progress, prospects, and problems.

The most potent opportunities seldom show up labeled as "projects," but arrive disguised as problems, issues, or murky messes. Tackling so-called B-HAGS (Big, Hairy, Audacious Goals), as Jim Collins describes them in *Built to Last*, involves juggling a full spectrum of slippery Objectives that can be difficult to define, let alone manage.

In the pages ahead, I'll walk you through a flexible thinking process, and show you how to sort through the fog of fuzzy ideas and develop sound strategies and executable plans. You'll see how these tools scale up and down to handle issues of any size and flex to fit multiple situations you may face. But first, let's review why most project plans are inadequate. See how many of these resonate with your personal experience.

Beware These Six Dangerous Planning Mistakes

I must admit that not all of the projects I've worked on were roaring successes. Some were total disasters. Reflecting back, I've learned this key lesson: *More often than not, the seeds of success or failure are planted during the early planning and team-building stage* (which sounds a lot like NASA Rule #15, doesn't it?).

Virtually every failed project suffered from one or more of the following six dangerous but common planning mistakes. These are not listed in any particular order of priority because, indeed, they often gang up together like a nasty pack of snarling junkyard dogs.

1. Tolerating Vague Objectives

"We don't know where we are going, but at least we're making good time!"

Projects that run this way usually end up going nowhere. In the rush to implement, not enough serious, upfront thinking goes into clarifying Objectives, Measures, and their interconnections. While Objectives may start off vague, there is no excuse for letting them stay fuzzy. Vague Objectives invite finger-pointing, blame, and predictable failure. Several chapters in this book demonstrate innovative ways to define, measure, and organize your Objectives.

2. Ignoring Environmental Context

"What we don't know won't hurt us."

Well, it just might. Projects unfold in unpredictable ways, but people sometimes think myopically and ignore how risk factors outside their project boundaries might affect them. While you can't control the wind, you can adjust your sails.

Chapter 8 shows how to examine environmental influences, and identify Assumptions that must be true for your project to work. You can then test them for probability and impact upfront and take preventive action to increase the odds of success.

3. Using Limiting Tools and Process

"This project management software can handle all our planning needs."

When your only tool is a hammer, the whole world looks like a nail. While I have healthy respect for Microsoft Project™, Primavera™, and enterprise systems, these programs become downright dangerous when used too early because they create a false sense of certainty.

Making a task list or booting up project management software isn't the place to start, even though this is commonly done. Don't get me wrong—you need these tools, but they are best used when it comes time to start breaking down tasks, not during the "fuzzy front end" when you are still firming up Objectives. Before firing up your PC, fire up your brain and flesh out your project strategy using the thinking system detailed in this book.

Chapter 4 offers ways to link project plans with program and strategic Objectives. Chapter 8 will then guide you in when to use software to spell out detailed work plans.

4. Neglecting Stakeholder Interests

"Everyone is aboard and fully supports this."

Projects are real-life dramas played out by multiple actors who bring their own agenda and varying degrees of interest and support. Without the buy-in from stakeholders involved in or affected by the project, projects suffer.

Stephen Haines, a leading systems thinker, said it best: "People support what they help create." Early stakeholder involvement reduces resistance, invites sounder solutions, and paves a smooth path for implementation. Stakeholder involvement doesn't mean you can always please everyone. Chapter 10 offers a stakeholder analysis tool to bring key players into your planning process and suggests multiple options for dealing with them.

5. One Shot Planning

"We're too busy doing to keep planning."

Like home-baked bread that grows moldy with time, project plans have a limited shelf-life. They are only as good as the information available when they were created. Over time, as conditions change, they must be updated to reflect new learning and progress.

Updating goes beyond monitoring costs and fine-tuning schedules. Updating means periodically stepping back and examining how the environment has changed, then revising core strategies as needed. The "Be Cycle-Logical" Principle in Chapter 9 explains how to keep your strategies fresh.

6. **Mismanaging People Dynamics**

"Of course my team will perform—they've been assigned to this project."

Project success requires the committed, coordinated action of many people. While some project managers run rough shod over their team, others tap into human dynamics and make projects a positive growth experience. Find a way, using tips in Chapter 10, to make your project a win for everyone—and you will have a sure-fire team.

Consider Your Own Experience

Think about the disappointing projects you have encountered. Did they suffer some of these same serious mistakes? Looking back with 20-20 hindsight, could better up-front planning and nimble execution have improved the results? Think also about the winners you've ridden to the finish line. What was different? Did your successful projects manage to avoid these common mistakes?

While I can't guarantee you perfect success in the future, I can promise that you will shift the odds in your favor by using the street-smart wisdom in the pages that follow.

The following chart offers a quick preview of the solution concepts covered in the pages ahead, and summarizes how they will address the six dangerous planning mistakes.

Planning Mistakes	Solution Concepts
1. Tolerating Vague Objectives	• Make Objectives clear and measurable • Identify logical levels and If-Then links • Define your strategic hypotheses • Define *why* before *what* and *how*
2. Ignoring Environmental Context	• Scan the environment for circumstances • Understand internal and external context • Identify risk elements • Make, test, manage, and monitor Assumptions

3. Poor Planning Tools and Process
   - Choose common planning model and language
   - Plan top-down, test bottom-up
   - Plan for the plan
   - Use the Logical Framework as a central planning tool

4. Neglecting Stakeholder Interests
   - Remember—people support what they help create
   - Involve people who matter
   - Understand the perspectives of others
   - Build consensus and commitment

5. One-shot Planning
   - Treat project documents as living plans, organic in nature
   - Be "cycle logical"—think, plan, act, and assess.
   - Iterate and update in predetermined learning cycles
   - Constantly refine the strategic hypothesis

6. Mismanaging People Dynamics
   - Build in payoffs (fun, learning, rewards)
   - Grow the team while growing the plan
   - Sharpen the who-when-what-how
   - Manage with emotional intelligence

Key Points Review

1. Fast-moving environments require twenty-first century ways to think, plan, and act. Traditional project management skills are necessary but not sufficient. Strategic Project Management has become a must-have body of knowledge for everyone in these rapidly-changing, complex times.

2. By mastering the principles of Strategic Project Management, you gain a lifelong transferable skill set to tackle just about any issue that crosses your path.

3. Many worthy projects are doomed from the start because of preventable planning mistakes. Avoiding these dangerous planning mistakes puts you on the right path early.

4. The seeds of success or failure get planted early. Smart initial planning and team-building is the key to project success. NASA's Rule #15 isn't just for rocket scientists. It applies to you too.

5. Executive sponsors need better ways to convey strategic intent to project leaders, who also need to lead their teams in understanding the full Objectives motivating the project. Using this process together bridges that communication gap.

6. The ability to turn strategic intent into well-designed, actionable projects is a potent competitive advantage for individuals and organizations alike.

7. Think outside the bar chart. The keys to doing so are in this book.

2

Building Strong
Project Backbones

If one link is broken, the entire chain is broken.

—Yiddish Proverb

As a consultant, my primary job is to empower my clients with powerful concepts and coach them to reach great solutions. All great solutions begin by asking the right questions. My major contribution to the field of Strategic Project Management is these *Four Critical Strategic Questions*, which I developed to make the Logical Framework Approach, (as you'll see in Chapter 3) easier to understand.

These seem like simple questions—that's exactly the point. They are indeed simple, but not simplistic. It took multiple refinements over several years in order to progressively simplify them while preserving their power to integrate multiple points of view. Albert Einstein famously said that if you can't say something simply, you don't understand it. I agree with Al.

The four following carefully crafted questions work wonders in virtually any situation. The first three are usually glossed over in the rush to answer the fourth.

Asking the Four Critical Strategic Questions

The call came from Keith, an Information Technology (IT) manager who had attended one of my strategy workshops at UCLA. He worked in a well-known company that needed to launch a critical initiative, but their task force had made little progress after several frustrating meetings. Keith invited me to facilitate their next discussion, which would be attended by a cross-section of company personnel with heavy representation from the IT Department.

There were a dozen key players in the conference room, each of whom looked frustrated when I entered. I listened to a lively technical discussion on the merits of Linux versus Windows, C++ versus Ajax/Java evaluations, and other technical issues. They were well into the *how* of the project, without being clear on the *what* or the *why*. Then a bald, geeky executive glared at me and asked, "Okay, you're the consultant. We're stuck. What should we do?"

I responded to the executive by tossing out this first question.

What Are We Trying to Accomplish and Why?

He and his team looked at each other as if to say, "We brought this guy in to get good answers, not to ask such simple questions." Yet, while hardly profound, this fundamental question is the perfect place to start—whatever your issue.

Surprisingly, the motivating Objectives behind projects are not always clear, or are badly communicated in a corporate memo or vague strategic plan. Sometimes my first question gets answered superficially by a catch phrase early in the game, but is seldom revisited, reconsidered, and revalidated.

The question of *what* the project should accomplish—and more importantly—*why* it needs to be done, deserves fine-tuned attention because those answers drive everything else. In the rush to decide on the *how*, *who*, and *when* of a project, people often gloss over the *why*.

This question posed to Keith's team cut through clouds of confusion. Numerous answers tumbled out, which I captured on the whiteboard. The discussion rapidly shifted from technical solutions to customer needs and expectations as well as to the operational benefits expected. Later, the team would organize these Objectives into a logical sequence.

Professionals today are often told *what* needs to be done, but are not really clear on *why* it is needed. Thus, they can easily become lost in the technical jungle of *how*. People first need to answer the whole "*What* are we trying to accomplish and *why*?" question before concentrating their best brain power on the *how*.

When Keith's team reached consensus on several major Objectives, I offered this next question.

How Will We Measure Success?

Their facial expressions suggested that I had revealed the magic formula that unlocks the universe. This question is significant because Measures flesh out and anchor what the Objectives really mean.

This question seldom gets the attention it deserves, due in part to the false belief that the answer must be obvious or else senior management wouldn't have mandated the project. One of Keith's team members provided a perfect example when he replied, "They said that our Goal is to deliver customer value; so, isn't it clear what constitutes success?"

Since it's easy to presume that senior management or "some other department" will decide whether or not the project is successful, tackling the question may seem to be irrelevant or a waste of time. However, until you define how success will be measured, even the most sincere visions are no more than highfalutin' fluff. As we sketched out specific Success Measures for each Objective, the mood in the room changed. The team felt a sense of progress that had been missing from earlier sessions. Now they were rolling along the right path, and the worry lines on Keith's furrowed brow began to soften.

What Other Conditions Must Exist?

When I posed this question, the geeky executive who had glared at me earlier began to smile. This third question puts your project, issue, or initiative into a larger strategic context. Asking this expands the analysis to include some of the outside factors which may disrupt your carefully crafted plans. All too often, capable, responsible professionals focus only on areas they *can* affect or control because it's seemingly irresponsible or inappropriate to worry about things they *can't* control. Asking this question forces us to think outside the artificial boundaries of the project scope and consider the project in its larger, often murky context.

They began sharing their concerns about other factors which would influence or affect the team's efforts: (1) How to provide necessary training; (2) how this system would mesh with processes already in place; (3) how to ensure sufficient resources; plus other critical issues that could easily have been missed. Later we turned these issues into Assumptions, and tested their validity in order to uncover potential problems early. With Assumptions captured, the last question could be answered with greater confidence.

How Do We Get There?

Now—but not before—was the time for the IT team to address the nitty-gritty details. The majority of project teams I have worked with tend to delve deep into the details much too soon, or get sidelined by premature technical arguments. They gloss over the first three questions in a rush to get moving. By ignoring or short-changing earlier questions, their neatly printed project plans are like the proverbial make up on a frog—lovely at first glance, but masking the ugly warts underneath. The value of the fourth question comes from consciously placing it in its only, truly functional place in the planning sequence: Last.

These Four Critical Strategic Questions form the heart of Strategic Project Management. Each needs to be asked and answered, *in exactly this order*. Of course, they are iterative and interconnected. It's smart to give first-cut answers and then cycle through them again and again, each time improving your project design. In Chapter 3, you'll learn about The Logical Framework, a simple strategic thinking tool which elegantly organizes your answers to these four questions.

Concepts from the Cornfield

In the movie *Field of Dreams*, Kevin Costner's character contemplates building a baseball park in the middle of an Iowa cornfield. He says to himself:

> "*If* we build it, *then* they will come."

These words capture a strategic principle that is both simple and profound: If-Then thinking. Understanding and applying this powerful principle will leverage your ability to produce project payoffs.

Planning is nothing more than imagining some future desired conditions, and then thinking backwards about the cause and effect steps needed to get there.

If-Then thinking (also called "cause-effect" or "means-ends" thinking) offers management language that lets you think top-down and backwards from future Goals to the present. In addition, you can think bottom-up and forward to the future, thus creating solid bridges between desired dreams and current reality. This phrase also illustrates the power of human vision and commitment—two ever-necessary competencies not to be set aside lightly.

Linking two Objectives into a logical If-Then relationship forms a *hypothesis*—a predictive statement of cause and effect that involves uncertainty. In plain language, a hypothesis is an educated guess that reflects our life experience, mental models and best judgment of how the world (or at least the project at hand) works.

Stringing multiple If-Then linkages together forms multi-level *strategic hypotheses*, a logic stream based on the generic formula "*If* A *then* B, *if* B *then* C, *if* C *then* D." Every project builds around presumed strategic hypotheses, whether or not they are consciously defined. When these hypotheses are fuzzy—meaning when causal linkages are unclear, undefined or illogical—your plan is a crap shoot. The learnable discipline of If-Then thinking will dramatically boost your odds of success because it forces rigorous systematic thought.

As this book unfolds, you'll appreciate how If-Then thinking is the key to integrating strategic intent into your project plans.

Reserve Your Reading Direction

As youngsters we were taught to read from the top of a page to the bottom, but in the diagrams that follow, it works best to read from bottom to top. That seems counter-intuitive at first, but you'll soon get comfortable with reading If-Then hypotheses from the bottom up.

You can diagram this basic "*If* we build it, *then* they will come" linkage as shown in Figure 2.1. (It works best to start at the bottom and read up.)

Figure 2.2 gives several examples of If-Then logic, visually displayed as linked hypotheses. Remember, start at the bottom and work up, connecting the phrases together with If-Then logic. Let's walk through the logic of the first example.

"*If* we organize a block watch program, *then* we can reduce crime; *If* we reduce crime, *then* we will have better neighborhoods."

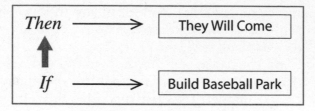

FIGURE 2.1   If-Then Logic

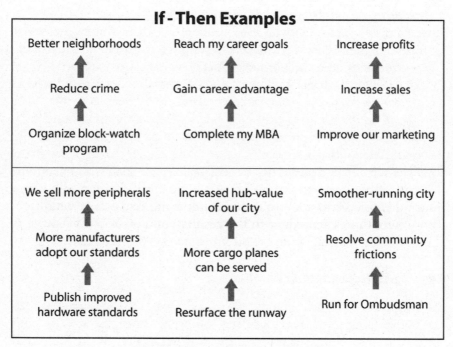

FIGURE 2.2   If-Then Examples

As you read Objectives chains from the bottom-up, grasp the thinking behind the linking. Observe how the higher Objectives tend to be global, general, and influenced by many factors other than the present project. It's best practice to design projects beginning with

Objectives at the top and working down, and to mentally test the soundness of our plan—and implement—by working bottom-up.

Making Strategy Simple

The essence of strategy—how to get to where you want to be—is embedded directly into If-Then statements, much like the chocolaty goodness baked into mom's hot-from-the-oven cookies. The approach to executing any corporate or project strategy can be expressed using If-Then logic. If-Then is a neutral language that crosses disciplinary boundaries, enabling front-line employees, accountants, and CEOs to share the same view of the world. Project players with different backgrounds and thinking styles can use If-Then to compare and integrate their mental models, and thus develop an informed and superior approach.

If-Then thinking is the basic formula for successful design and implementation of strategies, projects, and action initiatives of all types. Consider, for a moment, your project to be a carefully structured experiment. You design your project experiment by specifying a set of linked hypotheses or "educated guesses" believed to be true. During implementation, you'll determine the real-world validity of those hypotheses according to the results you get. You don't have to be a scientist to manage in a way that's strategic and scientific as well as street-smart. You may not win the Nobel Prize, but the quality of your results will be worthy of gold medals.

Why do I emphasize the importance of If-Then thinking? Because most project teams miss this crucial concept entirely. Project plans may turn into dozens of pages of tasks, but if you can't describe (with simple If-Then language) how your hard work ripples up to impact important organizational Goals, it probably won't make an impact. In short, it's hard to *achieve* what you can't *explain*.

Keep This Distinction in Mind

If-Then causal logic may seem obvious, but there is a subtle twist: Causal logic is different from the *sequential* If-Then logic commonly used in network diagrams, flow charts, Gannt charts, and computer programming. Here's the critical distinction: In sequential logic, A precedes B in time. A must happen before B, although it does not cause B. But with causal logic, A not only precedes B, *A causes B to happen*.

When building a baseball diamond in Iowa, sequential logic can identify the logical order of action steps: (1) Harvest the corn; (2) plow the field; (3) plant grass, and so on. It's true that "*If* we cut the corn, *then* we can level the surface," but such a statement expresses a time-based sequential relationship—you must do this before you can do that. Cutting the corn does not cause the surface to level itself; rather it simply precedes it in time. Gantt charts and network diagrams do a good job of showing sequential task logic and dependencies, but they seldom express causal logic.

Sequential logic, however, is rarely strategic. Hunkering down and completing all the tasks on a Gantt chart doesn't necessarily get you to the Goal. Many great ballparks, flashy products, and new systems have been built that remain largely unneeded, unwanted, and unused.

Being more precise, we have to admit that building a ballpark, stadium, or golf course does not, in itself, cause people to come. Having a winning team, creating successful promotions, and providing easy access are all factors that directly impact the strategic hypothesis. At the same time, it's true that "they can't come" *unless and until* "it's built." So, building the ballpark is a necessary prerequisite to people coming, but it is not sufficient, in and of itself, to *cause* them to come.

Observe, too, that the statement "they will come" is still a hypothesis, a deeply-desired view of how the world will respond to the project. Wrapped in that hope is the conviction, the desire, that *If* we build it, *then* they will come. This hope makes the heart of Kevin Costner's movie beat, but if you allow conviction to substitute for rigorous cause-effect reasoning, you're in trouble.

Why does Costner's character want them to come? What's the top-level Objective that drives his project? Costner's character was far behind on mortgage payments and slipping into foreclosure. So we can infer that "save the farm" was an even more important Objective. Let's extend the If-Then linkages up a level to capture the ultimate Objective, as well as down a level, to identify the steps necessary to build the ballpark.

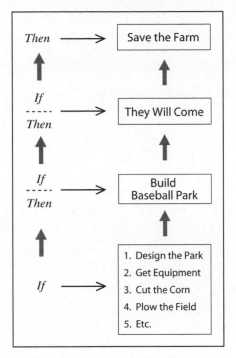

FIGURE 2.3   If-Then Strategic Logic

In Figure 2.3, our logic chain now goes like this as you read up from the bottom:

- *If* we design the park, get equipment, and so on,
  Then we can build a baseball park;
- *If* we build a baseball park,
  Then they will come;
- *If* they come (and pay),
  Then we can save the farm.

We've now constructed a four-level strategic hypothesis—the logical backbone of any project. Note how the linkages start with do-able tasks at the bottom and progress up to high-level Goals. These linkages—based on answers to the first question—provide a solid foundation for project design. (The complete LogFrame for the *Field of Dreams* example can be found at *www.ManagementPro.com*.)

Test Your Strategic If-Then IQ

Brainstorming to generate multiple answers to the first strategic question—*What are we trying to accomplish and why?*—produces a list of possible Objectives, but they are not in any particular order. Your team then needs to convert these scrambled objectives into a logically organized Objectives list, as shown by the two examples in Figure 2.4.

Get the idea?

To deepen your understanding of If-Then logic, I am going to give you several sets of scrambled Objectives, which you can unscramble and rearrange into a logical order. Stack the Objectives logically, top to bottom and bottom to top. You can start by finding the "highest" Objective and putting it at the top and work down, or start from the bottom and work up, or go both ways. It's best to actually sketch them out as shown in the previous examples, with arrows and spaces between each item, or reason them out verbally by stating the linking If-Then phrases.

Scrambled Objectives	Organized Objectives
Get great product idea	Improve profits
	⬆
Market new product	Market new product
	⬆
Improve profits	Develop new product
	⬆
Develop new product	Get great product idea

FIGURE 2.4   Converting Scrambled Objectives into a Logically Ordered List

Take a few minutes to solve these examples, starting with a couple of light-hearted ones and then moving on to the more serious. You can check your answers at the end of this chapter.

Example #1:
- Get rich and move to Fiji
- Find a mate for Orville the hamster
- Breed prize hamsters
- Become "the hamster giant"

Example #5:
- Get promoted faster
- Get an MBA degree
- Become a CEO by age 40
- Take part-time classes

Example #2:
- Meet lots of prospects
- Join an online dating service
- Find a soul mate
- Live happily ever after

Example #6:
- Write and publish articles
- Become a sought-after industry expert
- Increase my professional reputation
- Identify needs in my field

Example #3:
- Design a new expense reporting system
- Reimburse employees faster
- Have happier employees
- Implement a new expense reporting system

Example #7:
- Increase corporate profit
- Develop a new product
- Increase corporate sales
- Market product successfully

Example #4:
- Identify ineffective practices
- Have staff use standard procedures
- Develop and publish best-practice procedures
- Improve corporate productivity

Example #8:
- Develop portable land-mine detector
- Save lives and reclaim land
- Get research funding
- Deploy device in war-torn countries

Here's a final unscrambled example which shows an *illogical* strategic hypothesis—one with little probability of reaching the top of the If-Then chain.

- Live a life of luxury
- Win the lottery
- Buy a lottery ticket
- Drive to the 7-11

Note the virtual certainty of the lower-level If-Then link. You can indeed drive to a 7-11 to buy a ticket. That much is guaranteed. But "If buy ticket, then win lottery" is a huge leap with millions-to-one odds against you. As most lottery ticket buyers know, this If-Then hypothesis depends entirely on which numbered ping-pong balls pop into the chute at the lottery headquarters, a random circumstance outside of your control and totally unimpressed by your fervent desire to win a pot of cash.

Sorting Out Your Objectives

Let's dig deeper to explore finer points about Objectives. The motivation driving all projects is simple: To achieve desired Objectives. Some typical Objectives could be:

- Develop a new management system
- Reduce time to market
- Produce new knowledge
- Invent the perfect gizmo
- Increase data security
- Generate increased profit
- Reengineer core processes

Crafting meaningful Objectives begins with the careful use of language, using well-chosen *verbs* and *descriptive phrases*. (More explanation is in Chapter 4.)

Yet, defining Objectives is seldom straightforward because people interpret Objectives in unique ways based on their own technical background, thinking style, and vested interests.

To playfully make the point that words trigger different images in our minds, I ask my seminar participants, "Please bring me a great dog. Tell me what kind of dog you will bring me?" The answers ring out: "Poodle." "Doberman." "Pekingese." "Yellow Lab." "Mutt." "A dog just like Lassie." "My own dog Bingo." "Great Dane." "Chihuahua." On occasion, someone thinks to ask what kind of dog I consider to be great, which is the essence of Question #2.

Then in mock disappointment, I'll say, "Can't anyone get me a foot-long Coney Island hot dog in a warm bun lathered with mustard and relish?" They chuckle and the point is well made: Words are ambiguous, even when describing something tangible and real like a dog. The confusion escalates when dealing with the abstract and conceptual terms used in management.

Since no standard management vocabulary exists, a rainbow of terms is used to express what we will simply call "Objectives". Words like Goal, Purpose, aim, output, intention, Outcome, result, expectation, and vision are common examples. These terms may be perfectly clear to the person using them, but his or her colleagues may have very different definitions. Even worse, they may just be interchangeable buzzwords thrown around without making any meaningful distinction.

The concept in your mind's eye when you use terms like Goal or Outcome is not likely to match mine. But how often do teams take a moment to calibrate their terminology to ensure that meanings mesh?

Complicating the picture, all projects have multiple Objectives, ranging from those that are short-term, specific and easily achievable to those that are long-term and general and tougher to reach. Without a mechanism to clarify and logically organize Objectives, the situation is like our six blind men feeling an elephant. Each perceives just one part and misses the logical whole. No wonder the failure rate is so high.

Let's make a deal. From now on, we'll agree to use the word *Objective* as a generic term to describe any and all project intentions. In the next paragraphs, we'll get more precise and distinguish different types and levels of Objectives.

Link How You Think and Think How You Link

Project teams seldom define and examine the mental logic underpinning their efforts. That dangerous oversight leads to projects that deliver end products but fail to achieve business Goals. Examples abound of newly developed products that the market doesn't need; systems created that people don't use; and other well-intended efforts that fail to leave a mark. You can avoid this disconnect by recognizing four levels of Objectives, which are defined as follows:

Goal
↑

The high level, big-picture strategic or program Objective to which the project contributes.

Purpose
↑

The impact we anticipate by doing the project, the change expected from producing Outcomes.

Outcomes
↑

The specific results that the project team must deliver by managing Inputs.

Inputs

The activities and the resources necessary to produce Outcomes.

Put into words, the logic is:

- "*If* we manage Inputs, *then* we can produce or deliver Outcomes;
- *If* we produce or deliver Outcomes, *then* we will achieve a Purpose;
- *If* we achieve a Purpose, *then* we contribute to an important Goal."

Or, expressed more succinctly:

- "*If* Inputs, *then* Outcomes;
- *If* Outcomes, *then* Purpose;
- *If* Purpose, *then* Goal."

The logic between levels is not random or accidental; each level forms a link in the strategic hypothesis. Admittedly, the choice of words used to define each level in the project's hierarchy (Goal, Purpose, Outcomes, and Inputs) may seem arbitrary, but the concept each term expresses definitely is not. Each Objective has a particular and precise meaning. While the specific word is not important, the meaning attached to that word is crucial. If you wish, substitute your own terms—but be certain everyone on the team uses those terms in the same way.

Think of these various Objectives as rungs on a ladder. The logic that links each rung permits a disciplined approach to project design. By getting the implicit strategic logic out of people's heads and onto paper, you can *test* the soundness of any approach and fill in the missing gaps early in the game.

In general, project teams *manage* Inputs, which *produce* Outcomes to *achieve* a Purpose, which *contributes* to a Goal. Inputs and Outcomes are generally within the control of the project team, while Purpose and Goal are beyond their direct control.

Figure 2.5 gives several examples of bottom-up strategic hypotheses in various businesses.

In these examples, observe how the Goals tend to be global, general, and affected by many factors other than the project. Recognize the important distinction between Outcomes and Purpose. *Outcomes* are deliverables that the project team can control, make happen, and be held accountable for. *Purpose* is the expected impact from the deliverables, the aiming point which is beyond the team's direct control.

Strategic Hypotheses - Business Examples

Objectives	Weapons Systems	Disaster Recovery	Customer Service
Goal:	Military capability enhanced	Ensure company can operate smoothly despite unforeseen disasters	Better customer service
Purpose:	Weapons system deployed and ready to use	Recover quickly from a disaster	Employees use new procedures
Outcomes:	1. Weapons system built and tested	1. Emergency power systems in place 2. Data backed up in real time	1. New procedures developed 2. Staff trained in procedures
Inputs:	1.1 Design system 1.2 Build system 1.3 Test system	1.1 Install systems 1.2 Test systems 2.1 Identify critical data 2.2 Back up data in real time	1.1 Create task force 1.2 Develop procedures 2.1 Create training 2.2 Train staff

FIGURE 2.5   Strategic Hypotheses—Business Examples

When your key players grasp these distinctions, they can concentrate on delivering the right set of Outcomes, aimed at an important Purpose and Goal shared by senior management and critical stakeholders. Figure 2.6 applies the same logical progression to examples of personal projects.

Good project design requires that a project has a single Goal and a single Purpose, along with multiple Outcomes. Each Outcome can have several Inputs, which are the main tasks needed to get there. In addition, reaching a Big Hairy Audacious Goal usually requires multiple project thrusts to get there. Each requires its own LogFrame that is tied to a common Goal.

Programs consist of multiple projects that contribute to one common overarching Goal. Chapter 4 explores program management and how it benefits from the Objectives Tree tool that is presented in the next section.

Organizing Multiple Objectives Into Trees

Describing strategy using a single chain of linked If-Then Objectives is fine for getting a line of sight on stand-alone projects, but if the larger

Strategic Hypotheses - Personal Examples

Objectives	Career Planning	Improve Quality of Home Life	Become a Golf Pro
Goal:	Make money, have fun, and contribute in my career	Enjoy my family & give children safe place to play	Become the #1 golfer in the world
Purpose:	Increase my career mobility and market value	Create the ideal backyard environment	Become a tournament golfer
Outcomes:	1. New skills developed 2. Contact network expanded	1. Landscaping completed 2. New children's swing and playground put in place	1. Improve my golf skills
Inputs:	1.1 Attend seminars 1.2 Read business books 2.1 Be more active in community 2.2 Join Rotary	1.1 Hire contractor 1.2 Complete project 2.1 Design playground 2.2 Build playground	1.1 Get new glasses 1.2 Practice daily 1.3 Buy new clubs 1.4 Take lessons

FIGURE 2.6 Strategic Hypotheses—Personal Examples

environment is more complex, multiple other Objectives and projects naturally come into play. How does our system incorporate these?

Before answering, we introduce Objectives Trees, which are visual tools that organize multiple and parallel Objectives using our now familiar If-Then logic. We'll illustrate how If-Then thinking simplifies complex problem situations by showing its use in combating what was potentially the worst insect pest threat ever seen in the United States—the Asian Gypsy Moth invasion of the Pacific Northwest.

I first learned about the Asian Gypsy Moth (AGM) invasion in an urgent phone call from a senior entomologist in the Washington State Department of Agriculture (WSDA). While I couldn't imagine moths destroying more than a wool sweater, he soon convinced me otherwise.

"This isn't just any moth," James explained. "Asian Gypsies are the King Kong of the moth world. These voracious little pests threaten to wipe out the forests of the Pacific Northwest because they eat everything in their path."

He explained how these pests slipped into North America as tiny batches of larvae aboard ships coming from Siberia. When the ships unloaded their cargo in the ports of Washington, Oregon, and Canada, the moths entered the mainland and laid their eggs.

James continued to describe the severity and urgency of the matter. "The weather is getting warm. The moths, now in cocoons, will hatch and spread like wildfire. In a few weeks, the U.S. Forest Service will put eight helicopters into the air and spray over 130,000 acres to kill them—but they won't get them all. My team must then set out traps to find and destroy any they miss. We face a huge task. Our team needs to grow from just three people to almost 300 people in less than eight weeks. We must import, assemble and deploy 180,000 sticky-substance insect traps; hire and train trappers; then set up monitoring systems to find and destroy any remaining moths."

Whew! What a project! When they asked me to help them gear up fast, our first step was to sketch an Objectives Tree, as shown in Figure 2.7. This diagram offered a wide-angle perspective for planning how to find and destroy those dangerous moths.

The center column of linked Objectives illustrates how setting traps would ripple up the cause-effect chain and lead to saving the forests and protecting the quality of life in the Pacific Northwest. Note how this If-Then logic handles parallel Objectives. These center Objectives were

Objectives Tree for Combating the Asian Gypsy Moth Invasion

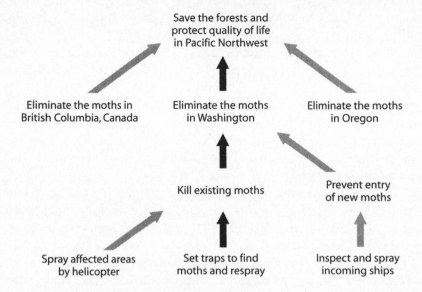

Save the forests and
protect quality of life
in Pacific Northwest

Eliminate the moths in
British Columbia, Canada

Eliminate the moths
in Washington

Eliminate the moths
in Oregon

Kill existing moths

Prevent entry
of new moths

Spray affected areas
by helicopter

Set traps to find
moths and respray

Inspect and spray
incoming ships

Responsible: U.S. Forest Service • Washington State Dept. of Agriculture (WSDA) • U.S. Dept. of Agriculture

FIGURE 2.7   Objectives Tree for Combating the
Asian Gypsy Moth Invasion

the responsibility of WSDA and became the focus of their LogFrame project plans.

This emergency effort would be coordinated with parallel efforts in Oregon and British Columbia, Canada. These other Objectives shown in the tree were outside the AGM teams' responsibility, but still vital to reach the Goal. From WSDA's perspective, these were Assumptions. (Keep in mind that your Assumptions may be someone else's full-fledged project, and vice versa.)

In properly constructed Objectives Trees, for any Objective, looking up the tree should answer the question "*why*," while looking down the tree answers the question "*how*." If you look carefully at the Objectives Tree figure and select, for example, "Eliminate the moths in Washington" you may ask: *Why* are we doing it? The answer: To save the forests and protect quality of life. *How* are we doing it? By killing existing moths *and* by preventing the entry of new moths.

(A note of caution: Don't confuse this *why* and *how* with those same elements in the LogFrame described later. In the LogFrame, those concepts are fixed at certain levels, whereas with Objective Trees, the *why/how* perspective floats freely as you climb move up and down the trees.)

As you can see, the Objectives Tree arrows all point upward and show the key program elements necessary to reach the vision of saving the forests by eliminating the moth.

Objectives Trees can clarify relationships, reveal missing elements, and help identify projects that we plan in greater detail with LogFrames. More often than not, developing the Tree will surface the need for related tasks that might otherwise be missed.

But be cautious: Objectives Trees are an imperfect tool because no single Tree branches out to tell the whole story. Trees are a less precise planning tool than the LogFrame because there are few rigorous definitions. In fact, it's not wise to label Objectives in the Tree hierarchy at all. Let's just call them all "Objectives"—our designated neutral term that covers all desires intentions, no matter how lofty or mundane. More precise labeling occurs when we create the LogFrame.

(You will find a completed LogFrame for the Asian Gypsy Moth project at *www.ManagementPro.com*. A Special Report entitled "Creating Objectives Trees" is also available there. There's no charge for these or other referenced resources.)

Key Points Review

1. All great solutions begin by asking the right questions. The Four Critical Strategic Questions keep your focus on solutions that are tied to the big picture.
2. The essence of smart project design is captured in two words: If-Then. Use this cause-effect thinking to form strategic, hypotheses and design sound strategies, projects, and action initiatives of all types.
3. Clearly identifying your underlying hypotheses forces rigorous, systematic thought and lets you design projects from a strategic, scientific, and management perspective.
4. Sharpening the strategic hypotheses of your project—the chain of If-Then connections—leads to common understanding and

agreement on how the project deliverables ripple up to impact business Goals.

5. Use Objectives Trees in order to clarify relationships among multiple Objectives in more complex environments.

Answers to If-Then Exercises

Example #1:
- Get rich and move to Fiji
  ↑
- Become "the hamster giant"
  ↑
- Breed prize hamsters
  ↑
- Find a mate for Orville the hamster

Example #2:
- Live happily ever after
  ↑
- Find a soul mate
  ↑
- Meet lots of prospects
  ↑
- Join an online dating service

Example #3:
- Have happier employees
  ↑
- Reimburse employees faster
  ↑
- Implement a new expense reporting system
  ↑
- Design a new expense reporting system

Example #5:
- Become a CEO by age 40
  ↑
- Get promoted faster
  ↑
- Get an MBA degree
  ↑
- Take part-time classes

Example #6:
- Become a sought-after industry expert
  ↑
- Increase my professional reputation
  ↑
- Write and publish articles
  ↑
- Identify needs in my field

Example #7:
- Increase corporate profit
  ↑
- Increase corporate sales
  ↑
- Market product successfully
  ↑
- Develop a new product

Example #4:

- Improve corporate productivity

  ↑

- Have staff use standard procedures

  ↑

- Develop and publish best-practice procedures

  ↑

- Identify ineffective practices

Example #8:

- Save lives and reclaim land

  ↑

- Deploy device in war-torn countries

  ↑

- Develop portable land-mine detector

  ↑

- Get research funding

3

Introducing the Logical Framework

Make no little plans: they have no magic to stir men's blood
and probably will, themselves, not be realized.
Make big plans: aim high in hope and work, remembering that
a noble, logical diagram, once recorded, will not die.

—Daniel H. Burnham, American architect
and urban planner (1846–1912)

The Best Solutions Tool You'll Ever Find

In the 1970s, I worked with an innovative management consulting firm called Practical Concepts Incorporated (PCI), whose visionary founder Leon Rosenberg first developed the Logical Framework, to help the United States Agency for International Development (USAID) more effectively plan, implement, and evaluate the thousands of projects in the U.S. government's multi-billion dollar foreign aid program.

The LogFrame has since been widely adopted by the international donor agencies of Great Britain, Canada, Australia, Denmark, and Germany. Parts of the World Bank and the United Nations. Several U.S. federal agencies (such as the Center for Disease Control) have adopted their own versions; some call it Logic Model.

My career mission is to expand the use of this methodology to corporate and technical arenas, through consulting, public seminars, and in-house workshops.

Private sector use is rapidly growing. Among our clients, Sony Electronics' TQM Black Belts found the tool valuable for internal consulting and quality improvement projects. DirecTV used the LogFrame approach to fight identity theft and turn high profile fraud cases over to the FBI. The Los Angeles County Assessor's office chose this approach for integrated planning to improve cross-department processes.

Application possibilities for the LogFrame are endless. Civic, voluntary and social organizations benefit from these same organizing principles. A New Mexico motorcycle club plans their annual children's toy runs this way. Girl Scout troops organize fund-raising campaigns. Churches develop after-school teen drop-in centers.

I first learned the power of systems thinking while coaching project teams in developing countries to design social and economic development projects. Working to solve difficult problems in complicated situations taught me to recognize the interconnection of issues and address them from a systems thinking perspective. The LogFrame makes that easy to do.

For example, a project to improve child mortality in Africa, may focus on nutritional education for mothers, but success also demands access to clean water and decent sanitation. *Strategy is all about managing webs of relationships.*

These projects typically dealt with hard-to-measure intangibles such as strengthening institutional performance, upgrading manpower skills, and changing cultural attitudes for the better. Your own projects may also involve processes, intangibles, and changes—tough topics to put your finger on. Bar charts cannot capture such intangibles, but the LogFrame does.

My greatest personal satisfaction comes from seeing my clients use what I teach them long after I depart from places like Thailand, which played an important role in refining these concepts. I was part of the original PCI team that trained Royal Thai

Government employees at the National Economic and Social Development Board.

Program attendees held senior government leadership positions, and many adopted the LogFrame as their way of doing business. The Bangkok Metropolitan Administration used LogFrame planning to move the world's largest outdoor marketplace—with nearly 15,000 vendors selling everything imaginable—to its new location at Jathujak. Dr. Sudjit Nimatkul, a program participant, applied these methods in his subsequent role as Governor of Phuket.

Many years later, I moved to Asia full-time to assist project teams responsible for executing USAID-funded projects. That's where I refined the RAP (Rapid Action Planning) process to develop impactful project plans which reflect on-the-ground reality and team dynamics.

I eventually went on to start my own consulting company and shifted my client base to corporations, government agencies, and research institutions. It soon became obvious that the challenges and issues they faced benefitted from using the same system thinking perspective.

Once you understand the inner workings of the LogFrame, you can better understand the interconnection of elements that comprise your project system, and manage it more effectively.

Systems Thinking: Conceptual Foundation of the Logical Framework

While the LogFrame matrix may initially seem intimidating, the ideas it captures are basic. The four strategic questions offer a user friendly way to learn and apply this tool. These questions are inherently embedded in the matrix and answering them helps you design your project in a way that connects all the dots.

The Logical Framework structure shown on page 45 appears as a 4×4 matrix. Each cell in the matrix organizes project information in a specific way, using standard management terminology. The various cells relate to each other by interlocking principles of good management and common sense. The cells interact—changes in one can affect the others—reflecting the dynamics of our thinking process and the complexity of the issues before us. The completed matrix can communicate a complicated project clearly and understandably on a couple of sheets of paper.

At first glance, the LogFrame looks like a bunch of connected boxes. But a closer examination reveals multiple types of thinking woven into the matrix logic. In this next section, you will see how the LogFrame invites, accommodates, and incorporates other best practice management disciplines.

Integrating Theory and Best Practice

The *Systems Thinking* perspective built into the LogFrame architecture recognizes that every project is part of a larger system, and we must understand how that larger system affects our effort. System thinking prevents the "elephant parts" problem.

Strategic Planning teaches us to begin with the end Objectives in mind, scan the environment, and systematically work backwards to develop our strategy.

Management by Objectives (as well as *Management by Results*) reminds us that Objectives exist at multiple levels and that they all need clear Measures of success to make them meaningful. The LogFrame requires separate success Measures for Goal, Purpose, and Outcomes, along with means of Verification.

The Scientific Method allows us to formulate any project as a series of linked If-Then hypotheses. Thus, every project can be considered to be a structured experiment, where implementation tests the validity of our educated guess hypotheses. (See the Implementation Equation™ on page 55).

Total Quality Management offers more specific tools for measuring Objectives and specifying the degree of quality required. This concept shows up in multiple cells.

Project Management provides the necessary body of knowledge to convert Inputs into Outcomes. The LogFrame puts project management tools in their proper place, to support Purpose and Goal Objectives.

Finally, *Team Building* occurs as a by-product when people use these tools together. It's remarkable how much real work gets done when people gather around a wall-sized grid or use collaborative LogFrame software to flesh out a design they all contribute to and mutually own.

Virtually any valid business methodology can be smoothly incorporated in the LogFrame structure. For example, the data for Return on Investment (ROI) analysis comes from estimating the economic value of the Purpose and Goal level achievement. Figure 3.1 shows the LogFrame matrix, and Figure 3.2 gives definitions of terms used in the LogFrame.

For small- and medium-sized projects, this may be the only planning tool you'll need. For projects of any size, this tool is the ideal starting point to help your team get going quickly and confidently as well as to build an iterative planning and implementation mindset.

Tackling the Four Critical Strategic Questions

The LogFrame captures, in various cells, the answers to the Four Critical Strategic Questions:

1. **What Are We Trying To Accomplish And Why? (Objectives)**
   The first column describes Objectives and the If-Then logic linking them together. The LogFrame makes important distinctions among various "levels" of Objectives: Strategic intention (Goal), project impact (Purpose), project deliverables (Outcomes), and the key action steps (Inputs).

2. **How Will We Measure Success? (Measures and Verifications)**
   The second column identifies the Measures of success for Objectives at each level. Here we select appropriate Measures and choose quantity, quality, and time indicators to clarify what each Objective means.

   The third column summarizes how we will verify the status of the Measures at each level. Think of the Verification column as the project's management information and feedback system.

Objectives	Success Measures	Verification	Assumptions
Goal			
Purpose			
Outcomes			
Inputs			

FIGURE 3.1   The LogFrame Matrix

Objectives	Success Measures	Verification	Assumptions
Goal: ▶ Big Picture Objective to which Project Purpose contributes	**Goal Measures:** Measures of Goal Achievement (quality, quantity, time)	Data sources to monitor and verify Goal	**To reach Goal:** External conditions needed to reach Goal and beyond
Purpose: ▶ Change expected from producing Outcomes ▶ Motivation for Project	**Purpose Measures:** Success conditions expected at end of Project (quality, quantity, time)	Data sources to monitor and verify Purpose	**To achieve Purpose:** External conditions needed to achieve Purpose
Outcomes: ▶ Specific Results expected from Project Team ▶ What good managers can make happen	**Outcome Measures:** Description of completed Outcomes (quality, quantity, time)	Data sources to monitor and verify Outcomes	**To produce Outcomes:** External conditions needed to produce Outcomes
Inputs: ▶ Activities and Responsibilities needed to produce Outcomes	**Input Measures:** Resource Budget and Schedule	Data sources to monitor and verify Inputs	**To obtain and manage Inputs:** External conditions necessary to obtain and manage Inputs

FIGURE 3.2   Definitions of Terms Used in the LogFrame

3. **What Other Conditions Must Exist? (Assumptions)**

The fourth column captures Assumptions; those ever-present, but often neglected risk factors outside of the project, on which project success depends. Defining and testing Assumptions lets you spot potential problems and deal with them in advance.

4. **How Do We Get There? (Inputs)**

The bottom row captures the project action plan: Who does what, when, and with what resources. Conventional project management tools like Work Breakdown Structures (WBS) and Gantt chart schedules fit here.

Grab a Front-Row Workshop Seat

Welcome to my workshop! Can a hands-on strategy workshop itself be considered a project? Absolutely. Workshops include all the elements of any project, including specific Objectives, defined timeframe, limited resources, new cast of players, and uncertainty. Mine have earned a reputation for being innovative because they center around the LogFrame and my "entertraining" style engages everyone as a contributor and participant in the process. As we proceed, you'll become convinced that the LogFrame is not a form to fill out, but a systematic thinking template that lets you logically design projects by asking, and intelligently answering, the four critical questions.

1. What Are We Trying to Accomplish and Why?

As you wrestle with this question, you may have written scopes of work, executive memos, or strategic plans to guide you. At other times, you start from scratch with a blank sheet of paper.

When I toss out this question at the start of my workshop, common responses include "Learn how to manage projects better," or "Learn how to meet Objectives," or occasionally, "Keep my boss from meddling." The common denominator of the various responses is "learning."

Most of the responses address the *what* part of the question, so I challenge them to answer the *why* part. Then I typically get statements like "Deliver successful projects" or "Improve my projects." So I diagram this If-Then linkage on a flip-chart pad, as shown in Figure 3.3.

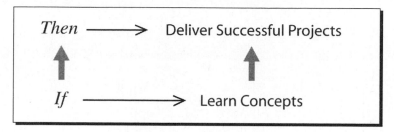

FIGURE 3.3 If-Then Grid

Does this If-Then logic make sense: If we learn the concepts, then we will deliver successful projects? Sure. This relationship is certainly logical, but the gap between these two Objectives seems too large— like rungs on a ladder that are spaced too far apart for safe climbing. Learning concepts won't necessarily deliver successful projects. I then ask my audience, "Is something missing? Does something else need to happen between learning and project success? What in-between Objective would make the linkages more logical?"

After some furrowed brows, they slap their foreheads in an *ah-ha* moment and exclaim, "Why, of course. We need to *apply* the concepts!" Exactly!

Inserting this intermediate Objective makes the If-Then logic more, well, *logical*. Our hypothesis becomes what is shown in Figure 3.4.

Inserting this intermediate Objective adds realism to our hypotheses and directs attention to the critical, after-workshop Objective that's necessary for successful projects. *Apply* now becomes the aiming point for designing and delivering a workshop that participants can, and will, put into action.

The Objective "Learn key concepts" requires a lower-level Objective describing workshop learning tasks and activities. The phrase "Conduct the workshop" will suffice for now. We'll break this out into specific tasks and schedule during Question #4.

Remember that every project under the sun is comprised of multiple Objectives. The Logical Framework tool helps distinguish these multiple Objectives, which show up at different levels in the cause-effect chain. The LogFrame organizes them into four separate and distinct levels, each with precise definitions. After applying these definitions, our strategic hypothesis looks as illustrated in Figure 3.5.

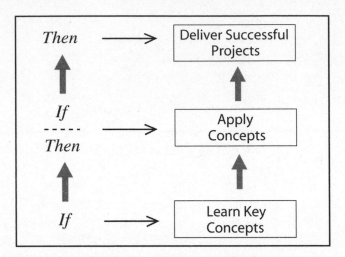

FIGURE 3.4   Logical If-Then Grid

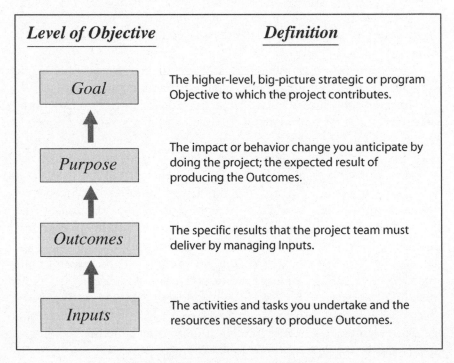

FIGURE 3.5   Strategic Hypothesis

Reading from bottom-up:

- *If* I conduct the workshop, *then* participants will learn key concepts;
- *If* participants learn key concepts, *then* they will apply them;
- *If* they apply concepts, *then* they'll deliver successful projects.

We've now constructed a first-cut of a four-level strategic hypothesis—the backbone of any project. Note how these "vertical" logical linkages start with Input activities and percolate up to higher-level Goals. You must climb up each rung in the ladder step-by-step, without jumping over any rungs.

Another important distinction is how this strategic hypothesis clearly distinguishes between Outcomes (the learning that happens during the workshop); Purpose (what occurs after the "project"—participants *apply* concepts learned); and Goal (the operational benefit expected from the training—better projects). Strictly speaking, Inputs are not Objectives. Rather, they are the tasks necessary to accomplish Objectives. These definitions are illustrated in Figure 3.6.

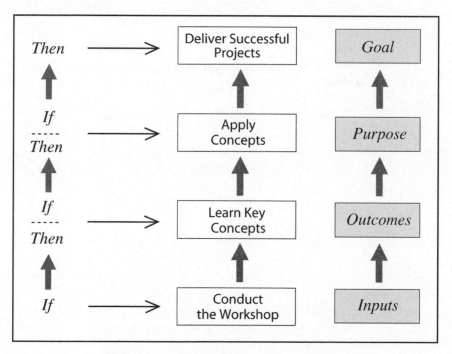

FIGURE 3.6   **The Various Levels of Objectives**

The value of this kind of thinking for your undertaking should be this evident, which makes it possible to test whether our project hypotheses hang together and connect to business goals. If-Then logic dissolves fuzzy thinking like morning fog evaporating under the stern gaze of the risen sun.

2. How Will We Measure Success?

Objectives, by nature, are ambiguous. They become crystal clear only when those involved agree how to measure them.

Each level of the LogFrame invites Success Measures which express how to recognize the successful accomplishment of each Objective. Success Measures consist of sentences, phrases, or bullet points that clarify exactly what each Objective means. These metrics describe, in advance, the conditions that you expect will exist when you declare the Objectives achieved. They should spell out Quality, Quantity, and Time—the three most frequent measurement dimensions:

- *Quantity*—How many/how much?
- *Quality*—How good? What standards or performance specifications?
- *Time*—By when or for how long?

In addition to these "QQT" categories, two other categories may come into play:

- *Customer*—Who are the customers/clients/users/beneficiaries?
- *Cost*—What resources are required?

Think of the LogFrame's Verification column as a summary of the project's MIS (Management Information System).

The Verification column defines the formal and informal data sources and methods necessary to track how well Measures have been (or are being) achieved validate the Measures. Typical means of Verification include physical observations, project team meetings, reports, survey results, analyses, tests, and/or whatever else confirms that the Measure has been met.

Let's add Measures to our workshop example, starting at the Goal and working top-down. As we proceed, notice how the interaction among the LogFrame elements enriches comprehension of how to make the project work.

Goal Measures

I encourage my attendees to define how they will measure the Goal "deliver successful projects." The usual responses that get mentioned are delivering on-time, within budget, and with quality. Reduction in problems encountered is an additional Success Measure, and all these are easily verified through project schedules and financial records. We then insert Goal Measures and Means of Verification into the LogFrame grid shown on page 53.

Purpose Measures

Purpose level Measures are the most essential of all because they describe the behavioral changes or conditions we aim for by delivering Outcomes. Purpose Measures describe *project success*, while Outcome Measures only describe *project completion*—an important distinction that is often lost.

I ask workshop participants to spell out Success Measures for the Purpose statement "Participants apply concepts after workshop." Let's get clear, "How many participants?"; What does "apply" mean?; and define "When?" and "How well?" In small work groups, they come up with possible QQT Measures like these:

- *Quantity?* They decide that at least 80 percent of participants is a reasonable figure.
- *Time?* They agree that within six weeks after the workshop is a reasonable timeframe. They also add a second six-month Measure to track the sustainability of the knowledge application over time.
- *Quality?* Quality, in this case, refers to specific after-workshop behaviors, such as briefing the boss, sharing workshop products, or using the tools on additional projects.

At the same time you define Measures, choose appropriate means of verifying them. If you cannot come up with good verifiers, the Measure needs to be modified.

Outcome Measures

Outcomes are defined as those deliverables your project team commits to make happen. Think of Outcomes as project scope, and Outcome Measures as performance specifications which spell out what the completed deliverables will look like. It's normally easier to visualize

Outcome Measures than Purpose Measures because Outcomes are usually more tangible. For example, the Outcome "Participants learn concepts" could be measured with, "By the end of the workshop, 90 percent of participants can apply the four strategic questions and define logical If-Then hierarchies."

Set your Outcome targets with an eye on your desired Purpose and its associated Measures. Target these at the magnitudes needed to achieve the Purpose-level impact you are aiming for. For example, if you only have 20 percent of people apply the concepts, it would not be necessary for 90 percent to learn them. Changes in the Purpose Measures affect the Outcome Measures, which is another example of interconnection between concepts in the LogFrame cell and how changes in one may affect others.

This dynamic and interactive interplay both, horizontally and vertically, promotes the disciplined thinking that creates superior projects. Give this thinking process the attention it deserves. By remembering NASA Rule #15 and using the LogFrame upfront, you'll avoid logjams down the line.

Now our project LogFrame looks like Figure 3.7 on page 53.

Input Measures

With Outcome Measures in place, Inputs and Input Measures (as discussed later) will begin to fall into place. Keep in mind that multiple outside factors will influence your projects, which is why the third question is also critical.

3. What Other Conditions Must Exist?

No project is a sure bet, even a workshop. Risk factors always exist, whether or not we recognize them. Most teams don't delve deeply enough into defining and testing their Assumptions at the start to surface the inherent risks. Assumptions are those uncertain factors which are necessary to complete the logical linkages, but which may be beyond the direct control of the project team. While we can ignore Assumptions, we cannot ignore the impact of ignoring these Assumptions.

Workshop participants form small groups again to identify the key Assumptions that link each pair of Objectives. We start by discussing what Assumptions are necessary to go from the Input

Objectives	Success Measures	Verification
Goal Deliver successful projects.	**Goal Measures:** Within next year: 1. Key project Objectives reached on time, within budget, and at required performance level. 2. Fewer problems due to ineffective planning or road blocks that could have been anticipated during planning (e.g., killer Assumptions).	 1. Schedule and financial records 2. Project logs
Purpose Participants apply what they learned following workshop.	**Purpose Measures:** 1. Within six weeks after training, 80% of participants have: • completed project designs they began during workshop • shared learning highlights with boss and team • explained selected course concepts to others • prepared a LogFrame for additional projects • scheduled in-house training or Rapid Action Planning (RAP) workshop • adapted selected concepts/tools to enrich their current approach 2. After six months, all participants' project plans have clear Objectives, Measures, Assumptions; all participants are using team process and involving key stakeholders in design.	 1. Follow-up evaluation after six weeks 2. Evaluation after six months
Outcomes: Participants learn key concepts and tools during workshop.	**Outcome Measures:** 1.1 At workshop end, >90% of participants can correctly: • identify and apply 4 key questions • identify LogFrame terms, set QQT Measures • construct logical *If-Then* hierarchies • identify and evaluate Assumptions 1.2 All teams develop an acceptable LogFrame for a case study in class within two hours. 1.3 LogFrame adds strategic value to participant thinking; all walk away with expanded capacity.	 1.1 In-class exercises, formal tests 1.2 LogFrame passes checklist 1.3 Ask participants

FIGURE 3.7 Partial Workshop LogFrame

activity "Conduct the class" to the Outcome "Apply the concepts." They typically identify such Assumptions as:

1. Participants are motivated to learn.
2. Instructor is competent to teach.

Further discussion enriches these initial Assumptions to become:

1. Participants want to attend, are motivated, and open to learning.
2. Instructor is effective with this group.

Note this iterative thinking process that applies to all parts of the LogFrame. First-stab answers get you going, but as you proceed, you'll come up with fine-tune phrasing that more precisely expresses your project intentions.

Examining Assumptions can be intimidating, and in some circles it is discouraged as "negative thinking" or "not our job." Many otherwise intelligent people are content with only dipping a toe into the Assumptions pool and quickly moving on, rather than diving in and swimming around.

Now let's identify the Outcome to Purpose Assumptions, those factors necessary to go from learning to post-workshop application.

1. Participants have the opportunity to apply concepts in their jobs.
2. Participants' bosses and organizational environments support and encourage application of concepts.
3. Participants can remember materials well enough to apply them.

To get from Purpose to Goal, we must assume conditions like:

1. Concepts are relevant—they work in practice and add high value.
2. The organization and its environment are reasonably stable.

Assumptions Complete the Hypothesis

Since Assumptions shine a bright light on possible pitfalls in our climb up the hierarchy, the benefit of spotting them early should be immediately apparent. Better to catch these potential deal-breakers upfront and decide how to handle them then rather than pay lip-ser-vice and have them sabotage you later.

Note that the concept of Assumptions forces us to expand our original hypotheses to reflect uncertainties in our logic chain. The enriched logic becomes "*If* / AND / *Then*" logic, as diagrammed in Figure 3.8.

Examine Your Strategic Hypothesis

This leads us to the core idea that distinguishes exceptional lead-ers and teams I have known from the rest of the crowd. The very best intuitively grasp and manage what I call *The Implementation Equation*™. This equation adds real-world realism by inviting Assumptions to join our If-Then logic, as shown in Figure 3.9.

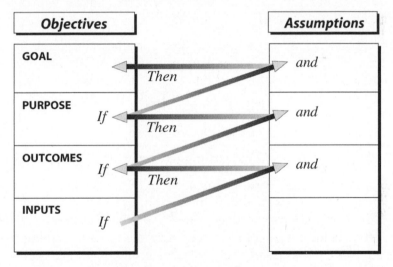

FIGURE 3.8   If / AND / Then Logic Expands the Hypothesis

The Implementation Equation™:

▷ *If* Inputs plus valid Assumptions, *Then* Outcomes

▷ *If* Outcomes plus valid Assumptions, *Then* Purpose

▷ *If* Purpose plus valid Assumptions, *Then* Goal

FIGURE 3.9   The Implementation Equation™

Every Assumption deserves up-close inspection with a skeptical magnifying glass. Simply stating an Assumption does not make it true. We must ask the following of each one:

- Is this Assumption reasonable? What are the odds it is valid? How do we know?
- What are the consequences for the project if it's not valid? How severe is the impact?
- How can we influence the Assumption in our favor?

Chapter 8 explores how Assumption analysis reveals risks and highlights potential problems. Addressed early enough, we can modify our game plan to head off trouble looming down the road.

4. How Do We Get There?

With Objectives, Measures, and Assumptions tacked in place, we can confidently turn to the Input level—the action steps to produce Outcomes. Project Inputs are defined as activities and associated resources (time, people, and money). This level—the land where bar charts dwell—is reasonably straightforward and familiar to anyone with project experience. Project management software doesn't help much at the higher levels of Objectives, but it works wonders here.

A clear Input task list, detailing the key steps to produce Outcomes, is the basis for implementation. In our workshop example, the Input list consists of the agenda, whose tasks and schedule are carefully tailored to produce the identified target Outcome. Resources include the people in the room, along with training materials (i.e., workbooks, markers, PowerPoint, and of course, coffee).

Figure 3.10 shows a complete LogFrame for the workshop.

Ingredients of the Grid

Let's complete this whirlwind tour by looking at all the Logical Framework elements together. If you didn't grasp all the key points and nuances, don't worry. The next four chapters will drill deeper into these four questions and associated planning steps. By the end of the book, you'll have seen enough examples to put the concepts to work for you.

Objectives	Success Measures	Verification	Assumptions
Goal: Deliver project successfully.	**Goal Measures:** Within next year: 1. Key project objectives reached on time, within budget, and at required performance level. 2. Fewer problems due to ineffective planning or road blocks that could have been anticipated during planning (e.g., killer Assumptions).	1. Schedule and financial records 2. Project logs	**To achieve Goal:** 1. Concepts are relevant; they work in practice and add high value. 2. Organization and its environment are reasonably stable.
Purpose: Participants apply what they learned following workshop.	**Purpose Measures:** 1. Within six weeks after training, 60% of participants have: • completed project designs they began during workshop • shared learning highlights with boss and team • explained selected course concepts to others • prepared a LogFrame for additional projects • scheduled in-house training or project launch workshop • adapted selected concepts/tools to enrich their current approach 2. After six months, all participants' roles in project have clear Objectives, Measures, Assumptions; all key stakeholders involved and all participants are using team process.	1. Follow-up survey 2. Evaluation	**To achieve Purpose:** 1. Participants have opportunity to apply concepts (nature of job is suitable). 2. Participants' boss and organization's environment support and encourage application of concepts. 3. Participants can remember materials enough to apply them.
Outcomes: Participants learn key concepts and tools during workshop.	**Outcome Measures:** 1.1 At workshop end, >90% of participants can correctly: • identify and apply 4 key questions • identify LogFrame terms, set QQT measures • construct logical If-Then hierarchies • identify and evaluate Assumptions 1.2 All teams develop an acceptable LogFrame for a case study in class within two hours. 1.3 LogFrame adds strategic value to participant thinking; all walk away with expanded capacity.	1.1 In-class exercises, formal tests 1.2 LogFrame quality checklist 1.3 Ask participants	**To produce Outcomes:** 1. Participants want to attend, are motivated and open to learning. 2. Needs of group can be met within course design. 3. Amount of time is adequate to cover topics. 4. Instructor is effective with this group.
Inputs: **Activities** 1.1 Establish objectives 1.2 Discuss core concepts 1.3 Fundamental questions 1.4 Preview of the Logical Framework 1.5 Vertical thinking–objectives and hypotheses 1.6 Horizontal thinking–measures and verifications 1.7 Identifying and reducing risk and assumptions 1.8 Apply to participant cases	**Schedule:** **Day One** 8:30-9:30 a.m. 9:30-10:00 a.m. 10:00-10:45 a.m. 10:45-11:50 p.m. 1:00-2:00 p.m. 2:00-2:50 p.m. 3:00-4:00 p.m. 4:00-5:00 p.m.		**To Obtain and Manage Inputs:** 1. Workshop facilities adequate to support learning Objectives. 2. Participants and instructor arrive on time, remain present and undistracted during scheduled time.

FIGURE 3.10 Strategic Project Management Workshop Design

Note how cells in the grid shown in Figure 3.11 integrate the project elements into a system through three types of directional logic:

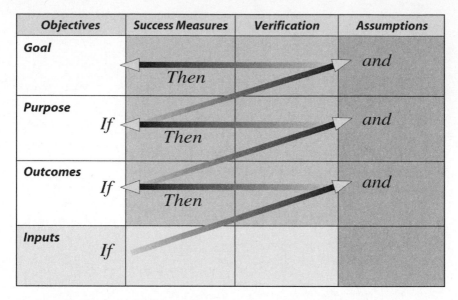

FIGURE 3.11   LogFrame Incorporates Multiple Types of Logic

1. *Vertical Logic* connects Objectives using If-Then thinking—so that our approach hangs together.
2. *Horizontal Logic* fleshes out Objectives at each level using Measures and Verifications—so we know how we are progressing.
3. *Zig-Zag Logic* pulls in Assumptions as we ratchet up the strategic hierarchy, using our now familiar If-Then thinking—so we can eliminate problems in advance.

Answering the Interrogatives

Take note of how the structure of the matrix elegantly incorporates answers to the standard "interrogative questions" like *who, what,* and *why*. Goal is the big picture program *why*, or the rationale for this and related projects supporting the broader strategy. Purpose is the project-specific *why*, or the reason for this particular effort. Outcomes are the *what* that we must produce. Inputs capture the *how, who* and *when*. (Figure 3.12 shows an Interrogative Chart.)

The interrogative concepts can help structure productive collaborative conversations between executive and project level staff, as this story shows. "Sheila" worked for a large, bureaucratic organization

Objectives	Success Measures	Verification	Assumptions
Goal **Why?**			
Purpose **Why?**			
Outcomes **What?**			
Inputs How? Who?	**When?**		

FIGURE 3.12   LogFrame Answers Interrogative Questions

and had an impressive background in corporate security. A month after attending one of my public seminars at UCLA's Technical Management Program, she called with the exciting news that she had been asked to head up a major corporate initiative to develop a security lessons-learned database for all employees. This project matched the sweet spot of her skill set. Sheila asked me to help her core team start smart by developing a LogFrame for this high visibility project. We scheduled a meeting.

But the week before, an angry Sheila called and read me a memo from headquarters essentially dictating the terms of her project. The memo specified that she would have a staff of two people, would finish within six months, and would deliver three interim milestones by specified dates.

She was justifiably upset at being micro-managed in an area where she was the expert. The notion that upper management could correctly identify what this project would require, without doing serious planning of the type advocated in this book, smacked of arrogance or ignorance as well as demoralized the implementers.

A suggestion to executives who define projects needs and then assign them to project teams: Communicate with project personnel so everyone understands and agrees upon the *whys* (Purpose and Goal).

Agree in general terms about the approach—the *what* (Outcomes)—then let the team figure out the *how*, *who*, and *when* (Inputs) as well as firm up the specific *what* it will take to deliver Purpose and Goal.

I never heard back about how Sheila's project went, but I can predict that it fell way short of what it could have been had there been productive dialogue between those who originated the idea and those who would make it happen.

A Rainbow of Applications

You now have previewed a potent planning process for designing projects of all types and sizes. Here are some work-related examples of projects that benefit from this approach:

- Preparing a strategic or operational plan for a company, division, or team
- Reorganizing a team and sharpening responsibilities
- Deciding how to implement new systems
- Evaluating and redirecting an ongoing project
- Reengineering a process to improve efficiency
- Conducting a paper study, or feasibility analysis
- Refining a rough concept into a proposal or action plan
- Analyzing a problem and developing a solution approach
- Planning new products and services from concept through delivery
- Organizing research and development
- Implementing initiatives identified through a balanced scorecard

This same thought process applies equally well to non-work and personal projects involving leisure, hobby, fitness, finance, family, and "honey-do's" around the house. Although the possibilities are endless, below are some additional ideas for the LogFrame use:

- Organizing church fund-raising events
- Managing a youth soccer team
- Turning your hobby into an online business
- Sharpening plans for professional development, learning, and career advancement

- Planning for promotion
- Writing and promoting a book
- Organizing a neighborhood Block Watch program
- Putting together a 25-year high school reunion
- Preparing for retirement
- Raising a loving and supportive family
- Completing an advanced degree part-time
- Remodeling your house
- Running for political office.

Key Points Review

1. The LogFrame tool provides a common framework, syntax, and vocabulary that equips your team to define and test the core strategic hypotheses of any project or plan:

$$\text{If A} \rightarrow \text{B, if B} \rightarrow \text{C, if C} \rightarrow \text{D; if D} \rightarrow \text{Bingo!}$$

2. Reduce problems early in the game by scrutinizing the Assumptions that are necessary for your strategic logic to be valid. While you can ignore Assumptions, you cannot ignore the impact of ignoring these Assumptions.

3. The four critical questions offer a simple and jargon-free way to learn and leverage the concepts in the LogFrame grid. These questions are inherently embedded in the LogFrame matrix, and answering those helps you cover all the important issues.

4. The Purpose level Objectives are the most essential because they describe the behavioral changes or conditions we aim for by delivering Outcomes.

5. The cells in the LogFrame grid connect in an integrated fashion using three directional types of logic.
    1. *Vertical Logic* connects Objectives using If-Then thinking.
    2. *Horizontal Logic* fleshes out Objectives at each level using Measures and Verifications.
    3. *Zig-Zag Logic* pulls in Assumptions, adding rigor to the If-Then thinking behind our strategy.

You may impress folks with your technical vocabulary, but if you want to speak the language of project success with your fellow team members, all concerned need to use the same vocabulary and the same logical framework. The four chapters in Part Two of this book will move you forward in learning this new language. As with any other language, to learn it you must use it. At first, you may speak haltingly and make mistakes. But by forming those new sounds, saying those new words, and thinking those new thoughts, they will soon become second-nature; and you'll gain the benefits that come from fluency in Strategic Project Management.

4

Aligning Projects With Strategic Intent

*The nice thing about not planning is that failure comes as a
complete surprise rather than being preceded by
a period of worry and depression.*

—Anonymous

Maybe you've seen the classic cartoon illustration depicting the joining of two turn-of-the-century railway lines—one stretching hundreds of miles from the West and the other stretching hundreds of miles from the East. Gathered together to celebrate, civil engineers, draftsmen, and linemen from both companies eagerly anticipate the great event of joining the last 30-foot section. But as the final rails are put in place, everyone is astonished and stopped dead in their tracks to see the tracks off-kilter by a ponderous 15 feet!

The team immediately scrambles to figure out where they got derailed. The draftsmen are seen arguing over their blueprints; the engineers hastily work their slide rules and transits; and the lineman crew bosses scratch their heads in bewilderment. How in the world did this happen? The argument continues, but one truth remains: Two sets of tracks stretch into the distance as far as the eye can see— but the twain shall not meet that day.

This disastrous railroad track metaphor exemplifies the "strategic disconnect" that often happens in organizations. One set of tracks represents the Strategic Plan built by the CEO and the executive leadership team. The other set of tracks represents the projects and processes intended to support the Strategic Plan. But as the cartoon shows, things don't always line up despite good intentions and smart, hardworking people on both sides.

This chapter explores ways to align your projects with strategic intent so you stay on track. We'll supplement the ideas introduced in the last chapter with a few other best-practice strategic planning concepts that can be used at any organizational level.

While the LogFrame is widely used on stand-alone projects, it adds particular value when applied to portfolios of projects. Even if your concern is with single projects, these ideas will help relate your project with your organization's larger themes.

To understand why disconnects happen, and how to reduce them, we will first briefly explore several aspects of strategy. I promise to keep this short because discussing strategy formation, cascading, and portfolio management can put even the most caffeine-buzzed person to sleep if the subject lingers too long.

Then I'll describe a "quick and clean" unit-level strategic planning process, and share how a client applied these concepts. As this case study will prove, time invested in smart early planning can produce breakthrough performance.

Strategy in a Nutshell

Conduct an online search at Amazon or Barnes & Noble for "strategy books" and you'll discover several thousand different publications. There are nearly as many different strategy variations as there are consultants who write books on the topic. But on the broadest levels, all the experts agree that strategy is what connects the present to the future.

Strategy is the particular means chosen to get from where you are to where you want to go, selected from multiple possibilities and reflecting your vision, mission, and values. An overall Strategy (big "S") usually consists of multiple strategic initiatives (small "s"), which are executed through programs, projects, and tasks.

While no list can be exhaustive, there exist some progressive and generic strategies with broad application. Several are, in fact, umbrella categories under which multiple specific strategies could be created. Consider how you might incorporate some of these progressive strategies for the twenty-first century:

- Flexibility (Southwest Airlines/Dell)
- Speed (FedEx)
- Horizontally Integrated—Related products/by-products (i.e., Arco's AM/PM Mini-Marts and ethanol plants)
- Networks and Alliances (Apple/IBM or Japanese Kiertsus)
- Value-Added—More Value for the Money (larger cereal boxes)
- Environmentally Improved/Green Products (i.e., solar heat; toxic waste clean-up)
- Mass Customization (Toyota)
- Simplification (Honda value analysis)
- Six Sigma (Motorola)
- Organizational Learning (GE, Peter Senge)
- Employee Morale/Family Benefits and Part-time Focus on Work (many firms)
- Management and Leadership Practices (GE)
- Outsourcing and Cottage Industries (many firms)
- Core Competencies — People, Technology, etc. (Sony)
- Market Tie-Ins/Preferred Customers (American Airlines)
- Cause-Related Marketing (McDonald's)
- Data Driven Marketing (Financial Services)
- Alternative Delivery Channels (Internet, Cisco)
- "Experiences " (Planet Hollywood, Adventure Travel)
- Value Chain Management (Wal-Mart)
- Social Networking (LinkedIn, Facebook)

Adapted from *Enhancing Your Strategic IQ* by Stephen Haines, Systems Thinking Press, © 2008. Used by permission.

Corporate strategy typically begins at the top and cascades down through strategic business units (SBUs) via a process of collective conversations that engage stakeholders in off-site retreats, negotiations, and meetings of all sorts. At the end of that process, the corporate strategy ends up as collections—or portfolios—of strategic initiatives. Programs and projects become the change vehicles for executing strategic intent.

My clients have applied LogFrame concepts in many different creative ways to support their organization's strategic and operational planning process. The concepts help formulate and document these vital conversations in a meaningful way. Use them as an adjunct to your existing strategic planning system.

Is Your Strategy Boxing You In?

But what determines whether a project is strategic or not? We recently reviewed a set of planning documents from a company that shall remain nameless. Believe it or not, they handled this determination with a simple check box on the proposed project form:

Is this a strategic project?

☐ Yes
☐ No

No further explanation was required or requested! But how did the proposer decide? Ouija board? Coin flip? Vested interest? Or was it solid analytic reasoning? My hunch is that this simplistic way of deciding boxed their organization in somewhere along the line.

My belief is that until you can describe how your project contributes to strategic intent—in clear and simple language—the chances of being right-on will be further off than those misaligned railroad tracks.

Fortunately, you now have a vocabulary for demonstrating clear connections—If-Then thinking. The language of strategic hypotheses offers a way to go beyond the jargon to show how proposed project Outcomes percolate up the chain and connect to a strategic Goal.

Try this: Take pen and paper and sketch out the logic for one of your projects. If you can't describe the If-Then links, you probably don't have a demonstrably strategic project.

As we'll soon see, Purpose is the lynch pin that connects project Objectives to strategic business Goals.

Juggling Portfolios and Programs

Project management is like juggling three balls—time, cost, and quality. Program management is like a troupe of circus performers standing in a circle, each juggling three balls and swapping balls from time to time.

—G. Reiss

Let's now turn to the way that corporate strategy is moved into project strategy via portfolio and program management.

Portfolio management involves screening candidate projects through a series of phases and gates, and funding those that appear to deliver the biggest benefit boom for the buck. In well-run companies like GE, it's a systematic and integrated system with smooth handoffs from corporate to business units to departments and functions. More commonly, it's an imperfect and choppy process with plenty of chances to drop the ball.

Admittedly, it's not always easy to align strategy elements with responsible organizational units. Nor is it simple to identify who owns and who supports what Objectives, as many involve multiple players.

Bits and pieces of overall strategy may be scattered among a variety of planning processes and documents, which miss the connective tissue. The logical fit that exists gets lost among the verbiage.

These plans, however, are seldom summarized in a single, succinct project strategy document. Planning may be ad hoc or use systems that are heavy on paperwork, but short on common goals or common sense, where confusion reigns. Many such systems roll on with a life of their own and serve the organization's bureaucracy, but aren't relevant or useful to line and project managers.

Some progressive organizations have added a one- or two-page LogFrame summary to long project proposals as a quick way to communicate intent. Others have added LogFrames into their Phase and Gate process.

There are better ways to cascade. Better ways would make the underlying logic crystal clear. If-Then language is well suited to do just that.

Grouping Projects by Common Purpose Themes

Any set of strategies involves multiple Objectives that can be set out in hierarchies that come together in some sort of a logical fashion. If they don't come together, that's an early warning of trouble coming!

As we saw in Chapter 2, Objectives Trees are a visual thinking tool which use If-Then logic to help us describe, develop, and test strategic relationships. These concepts can apply in multiple ways that are beneficial.

One example of using Objectives Tree at the program level by grouping is to group similar Purpose statements together. This greatly contributes to clarity in complicated situations.

Figure 4.1 shows a generic model in which the vision is supported by three major Goals, each with multiple Purposes. The case study below describes the practical power of "Purpose statements" to enhance corporate performance.

AEGON USA, a Fortune 500 company, is a major insurance holding company. After they acquired Transamerica and several other large insurance companies, they found themselves with overlapping

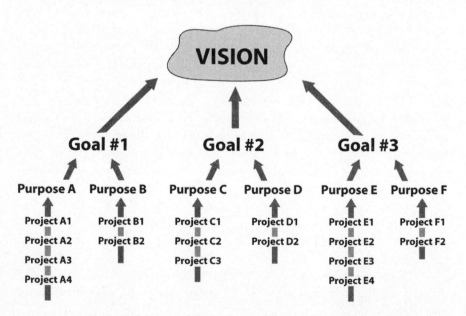

FIGURE 4.1 Objectives Tree Linking Projects to Vision

Technology Services divisions that they then needed to consolidate to reduce redundant services. AEGON identified 120 IT projects under way in several different locales, but the project plans lacked clarity and alignment with central strategies. Their geographically dispersed team members needed to collaborate, but their roles were unclear. After we trained their top 100 IT staff members in LogFrame planning methods, they put the tools to the test on their portfolios. In doing so, they discovered that most projects lacked clear Purpose statements—the *why* of the projects was not obvious.

After clarifying several Division Goals, a handful of common *Purpose themes* were identified. At that point, 120 projects were merged into 30 more meaningful projects that integrated the company's Goals with one another. Cross-connecting project teams were then organized around these Purpose themes. Working on larger puzzle pieces enabled them to standardize software, streamline help desks, consolidate over-lapping functions, and improve security. As a further result, communications improved, costs dropped, and service availability increased.

Every strategic thrust can be described and linked both up and down using If-Then language. This type of analysis can augment Goal cascading and portfolio management. When cascading is done by organization units without explicit causal relationships having been made clear somewhere in the process, the basic connecting threads and logic get lost. As a result, comments like the following are common from project managers: "We have a 40-page list of project tasks and no one has any idea of what we are trying to accomplish." This is a serious problem that is fixable when using top-down thinking and logical clustering.

Managing Multiple Bottom Lines

You can't win a game when you don't know how to keep score. Sports would be boring if there were no way of tracking who was winning.

How do *you* keep score? What's on your strategic scoreboard? What do you, your colleagues, your boss, and your boss's boss pay attention to? The ultimate test of any strategy is how well it delivers the measurable expectations we have in mind.

What gets measured gets managed. What you pay attention to and are able to manage, of course, varies by your job function, level, and responsibilities.

We all know what Measures command the most attention in most organizations: Financials and budgets. These are essential, no doubt, but if the strategies are not right, how much money is being left on the table? And what is being neglected that will eventually make the financials turn red?

The USDA food group chart reminds us to eat from a variety of food categories to stay healthy because excess reliance on just one category can make you sick. In a similar fashion, focusing attention on primarily the quarterly numbers can create organizational indigestion unless tempered with a long-term, big-picture focus. Many an executive has skimped on investing in research or training because it was perceived that these would not produce meaningful benefits in the upcoming quarters. Those myopic executives reasoned that by the time such investments bore fruit, they'd be out of there!

Contemporary management literature describes bottom lines, triple bottom lines, balanced score cards, and quadruple bottom lines. Let's up the ante by proposing a five-category model called "The Quintuple Bottom Line." The five Measures at the heart of this comprehensive model are:

1. *Financial Goals/Measures*—Rate of return, profits, sales growth, cash flow, savings, and compound Measures such as revenue per passenger mile (a key airline standard).
2. *Customer Goals/Measures*—Numbers, increases, type, quality, satisfaction, value-added, churn, and so on.
3. *Operational Effectiveness Goals/Measures*—Context specific, critical performance indicators (e.g., hotel occupancy, mean time between failure, and efficiency ratios).
4. *Employee Goals/Measures*—Number, skills growth, turnover, longevity, mix, satisfaction, and culture values-orientation.
5. *Community Goals/Measures*—Impact or involvement on local community (e.g. blood drives and United Way).

Not all Measures have equal importance at all levels. While the CEO keeps an eye peeled on all of these categories, your emphasis may be more selective.

Much of my consulting requests come from clients seeking practical ways to leverage their work unit's performance. These requests don't always come from the CEO. Plenty of motivated mid-level leaders want strategic tune-ups. So, here is an approach we have found valuable to sharpen strategy and create executable action plans for any organizational level.

Quick and Clean Strategic Planning at Any Level

In a perfect world, the organization planning process would deliver—on a silver platter no less—your menu of Goals, strategies, projects already cleanly sliced and diced and ready for action.

But in practice, leaders must often create that clarity themselves by applying a version of portfolio management at their own organization unit level.

This chapter section features a case study of a client organization committed to improving their performance and productivity by doing just that. Their actual work products are included to illustrate how this method adds value. As you read, consider how their approach could bring clarity in your situation.

While the exact steps are tailored to each case, implementation generally involves a series of well-designed and facilitated action-planning workshops of one or more days spread over several weeks. The process draws on existing plans and documents and is fully compatible with—and provides ways to operationalize—the formal planning requirements of virtually any organization. And if your company's process is messy—well, this practical process is quick and clean.

The portfolio concept applies at all organization levels. After all, doesn't your own work unit manage a portfolio of projects that shifts over time? And doesn't your own work (as well as life itself) consist of an ever-changing portfolio of Goal-seeking projects?

Hands-On Planning Example in a National Lab

The Los Alamos National Laboratory (LANL) is an 8,000-person research institute in New Mexico spread out over a rugged mountainous area. LANL's vision is to be the premiere organization in the world applying science to the solution of technical problems critical to national and global security.

Their multiple missions include: (1) To provide the core material science and technology base needed to maintain confidence in the safety and reliability of the nation's nuclear weapons; (2) to apply technical expertise to address a broad range of national security needs in energy, environment, infrastructure and conventional defense; and (3) to research materials to create new knowledge and lay the foundations for new technologies.

The LANL Geographic Information Service (GIS) team was comprised of 20 key players who provide various LANL customers with a variety of sophisticated maps, including topographic maps as well as specialized maps showing vegetation patterns, underground hydrology, wildlife, etc. These maps are not pulled off-the-shelf, but custom-created according to customer specifications.

The importance of GIS services became clear during the Cerro Grande wildfire that raced across the lab, burning 400 homes and threatening critical Lab facilities. GIS was quickly called into 24-hour operation and their maps helped emergency teams manage the fast-breaking situation. While the team delivered the necessary help through heroic efforts, the experience revealed serious short-comings in how they operated.

They recognized the urgent need to improve because in the future, GIS information will be critical to protect the groundwater, potentially threatened by a legacy of buried nuclear wastes.

Eight Logical Planning Steps

The following steps offer a logical game plan for unit level strategic planning and execution. They derive from my experience assisting hundreds of teams in diverse organizations worldwide. The first seven steps get things going, the eighth keeps things rolling with periodic strategic updates. As we walk through each step, consider how you might follow a similar path with your own collection of projects.

Step 1. Clarify the Planning Context and Issues

Begin with a basic question—What are your primary motivations and desired Outcomes from the planning process? To strengthen team-work? Shift directions? Attract new customers? Improve procedures? Get the boss off your back? Multiple Outcomes are possible. Define yours at the start.

Identify the boundaries of your effort by identifying the "system" for which you are doing the plan. Intact units are not the only choices—the system of interest could be a cross-functional group, a technology initiative, or various other configurations. (Sometimes it helps to define what is *not* included in your system of interest.)

The system of interest may thread through multiple organizations. On another project, I assisted the U.S. Advanced Simulation and Computing program (ASC) in developing a national strategic plan for supercomputer development. Their system of interest encompassed a broad network, which wove through parts of many different organizations and required integrating multiple planning documents with related technology blueprints.

GIS leaders Dr. John Huchton and his deputy Dr. Steve Koch had attended the Strategic Project Management seminar I conduct at the Los Alamos Management Institute, and immediately saw the applicability of the concepts. Dr. Huchton's primary Outcome was to make the unit operationally self-sufficient so that he could move elsewhere in the Lab. This meant putting in place action plans consistent with recently developed division and group plans, which were understood and supported by motivated, effective teams.

Step 2. Involve Key Players

Getting input from all key players is crucial. Because people support what they help create, you need to involve all key parties who have a stake in the process and its results. Begin by identifying and connecting with key internal and external stakeholders (customers in particular) to identify their concerns and needs. Many of these will translate into issues to tackle head-on, or at least to have on your radar.

Many different involvement roles are possible (e.g., giving input and opinions, joining planning team meetings, reviewing interim results, getting briefed on final results, and so on). Obtaining input can be as simple as meeting over a cup of coffee or it may involve structured focus groups and customer surveys.

Step 3. Scan Your Environment

Scanning your environment begins with examining all relevant business units' plans as well as those of your key outside organizations and your customer base. In most cases, there is no single guiding master document. Vital pieces may be scattered across numerous documents. Review these in order to extract Objectives and highlight those efforts that relate to yours. Without doing so, it's like leaving a puzzle with a missing part and expecting it to be a complete design.

If appropriate, conduct an external environmental scan of some sort to identify trends, events, and drivers that influence your future directions. This is often done at an enterprise-level.

Broad-brush scans of the larger environment examine the big picture and change factors that may impact your plans. This wide-angle scan seeks to identify the SKEPTIC factors—Societal, K(C)ompetitive, Economic/Environmental, Political, Technological, Industrial and Consumer/Client (adapted from the Haines Centre ABC Model)—and any change blips on the radar which may impact your project during its life. This broad-brush scan is often done during a larger strategic planning process and is optional for individual projects.

GIS leaders examined the Division and Laboratory documents and highlighted Objectives to which their team might contribute. They reviewed documents and extracted a list of some 15 Objectives, which would be turned into strategies by the larger team during the hands-on action workshops.

Steps three through seven involve bringing together the core team (including key technical and administrative staff), in a workshop setting. Agendas for these sessions are custom-designed, and provide skills training followed by application to the identified issues. The GIS project agenda consisted of a concentrated two-day RAP (Rapid Action Planning) workshop for all staff with a one-day follow-up six weeks later.

For best results in this process, engage a skilled external consultant. An outside facilitator who is expert in action-planning workshop design and facilitation keeps the process moving. Choose a consultant who is a process expert, not a content expert. "Outside" may also mean someone who is an internal organization consultant with the right skills, but is not part of the immediate group.

Step 4. Revisit Your Vision/Mission/Values

Why should a team develop their own vision, mission, and value statements (VMV) when these already exist for the parent organization?

The reason is simple: Consciously choosing and shaping their own unit-level VMVs lets people better appreciate how what they do delivers real value to their customers and to each other.

For most employees, it's not easy to identify how their individual efforts contribute to critical high level missions such as, in this case, stewardship of the nuclear stock pile. There is a huge gap between such a broad mission and their day-to-day work. But writing home-grown, localized statements stimulates rich discussion, which usually leads to stronger engagement and personal commitment. Group-level Mission and Vision statements, of course, must derive from and support the larger organization statements.

Vision can be defined as *what we wish to see in the future that we can affect*; and Mission defined as *how we will get there*.

GIS Vision (What We Want to See)
Decision-makers use GIS-provided information in making informed decisions that support good environmental steward-ship of the LANL reservation.

GIS Mission (How We Will Get There)
Efficiently provide various decision-makers with GIS-related maps and information that meet their needs.

Note that the connecting logic between Mission and Vision is a direct causal relationship and a linked operational hypothesis that says, "*If* we efficiently *provide* information, *then* GIS decision-makers can *use* the information."

Values are given lip-service and glossed over in many companies because they seem a given, or because values seem fluffy, or because even discussing them may feel awkward. Again, the benefit is to make these come alive with meaning for those involved. Values discussions deserve time—especially for new groups just getting their bearings are those aiming to shift operations norms.

Beginning from Lab-wide values, the GIS team crafted a set of agreed upon values that would become their operating norms in delivering Vision/Mission as well as for making GIS a great place to work. Their list of one dozen included:

- Take responsibility
- Continuously improve
- Have fun

- Focus on the customer
- Respect each other
- Strive for excellence

A further refinement of values involves defining the specific behaviors that constitute the spirit of the value. What, for example, does "respect each other" mean on a day-to-day basis? Converting these into a set of observable behaviors (we "do-this" but "don't do this") builds a shared code of conduct that translates into improved interpersonal behavior and operational effectiveness. Exercises like this generate enormous energy and enthusiasm and build a high-performance, customer-oriented culture.

Step 5. Sharpen Your Goals and Measures

You can't manage what you can't measure. The measurement discussion is one of the most enlightening any group can have. Success Measures at the until level usually concentrate in one or more of the big five areas. They are chosen to reflect the key Goals that, when achieved, optimize the group's value-adding contributions to their customers' Goals.

GIS-selected key success Measures incorporated their mission, vision, and values; and thus, they turned these concepts into operational tools—not just verbal window dressing. Five clusters of Measures were chosen, along with specific indicators for each. (See box on next page.)

These Measures resemble the well-known balanced scorecard approach, which includes customer, employee and key internal operational Measures. Balanced scorecards, however, usually ignore VMV Measures and are seldom strategic in their derivation. But the major difference that makes this process so potent comes in the next step.

Step 6. Develop Core Strategies

This is the most creative part—coalescing the various Goals into a manageable set of strategies which collectively deliver the measurable

GIS Success Measures

1. Customer satisfaction with quality of GIS products and services (reflects GIS Vision and customers).
   • Increased percent of customers rate as "excellent"
   • Growing number of requests from current customers
   • Increased number of new customers
2. Efficiently provide our customers with needed services and products (reflects GIS Mission and customers).
   • Reasonable cost to deliver various products
   • Meet promised schedule a certain percent of the time
3. Greater team cohesiveness, effectiveness, and living our values (reflects employee values).
   • Reduced voluntary turnover
   • Increased staff morale
4. Effective and consistent utilization of best practices change (reflects key operational needs).
   • Increased percent of projects use standard conduct of operations
   • Ability to accurately predict time/cost to deliver a GIS map
5. Increased Division and Laboratory awareness of GIS Team services and products (reflect customers).
   • Increased number of senior-level managers and possible users who are aware

results. Developing strategies is as much art as science, requiring thoughtfully organized Objectives into meaningful and manageable clusters.

There seldom exists a one-to-one relationship between Goals and strategies, which is partially because of inconsistent language use and because an Outcome for the CEO may be a Goal for those lower in the hierarchy. The preliminary list of 15 GIS Objectives pulled from various documents was blended into a set of eight strategies. (When terminology and perspective differences are reconciled, different Objectives statements from various documents often collapse into one Strategy.)

Chosen strategies should provide solutions to current problems and build future capacity.

In this case, GIS team member skill levels varied widely and employees used very different approaches to providing customers with maps. Some approaches were effective and time-efficient, while others were ad hoc and inefficient. There were few standard procedures, so they could not model best practice. As a result, *Conduct of Operations* became the top priority new strategy.

A related problem was that team members worked in geographically dispersed customer premises and seldom were physically together. Team cohesion and knowledge-sharing were low. So, *Team Networking* emerged as a vital strategy to strengthen team bonds. These two examples show how *analysis of problems leads to shaping specific solution strategies.*

GIS described their eight core strategies with a short title and brief elaboration.

1. *Conduct of Operations*—Improve formality of team operations and standardize procedures.
2. *Team Networking*—Improve team dynamics through periodic get-togethers and networking with colleagues.
3. *Continuous Process Improvement*—Continually improve team processes and services.
4. *Marketing*—Enhance team visibility and expand the customer base via web pages and information programs.
5. *Customer Feedback*—Monitor customer satisfaction through surveys and analysis of lessons learned.
6. *Customer Education*—Educate customers about the products and services we offer.
7. *Data of Known Accuracy and Lineage*—Ensure that maps have appropriate meta-data tags attached so customers are aware of limitations.
8. *Employee Development*—Enhance development of skills through formal and informal means.

Now comes the pay-off step: *Analyzing strategies in relationship to Success Measures.* This insightful step helps you zoom in on the right set of strategies for maximum impact on Measures. The Strategies-Measures matrix offers a new lens to analyze what matters most—leading to thoughtful iteration, and refinement to uncover hidden synergy.

The generic form of this matrix is shown in Figure 4.2, while Figure 4.3 shows the matrix with the GIS Measures and strategies.

KEY SUCCESS MEASURES	CORE STRATEGIES						
	1.	2.	3.	4.	5.	6.	7.
1. Financial: · ·							
2. Customers: · ·							
3. Operational Effectiveness: · ·							
4. Employee: · ·							
5. Community: · ·							

FIGURE 4.2   Generic Format of the Strategies-Measures Matrix

KEY SUCCESS MEASURES	CORE STRATEGIES							
	1. Conduct of Operation	2. Team Networking	3. Continuous Process Improvement	4. Marketing	5. Customer Feedback	6. Customer Education	7. Data of Known Accuracy & Lineage	8. Employee Development
1. Customer Satisfaction with quality of GIS products and services								
2. Efficiently provide our customers with needed services and products								
3. Greater team cohesiveness, and living our values								
4. Effective and consistent utilization of best practices								
5. Increased Division and Lab awareness of Team services and products								

FIGURE 4.3   GIS Strategies-Measures Matrix

✓✓ = Major Impact   ✓ = Some Impact

KEY SUCCESS MEASURES	CORE STRATEGIES							
	1. Conduct of Operation	2. Team Networking	3. Continuous Process Improvement	4. Marketing	5. Customer Feedback	6. Customer Education	7. Data of Known Accuracy & Lineage	8. Employee Development
1. Customer Satisfaction with quality of GIS products and services	✓✓	✓	✓✓		✓	✓		
2. Efficiently provide our customers with needed services and products		✓		✓	✓	✓		
3. Greater team cohesiveness, and living our values	✓		✓				✓	✓
4. Effective and consistent utilization of best practices	✓✓		✓			✓	✓	
5. Increased Division and Lab awareness of Team services and products				✓✓	✓			

FIGURE 4.4   Testing the Impact of Strategies on Measures

In Figure 4.4, checkmarks in the matrix cells show the estimated degree of impact of each strategy on each Success Measure. The matrix provoked valuable discussion and helped them converge on the optimum set of strategies to deliver Measures throughout the project life cycle. The chosen cluster of GIS strategies would increase current effectiveness while also building future capacity.

After completing their work on a much-erased and rewritten whiteboard, the team reached a consensus conclusion and celebrated out loud: "We are covered!"

If you develop a Strategy-Measures matrix like this example, you'll establish a strong framework for achieving superior performance and delivering outstanding customer value.

Step 7. Turn Strategies Into Execution Plans

With a coherent set of strategies defined, the next step was creating action plans and building unified implementation teams, both of which can occur simultaneously when using the Logical Framework tool.

During the first GIS workshop, participants learned how to use the LogFrame and then formed sub-teams of two or three people to begin developing plans for each strategy. The LogFrame helped members to wrap their minds around a complex issue and develop a solid plan. Between the first and second workshops, they met on their own to continue the work. Six weeks later, these preliminary project designs were brought back for consultant review during a one-day follow-up workshop.

A copy of Conduct of the Operations Logical Frameworks strategy can be found in the Appendix (You can view the GIS Team Networking design on the web site *www.ManagementPro.com*).

The LogFrame, of course, can be used on its own for discrete projects or strategies without going through the prior strategic planning steps.

Implementing new strategy involves change to create the future. But at the same time, today's operational work must get done. To avoid overwhelming the teams, GIS prioritized and staggered the start of each strategy rather than initiating them all at once. "Strategy owners" volunteered to manage each strategy. Two new "strategy starts" per quarter were scheduled, as shown in Figure 4.5, the implementation matrix.

The hands-on approach generated a strong sense of ownership, which translated into implementation momentum. A couple of months after the workshops, Dr. John Huchton felt comfortable that GIS was self-sufficient and took another Lab position as planned. The workshop products gave the new leadership team the

KEY SUCCESS MEASURES	CORE STRATEGIES							
	1. Conduct of Operation	2. Team Networking	3. Continuous Process Improvement	4. Marketing	5. Customer Feedback	6. Customer Education	7. Data of Known Accuracy & Lineage	8. Employee Development
Strategy Owner	Ortega	Red Star	Bennett	Koch	Gebhardt	Oudejans	Woodward	McKown
1st Quarter	✓	✓						
2nd Quarter			✓		✓			
3rd Quarter				✓				✓
4th Quarter						✓	✓	

FIGURE 4.5 Prioritizing for Implementation: Project Starts

foundation needed to smoothly take over and manage the program successfully.

Achieving organization excellence is an ongoing process, not a one-shot workshop event.

Step 8. Follow Up and Continue the Process

Build an annual implementation calendar that includes periodic review and refinement. Update your project plans as conditions change. By intelligently linking this with other processes and systems, you will establish your own practical strategic management system and harvest the fruit of exceptional performance.

Management consultants like me get warm and fuzzy feelings when a client letter comes out of the blue and reports a success story. GIS team member Tony Tagliaferro made these observations in an e-mail sent to me a year later.

> During these workshops, the folks in the GIS group came together and focused on a specific direction. We had become overwhelmed and disillusioned by the weight of the organization and allowed the bureaucracy to make us feel powerless and not able to get things done. But after the workshop, we felt empowered and in control. Our perception of upper management improved and things went smoother. We worked better as a team. Our morale and performance improved dramatically.

Tony's letter confirmed what a motivated group of men and women can do when given the right tools and empowered to shape their destiny. The LogFrame tools you'll learn to use in the chapters that follow will help you create and enjoy successful solutions for you, your team, and your customers. The process may get bumpy at times, but it's worth it to get the right ingredients in place to smooth out your system.

Key Points Review

1. The LogFrame can be the cornerstone of any unit-level management system. However, this presumes that there is a sound, overarching strategy to begin with. Since this is not always true, use the Quick and Clean planning steps.

Summary of Quick and Clean Strategic Planning Steps

1. *Clarify the Planning Context and Issues*—Be clear about your expected planning Outcomes and identify current issues to include.
2. *Involve Key Players*—Decide who to involve in your process to build buy-in and stay-in.
3. *Scan Your Environment*—Identify what's changing in your environment; and analyze division and department plans to extract Goals your group shares or owns.
4. *Revisit Your Vision/Mission/Values*—Turn these "fluff" statements into high-performance tools that energize staff and build shared commitment.
5. *Sharpen Your Goals and Measures*—Develop a meaningful performance scorecard that identifies how you deliver customer value.
6. *Develop Core Strategies*—Turn Goals into strategies, and test those strategies for impact against Measures to ensure smart choices.
7. *Turn Strategies into Executable Plans*—Using the Logical Framework. Let the responsible players flesh out implementation plans.
8. *Follow Up and Continue the Process*—Build momentum by reviewing and updating the plans while strengthening the planning process itself.

2. To add clarity to large or confusing portfolios, group projects by their Goal and Purpose. Projects with no clear Purposes are candidates for elimination.
3. Be clear about the Measures that matter in your organization unit. Pick meaningful Measures guided by the Quintuple Bottom Line categories.
4. Strong benefits come from developing a strategy and Measures matrix.

This Part One overview, should give you an initial understanding of how Strategic Project Management concepts add value. The four chapters in Part Two drill down to explore the Four Critical Strategic Questions in detail, and illustrate how to apply them at the project level.

Part Two

Mastering the Four Critical Strategic Questions

The LogFrame matrix (see Figure II.1) organizes the answers to these four questions in relationship to each other. Each provides pieces of the project puzzle solution.

The following four chapters explore how these four questions work together as an integrated thinking system. By understanding them at a deeper level you can use them to the fullest extent.

- *Chapter 5* explores *Question #1* and guides you in defining and aligning project Objectives. Linking your project clearly to the corporate-level Objectives builds a strong foundation to get you to the results you want.
- *Chapter 6* addresses *Question #2* and assists you in pinning down what success means. Being able to describe what success looks like in advance grounds your project in the real world and shapes agreement.
- *Chapter 7* answers *Question #3* and leads you through a process to identify and reduce risk. After you clarify major Assumptions, you can then evaluate their validity and adjust your project as needed to avoid anticipatable problems.
- *Chapter 8* discusses *Question #4* and helps you flesh out the work plan tasks, budget, and schedule. By answering the prior three questions you increase confidence that these action steps will deliver the end results you need.

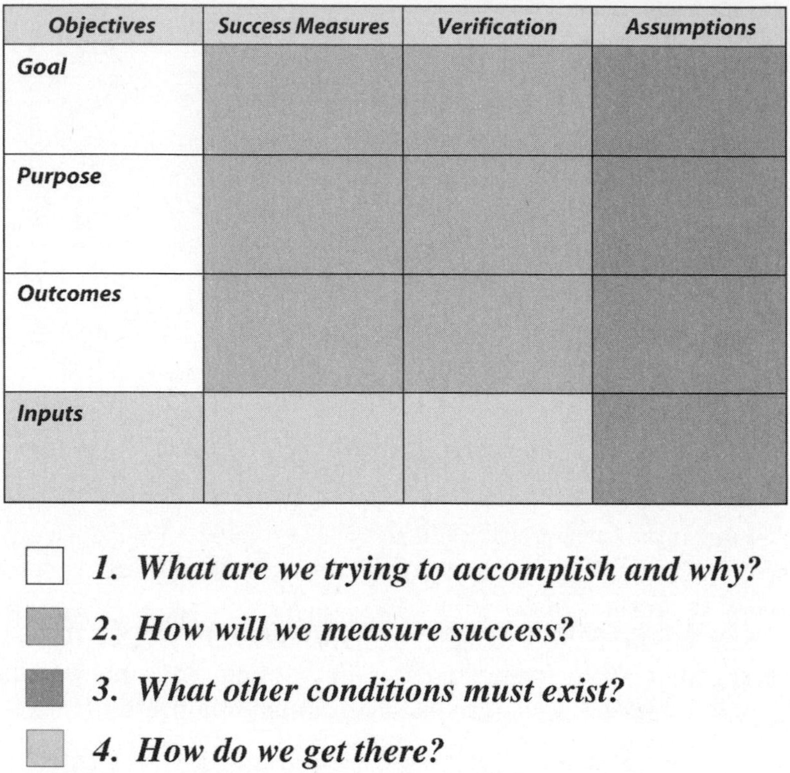

Objectives	Success Measures	Verification	Assumptions
Goal			
Purpose			
Outcomes			
Inputs			

☐ *1. What are we trying to accomplish and why?*

▨ *2. How will we measure success?*

▮ *3. What other conditions must exist?*

▢ *4. How do we get there?*

FIGURE II.1   The LogFrame Matrix Organizes Answers to Critical
Strategic Questions

These simple questions provide powerful ways to guide your team's discussion and concentrate your attention on what matters most in designing and implementing your project.

5

Question #1—What Are We Trying to Accomplish and Why?

Management by Objectives works—if you know the Objectives.
Ninety percent of the time you don't.

—Peter Drucker

Define and Align Objectives

Objectives	Success Measures	Verification	Assumptions
Goal			
Purpose			
Outcomes			
Inputs			

FIGURE 5.1 The LogFrame Matrix Helps Organize Objectives in Relationship to Each Other

Shoot for the Moon

In 1962, President John F. Kennedy committed the United States to landing a man on the moon and returning him safely by the end of the decade. America's grandest achievement was realized in July 1969 when Apollo 11 completed man's first lunar landing. This was also a grand moment for me, the youngest accredited reporter at Cape Canaveral covering this historic event for a Seattle underground hippie newspaper, *The Helix*. Barely old enough to shave, I sat in the wooden press bleachers among a row of journalists from the world's leading publications, including *Time* Magazine, *Le Monde*, the *New York Times* . . . and *The Helix*!

The evening before launch, the press was escorted to just 50 yards from the majestic Saturn V launch vehicle. Being so near this 363-foot tall triumph of technology and imagination bathed in bright Xenon spotlights made me proud to live in a nation with such a daring vision and go-for-it spirit.

The countdown proceeded through the night and into the next morning until the final seconds . . . 3-2-1. *Ignition!* The massive engines erupted in a fiery plume and the rocket slowly ascended. Even from the press bleachers, two miles away from the launch pad, you could feel the air pulsating from the powerful Saturn first stage engines. I still get goose bumps recalling the thrill of take-off as the press cheered with excitement; and Dr. Wernher von Braun, watching his dream take flight shouted, "*Go baby go!*"

Kennedy's bold challenge came during the Cold War, the global psychological-political game that the United States seemed to be losing. In 1957, the Soviet Union surprised the world by orbiting Sputnik 1, a three-pound basketball-sized satellite that shocked America into action. Though Kennedy called landing on the moon his Goal, his true intention was a higher, unspoken Objective. Landing on the moon would demonstrate the superiority of the Western system and help the United States win the Cold War. Figure 5.2 shows this progression in an If-Then chart.

Why is this example significant? Because behind every project rests a higher level motivation of interest to senior leaders. This Objective often gets lost in the hand-off and may not be obvious to those doing the work. If you are a project manager, it's helpful

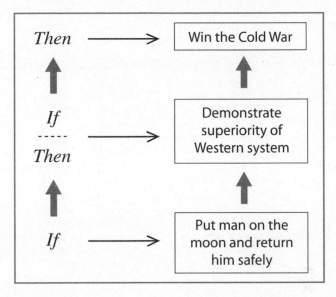

FIGURE 5.2   From Landing on the Moon to Winning the Cold War

to understand the Purpose and the Goal so that you can more intelligently deliver the Outcomes that will get you there. If you are a senior executive, make sure the Purpose is clear, so that project teams aim their efforts towards Purpose achievement—not just Outcome delivery. The LogFrame's Objectives column helps line up project Objectives so they mesh with the broader corporate strategy.

Linking Objectives Into Logical Levels

Whether you aim for the moon or someplace closer to home, making the logical links explicit builds the business case. Making the linkages clear is especially valuable in emergent or initiated-from-the-middle projects when you have to sell your ideas to others or get funding.

The Logical Framework tool helps distinguish and link multiple project Objectives. The right column in Figure 5.3 elaborates on previous LogFrame definitions.

Level of Objective	Definition	Elaboration
Goal ⬆	The higher-level big picture strategic or program Objective to which the project contributes.	• This is the 10,000-foot helicopter view. • Overarching umbrella for multiple projects. • Anchors project to strategic intent.
Purpose ⬆	The impact or behavior change we anticipate by doing the project; the expected result of producing the Outcomes.	• Desired change expected after Outcomes produced. • "Linking pin" Objective that's usually missing.
Outcomes ⬆	The specific results that the project team must deliver by managing Inputs.	• Deliverables, end products, and processes we can manage. • Team held responsible for delivering Outcomes.
Inputs	The activities and tasks we undertake and the resources necessary to produce Outcomes.	• Implementation plan and schedule. • Project management software helpful here.

FIGURE 5.3   Linking Multiple Objectives Into Logical Levels

Again, our strategic shorthand (reading the Objectives from bottom to top) is:

- *If* Inputs, *Then* Outcomes
- *If* Outcomes, *Then* Purpose
- *If* Purpose, *Then* Goal.

In any context, Objectives at an even higher level than the Goal may also exist. The standard LogFrame format includes just four levels, but you can add additional levels to tie the project into a high-level Objective or more clearly illuminate the If-Then logic. Call this higher Objective a super-Goal, vision, or whatever term you prefer. (I have field-tested terminology variations and concluded that substituting Outcomes over the original term Outputs enhances understanding and makes it easier to dovetail LogFrames with systems thinking terminology.)

Feel free to tailor the LogFrame structure to fit your needs. What's important is to have clear meanings for all of your terms as well as to pressure-test the integrity of the If-Then logic.

Avoid the Muddle of Messy Meaning

A Human Resources (HR) department needed to align their goals with a headquarters-issued set of ten overarching Goals. Unfortunately, each of these ten Goals was accompanied by "Success Measures" and several "sub-Goals." But there was no rhyme, reason, nor meaningful distinction among the three terms. It was a hodgepodge.

Sub-Goals (or anything lower in the casual chain) should be the *means* to Goals, (the *"If"* of the higher level *"Then"*), while Measures should describe conditions that will exist when those Goals are met. The muddled use of terms made aligning HR Goals with them impossible. Make sure that everyone speaks the same language by agreeing on what your key terms mean and using then in a consistent way.

Task Force Start-Up

A team of scientists from the Los Alamos National Laboratory (LANL) and Sandia National Laboratories (SNL) faced the daunting task of organizing a task force of experts to solve a critical national security problem. This Offsite Recovery Project (OSRP) needed to find a permanent disposal site for some 20,000 "sealed-sources." These small, neutron-emitting radioactive sources had been issued to universities and private companies for research, medical diagnostics, and geological exploration.

Many sealed-sources were no longer needed for their original mission, but there was no convenient process for their owners to safely dispose of them. Some had actually been found abandoned in sheds and landfills—posing a serious health, safety, and security hazard. The really scary part was that, in the wrong hands, they could be used to make dirty bombs.

Since these were considered to be civilian rather than military waste products, they could not be buried in existing disposal sites because of bureaucratic constraints. Thus, a new site would have to be found somewhere in a state willing to accept them—not an easy task. In addition, no disposal standards existed for this class of device, so new standards would have to be developed as part of the project and be approved by the Nuclear Regulatory Commission.

The OSRP study team included multiple players from other national research laboratories and from the private sector. A robust planning approach was crucial, given the wide variety of perspectives among the strong-minded, opinionated players as well as the technical and political complexity of the problem itself.

Some serious institutional barriers and competitive issues needed to be overcome before productive work could begin.

The project director chose the Logical Framework tool to get a smooth start. This common language helped a diverse team work together to unravel a complex problem into solvable chunks; and it put a spotlight on some of the critical external factors shaping the success of this Assumptions-driven project. Their initial LogFrame plan served to shape a common vision and guide the process of defining the task details necessary to achieve the Goal. They added a fifth level to their LogFrame to show the cause-effect ripples of their strategy up to an important national Goal.

In the Objectives column of their initial LogFrame shown in Figure 5.4, note the verbs in bold.

Be assured that by the time you read this book, the most dangerous sealed-sources will be in safe hands. We'll return to this example in the next chapter to show how the team added Measures to their Objectives. (This project's complete LogFrame can be viewed at *www.ManagementPro.com*.)

The main value this process added to the OSRP team was the ability to keep sight of the higher level Objectives and avoid prematurely jumping to solution-finding before understanding the full dimensions of the problem.

Turning a Problem Into a Set of Objectives

A problem is simply a project in disguise. Projects masquerading as problems must first be converted into Objectives before advancing to solutions. Spend some time carefully diagnosing the problem because

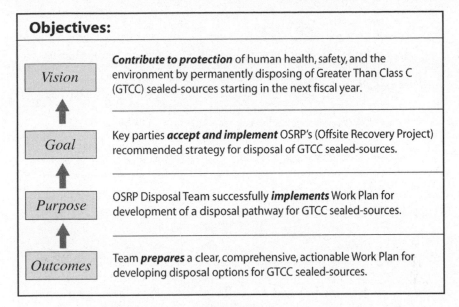

FIGURE 5.4   The OSRP's Hierarchy of Objectives

the way you define it shapes the range of solution options. Don't get sucked in by an over-simplified definition, catch phrase, or symptom. Get at the root causes. Find the right problem to solve.

A classic story, first told by systems thinker Russell Ackoff, proves the point that unless you zoom in on the right problem, you risk solving the wrong problem. Tenants in an aging 20-story Chicago office building complained about the long wait for elevators in the lobby. Karen, the owner of the building, was worried that her small business tenants would move to a newer space. Consequently, she hired a consulting engineer to solve the slow elevator problem. The elevator was too old for upgrading, so the consultant recommended a new elevator system. The owner gulped at the $300,000 price tag—fearing that she could not increase rents to cover the cost without losing tenants.

Fortunately, Karen got a second opinion from a different consultant. Rather than automatically accepting the problem as "The elevators are too slow," this creative consultant suggested that the real problem was that "Tenants get bored while waiting." His recommended solution: Entertain and distract tenants so they wouldn't mind the long wait. Following his advice, the owner renovated the

Solution #1 Objectives	Solution #2 Objectives
Goal: Keep tenants happy	*Goal:* Keep tenants happy
Purpose: Reduce wait time	*Purpose:* Keep tenants from boredom while waiting
Outcomes: New elevator installed	*Outcomes:* Lobby renovated
Inputs: Install elevator @ $300,000	*Inputs:* Install monitor and mirrors @ $30,000

FIGURE 5.5   Two Alternate Solutions to Reach Goal

lobby, installed television monitors tuned to CNN, and mounted mirrors by each elevator so people could preen themselves. Problem solved at a fraction of the cost. Total cost: $30,000. The tenants enjoyed the upgrade at a cost the landlord could afford and everyone was happy.

This story illustrates two very different strategies to reach the same Goal, as illustrated in LogFrame language in Figure 5.5. Problems usually look different through the eyes of different stakeholders. To zoom in on the right problem to solve, get alternate points of view. State the problem in different ways, and examine its various facets. Try inverting each problem statement into an Objective.

Stakeholder collaboration during problem analysis builds shared understanding, generates better solution approaches, and greases the skids for smoother execution.

Ask Your Stakeholders

- What do you see as the problem?
- Why is this a problem and for whom?
- What causes the problem?
- What are the consequences if we ignore the problem?
- How will you know when the problem is gone?
- What benefits will a solution bring?
- What might an ideal solution look like?

Many proven problem analysis methodologies are available, such as the well-known Fishbone Analysis, the Five Why Questions, basic TQM tools, LEAN Value Stream Mapping, and Six Sigma processes. No matter which methodology you use, it pays to involve your stakeholders early and often in problem identification and analysis.

Terry's Tips for Clear Objectives

Apply these proven tips to make your Objectives stand up straight and salute.

Tip #1. Select Just the Right Words

Precise language leads to clear Objectives. While your project Objectives may already be described in a work scope or corporate memo, their clarity and quality of the logic behind them can vary tremendously. Some are coherent, while others seem to have been written while under the influence.

Take any given set of Objectives as a starting point only. As you wrap your mind around the situation, you may find that a subtle restatement captures the underlying intent much better. Brainstorm multiple possibilities. Since brainstorming is an imperfect process, your possibility list needs to be reviewed and reworked. Before solidifying which words best describe your Objectives, generate a dozen different answers to Question #1: *What are we trying to accomplish and why?* Experiment by choosing different words and sense their nuances. Savor various wordings, rolling phrases around in your mind—sensing any sour, bitter, or bland constructs with an aim to crystallize and sweeten them for the benefit of all.

Here's the key to well-formed Objectives: State each Objective in a sentence or phrase using chosen verbs and descriptive phrases. Selecting just the right words is as important as selecting just the right person for a job. So, choose well!

Figure 5.6 offers a master menu of Strategic Management verbs so you can pick those just-right, on-the-mark words that best express your true intentions.

During the early stages of project initiation, Objectives may be ragged, suggesting a general intent or direction but without real

Master Menu of Strategic Management Verbs

- Accelerate
- Accomplish
- Achieve
- Activate
- Administer
- Amplify
- Analyze
- Apply
- Assemble
- Assess
- Assist
- Attain
- Begin
- Build
- Certify
- Change
- Commercialize
- Compare
- Complete
- Compute
- Conduct
- Consolidate
- Construct
- Convert
- Convince
- Coordinate
- Create
- Decide
- Decrease
- Deduce
- Define
- Deliver
- Demonstrate
- Design
- Destroy
- Detect
- Determine
- Develop
- Diagnose

- Direct
- Discover
- Dispose
- Dissolve
- Document
- Educate
- Elevate
- Eliminate
- Encourage
- Enhance
- Enjoy
- Enlarge
- Enlighten
- Enlist
- Ensure
- Envision
- Erase
- Establish
- Evaluate
- Examine
- Execute
- Expand
- Explain
- Explore
- Fabricate
- Facilitate
- Finalize
- Identify
- Implement
- Improve
- Improvise
- Incorporate
- Increase
- Initiate
- Install
- Institute
- Institutionalize
- Integrate
- Introduce

- Invent
- Investigate
- Lead
- Launch
- Link
- Maintain
- Manage
- Market
- Maximize
- Merge
- Minimize
- Modify
- Obliterate
- Obtain
- Operate
- Optimize
- Organize
- Outline
- Persuade
- Plan
- Predict
- Prepare
- Prevent
- Produce
- Program
- Project
- Promote
- Prove
- Provide
- Publicize
- Qualify
- Quantify
- Recommend
- Reduce
- Reengineer
- Remediate
- Report
- Reorganize
- Research

- Resolve
- Respond
- Reverse
- Review
- Revise
- Revitalize
- Revolutionize
- Roll out
- Satisfy
- Save
- Schedule
- Search
- Select
- Sell
- Simplify
- Slow
- Solve
- Speed up
- Spin off
- Stabilize
- Stop
- Store
- Streamline
- Strengthen
- Structure
- Submit
- Support
- Survey
- Synthesize
- Systematize
- Teach
- Test
- Train
- Transform
- Understand
- Update
- Upgrade
- Utilize
- Validate
- Verify

FIGURE 5.6   Master Menu of Strategic Management Verbs

clarity. That's okay. By applying your answers to the four strategic questions, they will become well-formed. After reworking your Objectives, validate your interpretation with stakeholders and invite suggestions as you test iterate until consensus.

Tip #2. Unravel Narrative Gobbledygook

Early in my career, when I was a program analyst for the U.S. Department of Transportation in Washington D.C., draft Requests for Proposals (RFPs) would sometimes cross my desk. These contained work statements for research studies that would be contracted out to industry and academia. While most made sense, some were convoluted and confusing—loaded with bloated bureaucratic paragraphs that left me scratching my head and worrying about how our tax dollars were being spent.

One day, over lunch with the author of an especially suspect RFP, I asked what the real intent was. He confessed that this study would break new ground. The government was not sure what they wanted, but didn't want to come out and admit it. He hoped that by putting enough good-sounding gobbledygook in the RFP, some smart consultant would figure out what was needed!

Later, as a management consultant responding to RFPs, I learned a great technique for uncovering the strategic logic buried in convoluted narrative language. Try out the method described below if you want to separate the extraneous words from the strategic essence in written descriptions.

Certain linking words suggest that an If-Then relationship exists:

- To
- In order to
- So that
- Through

- By
- Thus
- That will
- That

For example, "Develop a new customer order system that reduces errors in order to enhance customer satisfaction," includes three linked Objectives. Can you recognize and express them as If-Then statements? (See answer at the end of this chapter.)

A great way to connect the dots among Objectives contained in a work scope or strategic plan is to go through the document and highlight all of the Objectives you can find (clue: look for verbs). If it's a lengthy document, don't be surprised to discover redundancy, with the same ideas repeated using slightly different words. Look for key verbs and phrases, and then search for the connecting words that indicate If-Then links. With that done, you can recognize the cause-effect relationships and identify the underlying strategic hypotheses using Objectives Trees and LogFrames.

It's likely that your project background documents may use terminology different from those in LogFrames, or may use similar terms without clear definitions of their meanings.

Their meanings may be quite different. Don't be misled by sloppy use of terminology—just because something is labeled *Goal, Objective, Purpose,* or *Outcome* does not make it so.

For example, "The project Goal is to develop a safety training program" is not strictly correct. In our logic, the Goal of such a program would be "Fewer accidents" or "Increased safety." Developing a safety training program is an Outcome by definition because it is something you can make happen. Purpose, in this case, might be "People practice safe behaviors."

You are free to use any terms and meanings you like. Whatever terms you choose to use, consider creating a reference document so that everyone uses the terminology consistently. (The Appendix to this book includes a Glossary of Terms and Usage, which you are free to adapt as your standard terms).

Tip #3. Tweak and Fine-Tune

Corporate objectives and mandates that slide down a chain of command or arrive in a memo are too often treated like commandments carved on stone tablets. But they are seldom fully thought out in the first place and should not be taken as gospel.

If there is a project charter or a scope of work, use it as a starting point. Recognize that, like the first bid in an auction, its real value is to get you into the game. Most of them smell of "preliminary draft" and could usually benefit from going through several iterations to get them squeaky clean. Treat the original problem statement and/ or scope of work as molded in soft and malleable clay rather than as cast in concrete.

A LogFrame at this early stage will give you ideas on how to proceed. Do not hesitate to go back up the chain of command regarding that preliminary plan with a suggestion for doing something a little differently than what was asked for. Those who originated the requirement may not have thought through their needs, or the requirement may have become garbled as it was passed along. By investing some quality thinking time, you may have a better understanding of what's required or what's possible than the person who made the request. So, speak up!

Tip #4. Avoid the "Joe's Correct" Syndrome

Keep an open mind about how to best state your Objectives, especially for complex projects. Avoid "premature cognitive commitment," which is what psychologists call the all-too-human tendency to lock onto statements that sound good and stop making refinements. I call this the "Joe's correct" syndrome.

"Joe's correct" syndrome is a common occurrence when groups brainstorm about project Objectives. Joe is usually a senior manager or respected informal leader who suggests something to which everyone shouts, "Yes! Joe nailed it. That's right!" Joe's words then become written in stone, even though better language might have emerged with more patience. No one suggests any tweaking because of "group think" dynamics. Joe himself may later realize that his first stab was a little off-course, but he hesitates to suggest a change because everyone seems sold on his idea. After receiving all of that praise and hook-line-and-sinker commitment, he doesn't want to admit that his idea needs improvement.

Exploring Distinctions Among LogFrame Levels

To fully appreciate the Logical Framework's power, let's explore each level separately and examine the distinctions among the Objectives, and offer some secondary questions that may capture the right nuance.

Goal: The Big Picture Impact

The Goal is the big picture context—the overarching corporate or strategic Objective to which your project, and usually other projects, contribute.

Some typical Goal examples:

- Delight our customers
- Become the top provider in the market
- Increase corporate profits
- Ensure reliability of the nuclear stockpile
- Foster a climate of innovation
- Be the global leader in safety education

These secondary trigger questions can help you get to the primary Goal of a project:

- What is the higher corporate or strategic Objective to which this project contributes?
- Why is the project's impact important?
- What should happen after we achieve the Purpose?
- What is the big picture reason for doing this project?

The project Goal is often a given, but worthy projects also begin bottom-up as a hunch, gut feeling, or gleam in the eye of a visionary. In these cases, you begin without clear connecting logic and it may take some time to develop, coax out, or infer the most appropriate Goal. In corporate situations, it can be smart to plug in a hot button Goal statement for your emerging strategy.

The LogFrame matrix usually shows four levels, but as the OSRP project demonstrated, Objectives above the Goal can be included to illustrate a higher level of impact. The higher up the hierarchy we climb, the more long-term, general, and "vision-sounding" these Objectives become. Alternately, to maintain conceptual parallelism or to dovetail with the levels in your corporate strategic plans, you can insert a level between Purpose and Goal and call it a sub-Goal. You can chop your strategic salami in thinner slices, as long as the structural foundation of If-Then logic hangs together.

Purpose: The Project Sweet Spot

Purpose is the vital, often missing focus that expresses the desired result or the impact we expect the project deliverables to produce. It describes *expected change* in system behavior, whether the system of interest is a core process, a new organization unit, or target customers. Purpose floats a level above that which we can directly control—the Outcomes. It's a subtle concept, often hard to grasp because we are so conditioned to thinking of activities and Outcomes.

Consider these examples:

Outcomes Statement	Corresponding Purposes
System built or delivered.	Customers *use* our system.
Process improved.	Improved process *used*.
System developed.	System successfully *implemented*.
Staff trained in safe procedures.	Staff *operates* machinery safely.

Choosing a Purpose statement is the most critical part of project design. Here are some trigger questions you can ask to articulate the Purpose:

- Why are we really doing this project?
- What would the clients or users like to see happen because of this project?
- If this project were a success, how would we know?
- What impact are we trying to achieve?

Aim for project Purpose—the project's sweet spot and motivation. Designing projects from the Purpose perspective helps you determine what set of Outcomes you need to reach that Purpose. When you identify a project Purpose and then define the Outcomes needed to achieve it, you are hypothesizing: "*If* we can produce these Outcomes, *then* we should achieve this Purpose." In other words, select the set of Outcomes you believe will cause the Purpose to happen. Structure your project design around the essential hypothesis of—*if* Outcomes, *then* Purpose.

Don't get tangled up in the terms and stumble over whether a project Objective should be called a Goal or a Purpose or a duck-billed platypus. Just keep the if-Then linkages in logical alignment. Confusion often crops up between Goal and Purpose relationships. To determine which is which, test which direction the If-Then relationship between them makes the most sense.

Purpose Drives Outcomes

Purpose describes the change in behavior of the project users or in the system of interest. Remember, Purpose hovers over a level above our direct ability to deliver or control.

Purpose is the glue connecting Outcomes to strategic Goal. When executive sponsors and project teams take the time to jointly define this relationship in words and Measures, the odds of success sky rocket. For example, if you are responsible for putting in place a new reporting system, the following might be your first-cut hypothesis:

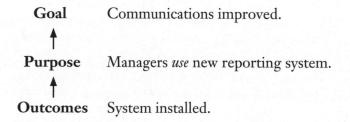

Goal   Communications improved.

Purpose   Managers *use* new reporting system.

Outcomes   System installed.

How confident are you that this single Outcome is enough to achieve this Purpose? Hmm . . . haven't we all seen systems that are built but never used? It seems that an additional Outcome is necessary. Adding this second Outcome adds confidence in reaching the Purpose and strengthens the strategic hypothesis.

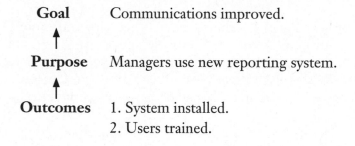

Goal   Communications improved.

Purpose   Managers use new reporting system.

Outcomes   1. System installed.
                2. Users trained.

Iteratively testing and refining the Outcome-to-Purpose link to determine whether or not you have the right set of Outcomes to achieve the Purpose calls for systems thinking and mental flexibility. Examine the Outcome-to-Purpose link and evaluate whether or not you have the necessary and sufficient set of Outcomes to achieve the Purpose. Are other Outcomes needed? Are they collectively sufficient? Are they all necessary? Are some nice to have but not must-have? Are these Outcomes the best choices? What other sets of Outcomes might be better? Continue this dynamic mental modeling process until you come up with what feels like the appropriate Outcome chunks.

In many cases, multiple project thrusts (each with their own Purpose) are needed to reach the Goal. If so, develop a separate LogFrame for each. For example, reaching the single Goal of increased profit margins may require twin Projects (and Purposes) to reduce costs and increase sales. When each LogFrame expresses only one Purpose, it's easier to align project Outcomes. Multiple Purposes dilute the project focus and muddle the design.

If you seem to have more than one valid project Purpose, first check to see whether or not there is a causal relationship between your candidate Purpose statements. Perhaps you can summarize the multiple Purposes in a single, more global statement.

Many times, what sounds like different Purposes is actually the same thing but using different words. To discover if this is the case, ask how you would measure each one. If the Measures are the same, so are the Objectives. Many times statements that initially sound like different Objectives actually say the same thing. Or one may be a valid Measure of the other.

For example, consider these two possible Objectives of a safety program "Improve employee safety" and "Reduce accidents." Which is better? In fact, accident reduction is a perfect Measure of employee safety.

The most frequent mistake LogFrame beginners make is to choose a Purpose statement that merely restates or summarizes one or more Outcomes. Purpose is the synergistic *result* of Outcomes, not a re-description or summary of them.

Outcomes: What the Project Will Deliver

Project Outcomes describe what the team can, must, and commits to make happen to achieve Purpose. They can be functioning systems or processes (i.e., recruiting process operating) as well as completed end products (i.e., prototype built) and delivered services (i.e., people trained). They describe the specific end-results (or deliverables) expected from implementing a series of activities or tasks.

Use these questions to help solidify required Outcomes:

- What are our main project deliverables?
- What do we need to make happen in order to achieve the project Purpose?

- What are the end results for which the project team can be held accountable?
- What processes do we need to put in place to achieve Purpose?

Be careful not to lock into a rigid set of Outcomes too early. Instead, allow the mix of Outcomes to intelligently evolve. That's not being a flip-flopper—that's being smart! As a loose rule of thumb, try to structure your projects to include three to seven Outcomes.

Here's a tip to formulate Outcomes: Describe them as they will exist on the day they are completed, using the *past tense* form of the verb. For example, use "System developed," not "Develop system"; or "Users trained," not "Train users." While your fifth grade English teacher might frown, this makes Outcomes easier to visualize in your mind and distinguishes them from activities.

Remember, Input activities are the action steps to produce Outcomes; and Outcomes describe what you have after the activities are completed.

The set of Outcomes constitutes "a management contract," an agreement and commitment between the project team and the customer or sponsor to deliver these Outcomes, given appropriate resources. This establishes accountability and defines the project manager's primary job—to produce Outcomes aimed at achieving Purpose.

Figure 5.7 shows some more examples of Inputs and Outcomes.

Test for Necessity and Sufficiency

Outcome-to-Purpose logic is the heart of your project and consti-tutes your best-guess hypotheses, given present knowledge and an integrated strategy for reaching Purpose. Each Outcome is a neces-sary ingredient in the recipe for a successful Purpose. But they are usually not sufficient. The other factors—which are also necessary but outside your control—will be expressed as Assumptions.

Sometimes it's not immediately apparent just what Outcomes are needed to reach Purpose. So start with the ones you are sure about. As your thinking progresses, some additional Outcomes required should coalesce in your mind. To optimize your ability to zoom in on the right Outcomes, let's first study how an artist uses successive approximations and iterations to create a masterpiece.

Inputs (Activities)	Outcomes
• Train users	• Users trained
• Improve skills	• Skills improved
• Determine best methods	• Best methods determined
• Build new office	• New office built

FIGURE 5.7 Distinguishing Inputs and Outcomes

Sculpting Your Project Masterpiece

Initial project planning at the fuzzy front end brings to mind the image of a sculptor pondering a large slab of unformed clay or block of granite. The artist begins with a general strategy based on the shape of the artist's inner vision and works to release the masterpiece from the granite block for all to appreciate. A project planner is much like the artist with a vision, but the planner's intent is to lead a team in drawing out ideas and creating a plan that all can use.

The artist's tools are his or her hands, mallet and chisel, and a variety of shaping implements that turn the vision into reality. The project planner's tools are his or her ideas, human resources, and physical assets. His or her initial project statement jottings sketch out the Goal, the Purpose, and Outcomes, as well as some initial Input tasks. These are in draft form because still more granite needs to be chiseled away. At this point it still smells of a hunch. The purification of validation will come later.

Now look again at the basic LogFrame grid. Mathematicians talk about "elegant proofs"—concise, logical descriptions of precise numeric relationships that leave no room for ambiguity. That is what the LogFrame provides—an elegant, concise framework with which one can build the simplest to the most complex projects from start to finish, providing a path through the jungle of complications and changing conditions. This rigor should not be confused with rigidity—locking in a project design too early or printing the blueprint too soon is dangerous.

It's worth repeating the importance of keeping some flexibility to avoid prematurely committing to a solution before several alternatives are considered. Even well-meaning early solutions can fall far short because they become focused on limited solutions.

With that, we can more easily see the tremendous value and exciting potential of using the LogFrame constructs. It's preprogrammed to provide you with the most essential tool thinking templates in the box. More than a tool, in a figurative sense, it is a discovery map with the ability to unearth clues to the location of buried treasure.

The metaphor of a hidden treasure rings true with the sculptor's vision, such as Rodin's, which enlightens us to the hidden beauty that was once unseen. At the outset, the sculptor sees what does not yet exist, and gradually determines what needs to be removed at the first and subsequent whacks. *The Thinker*, as an example, was once hidden inside the slab of granite, but it took a real-world visionary with artistic know-how to see it initially and courageously chisel away again and again so that all could see it eventually and be inspired.

How well do you sculpt ideas? Whether or not you have natural talent, the four question concepts in the book can serve as a step-by-step manual to walk you through the process—almost as simple as a Color by Numbers painting (but with rigorous thinking required).

Example: First Cut Chunking of IT Project Objectives

The best way to get started is to establish an imperfect, first-cut answer to Question #1. Here's an example for an IT project that led to a very spirited discussion of just what the Goal and Purpose mean.

Goal ↑	New processes and systems enable staff to achieve strategic Goals.
Purpose ↑	Staff adopts use of newly established processes and systems.
Outcomes	1. Project structure established and followed.
	2. Business processes redesigned.
	3. Software solutions identified and developed.
	4. Processes redesigned in context of software environment.
	5. Roll-out plan in place.
	6. Training and communication plan in place.
	7. Solutions implemented.

Note that the Outcomes are more or less chunked by phase and appear in logical sequence. The Measures discussion, which comes into play with Question #2, fleshes those out and transforms the project from a theoretical one into a real one where the end results are real-world changes.

Also notice the past tense form for the Outcomes. Instead of "redesign business processes," it should be stated as "business process redesigned." Past tense Outcome language is important for two reasons. First, the present-tense form is an activity and, as such, is a summary of many tasks leading to the Outcome. Second, we can more easily describe what "business process redesigned" means by answering which processes and defining the meaning of "redesigned."

Only by being clear and descriptive about Objectives and logical hierarchies can the true elegance of the project design emerge.

Smart and deliberate initial Objectives setting lays the groundwork essential to strategic success.

Knowing what you want to accomplish and why sets the stage for planning the remainder of your project masterpiece.

Key Points Review

1. Projects masquerading as problems must first be converted into Objectives before you can proceed to project solutions. Carefully diagnose the problem. Don't be deceived by an oversimplified definition, catch phrase, or symptom. Get at root causes, and find the right problem to solve.

2. While vague, fuzzy Objectives can provide cover—they do not provide focus. Establish clear Objectives with a careful use of language. State your Objectives in concise language, using well-chosen verbs and descriptive phrases. Remember: separate Objectives for Goal, Purpose, and Outcome levels.

3. Keep in mind the important distinction between Outcomes and Purpose. Outcomes are what the project team can deliver or make happen. Purpose is the synergistic impact expected from the set of Outcome deliverables.

4. Purpose is the vital, often missing focus. It's the glue of a project and should be the primary aiming point. Purpose expresses the important result or impact we expect the project to produce.

Purpose floats a level above that which we can directly control—the Outcomes.

5. The set of Outcomes constitutes a management contract—an agreement and best-effort commitment to deliver the Outcomes with appropriate resources. This establishes accountability and defines the project manager's job—to produce Outcomes aimed at achieving Purpose.

6. Time spent examining and challenging presumed If-Then linkages is well-invested to avoid wishful thinking, ideology, ignorance, or baloney masquerading as logic.

The four chapters of Part Two include Application Steps at the end of each chapter to activate each critical question. Use these to jumpstart your efforts. By following Step #1, you will have created a strong but flexible backbone for your project.

Application Step #1

Question 1—What Are We Trying to Accomplish and Why?

For the best results with this and other steps, invite a few core team members to gather around a whiteboard. You can also do this on your own. To define and align Objectives, follow these steps:

1. Create a draft list of Objectives. Take from a work scope, if one exists; otherwise brainstorm.

2. Group your Objectives into those you can make happen and those you cannot. The former will become Inputs and Outcomes, while the latter will be Purpose and Goal level Objectives. But they are all still in the draft.

3. Review for logical If-Then relations among them. Discard redundant statements and incomplete thoughts.

4. Tentatively select the highest Objective and make it the Goal. Identify one or two Outcomes that you know will be necessary. Then fill in a connecting Purpose statement. When adding Measures (our next step), you will discover insights to refine all the Objectives until they feel right.

5. Test the logic of your strategic hypothesis (Outcome to Purpose to Goal Linkages). Make sure this project backbone is solid. Be willing to tinker with it. If time allows, set it aside for a few days and review it with a fresh eye to improve the wording.

Answer to Example Question on page 97

Enhance Customer Satisfaction

↑

Reduce errors

↑

Develop a new order system

6

Question #2—How Do We Measure Success?

What's easy to measure isn't always important;
what's important isn't always easy to measure.

—Albert Einstein

Develop Success Measures and Verifications

Objectives	Success Measures	Verification	Assumptions
Goal			
Purpose			
Outcomes			
Inputs			

FIGURE 6.1 The LogFrame Helps Define What Success of
Each Objective Means

110

Winning the Peace After Winning the War

My appreciation of the Logical Framework's power to tackle the big hairy audacious goals multiplied after I served as a consultant to His Excellency the Wali of Dhofar in the Southern Region in the Sultanate of Oman. Oman is a small Arab country tucked beneath Saudi Arabia on the edge of the Arabian Sea. While this example may seem far from your field of work, it shows how this approach can organize people to plan and execute an ambitious and complex change strategy.

In the mid-1970s, Oman was wracked by Chinese-backed insurgents from Yemen who enticed some of the local population to rebel against the government. Following years of fighting, the war ended after the government finally found a compelling way to convince the rebels to lay down their arms and surrender: They paid them in cash.

Having won the war, His Excellency then shifted his attention to "winning the peace"—a much tougher proposition. At the time, Oman's population consisted primarily of nomadic herdsmen without permanent homes. The herdsmen had to constantly move their cattle in search of scarce water, whose location varied with shifting rainfall patterns.

The government's strategy was to put in place a community infrastructure that would encourage stable villages to become established. His Excellency believed that by drilling deep wells and creating several dozen year-round water sources, herdsmen would settle down in permanent locations.

In each community, the government would also put in place Outcomes such as schools, health clinics, mosques, and markets. This new physical and institutional infrastructure would, when accepted and used, produce a stable environment for social, economic, and political advancement. In brief, the logic was as follows:

Goal	Stable environment for social, economic and political advancement.
↑	
Purpose	People accept and use infrastructure, and settle down permanently.
↑	
Outcomes	Institutional infrastructure built (wells, schools, mosques, and so on) in permanent village locations.

This approach had never been tried before and there was no guarantee of success. But without the ability to track progress using well-chosen Measures, the government wouldn't know if the strategy was working or if the insurgency was in danger of erupting again.

Over a six-week period, I guided government staff in creating a master Logical Framework, which was exquisitely hand-drawn by Indian draftsmen on a six-foot tall vellum document (both in English and Arabic). This was another gigantic grid that should be recorded in project management history! Between working sessions, our project team staff would gather baseline data, consult with local officials, and travel to remote villages by helicopter, armor-plated Land Rover, or camel.

His Excellency joined us during the final session when the team briefed him about the win-the-peace strategy using the LogFrame. The three-hour discussion that followed targeted communication around meaningful issues. His Excellency accepted responsibility for influencing certain Assumptions beyond the team's control. The good news: The program was successful; and today, Oman remains a progressive and moderate Arab nation.

We'll return to the Oman story later, after making some important points about Measures.

Four Tips for Meaningful Measures

Measures are the instruments on your project dashboard so choose those needed to intelligently guide your project journey. Don't fall into the trap of measuring only that which is easy to measure. Measuring Inputs and Outcomes is most straightforward, *but progress towards Purpose and Goal is what really counts*. The best Measures meet these criteria:

1. *Valid*—They accurately measure the Objective.
2. *Verifiable*—Clear, non-subjective evidence exists or can be obtained.
3. *Targeted*—Quality, quantity, and time targets are pinned down.
4. *Independent*—Each level in the hierarchy has separate Measures.

Tip #1. Choose Valid Measures

Valid Measures capture the essence of an Objective such that changes in the status of Measures accurately reflect changes in the status of the Objective. Let's assume that you manage an internal corporate service function, such as Personnel or Finance. Given the Purpose stated in the LogFrame in Figure 6.2, which four of these nine Measures seem most valid?

Objectives	Success Measures	Verification
Purpose An effective and responsive organizational unit	1. Fully staffed 2. Achieves objectives in annual plan 3. Comfortable and efficient facilities 4. Operates within budget 5. People arrive at work on time 6. Meets customer expectations 7. High morale 8. Provides results within "X" days of request 9. Admired by the boss	

FIGURE 6.2   Clarifying Purpose with Measures

The even-numbered Measures are most valid. We can reasonably conclude that an organization that achieves its Objectives operates within budget, meets customer expectations, and provides results within "x" days, is indeed effective and responsive. None of the odd-numbered Measures pass the validity test.

Admittedly, the unit may need to be "Fully staffed" (#1) and have "Comfortable and efficient facilities" (#3). However, you cannot observe that its status of being fully staffed with comfortable and efficient facilities concludes that it is effective. Note this subtle distinction: Being fully staffed and having the right facilities may be necessary to be effective, but they are not a Measure of effectiveness. As such, these would be Outcomes, not Purpose Measures.

"People arrive at work on time" (#5) may be vital in some contexts (i.e., aircraft crews, pro ballplayers, or bank officers who unlock vaults), but it is less vital in creative or professional work. Google employees, for example, have the freedom to show up when they choose, as long as they perform.

Another distinction: "High morale" (#7) may be present in an effective unit, but its presence does not prove a state of effectiveness because high morale can occur for many reasons (great pay, barrels of fun, friendly folks, and daily donuts—to name a few). There is some correlation, but not causation.

Finally, being "Admired by the boss" (#9) never hurts, but some bosses may admire for reasons that do not include effectiveness.

Tip #2. Make Your Measures Verifiable

Decades before the expression GIGO (Garbage In-Garbage Out) entered our vocabulary, the Measurement/Verification problem was summed up as follows:

> The government ministries are very keen on amassing statistics. They collect them, raise them to the nth power, take the cube root, and prepare wonderful diagrams. But you must never forget that every one of these figures comes, in the first place, from the village watchman, who just puts down what he damn well pleases.
> **—Sir Josiah Stamp, 1911, English economist (1880–1941)**

The village watchmen, and their modern-day equivalents, will be found in the Verification column. This third LogFrame column identifies processes and mechanisms for determining the status of Measures in column two. Today's versions of village watchmen range from no-tech to low-tech to high-tech. Here are some examples:

- Staff meetings
- Decision meetings
- Financial reports signed
- Industry financial comparisons
- Direct observation of behavior
- Instrument reading or test results
- Employee/management meetings
- Industry surveys
- Customer surveys
- MIS reports
- Letters of agreement
- Completed documentation
- Evaluation meetings
- Focus groups
- Industry certification
- 360-degree feedback

Measurement demands objective and verifiable evidence, not subjective interpretation. Personal opinion is no substitute for verifiable Measures. Here's a practical rule of thumb for whether Measures are objectively stated: If being truthful, both a project skeptic and an advocate would agree on the degree of achievement, based on the data presented.

Choose your Measures and Verifications carefully and avoid highly subjective ones. The usefulness of a Measure is determined by how efficiently you can gather accurate data to verify it. A project to train in-home healthcare nurses initially chose "Observe nurses in practice" as a means of Verification, but management later realized that it was too expensive and unreliable to send people along to watch nurse performance. The team substituted "record of complaints" as an easy-to-track proxy.

Let's add means of Verification to the valid Measures of our earlier example, as shown in Figure 6.3.

Think of the Verification column as your project management information and learning system. It forces you to define and concisely summarize how information will be generated, tracked, analyzed, and reported. Look first for already existing and easy-to-use methods, and then supplement those as needed. Remember to collect not only data that shows progress but also offers clues that warn when you are off-track. Having your project team discuss the most effective means to verify your Measures should stimulate creative thinking about how the team will perform, learn, and evolve over time.

Just because you *can* measure something doesn't mean you necessarily should. Give careful thought to choosing the most appropriate indicators. Some indicators may give the information you would

Objectives	Success Measures	Verification
Purpose An effective and responsive organizational unit	1. Achieves objective in annual plan	1. Quarterly & annual reviews
	2. Operates within budget	2. Monthly budget reports
	3. Meets customer expectations	3. Periodic customer survey
	4. Provides results within 'x' days	4. Tracking logs

FIGURE 6.3 Adding Means of Verification Makes Measures Trackable

ideally like to have, but the means of getting this might be impractical, too complex, or too expensive. Ask these questions to refine your information needs:

- *What* kind of data will be collected? How and how often?
- *Where* specifically will we collect this data, and who will do it?
- *How* will data be turned into usable information?
- *How* will that information be used? By whom?
- *Who* else will it be shared with?
- *How* will it be analyzed and reported? By whom?
- *What* is the most cost-effective means of Verification?

Tip #3. Target Your Measures

The process of putting numbers and dates on Measures is called *targeting*. Begin with the basic indicators and then elaborate on the required Quantity, Quality, and Time (include Cost and Customer Measures, if appropriate). Note this progressive targeting:

a. **Choose the Basic Indicator**
   Level 1 and 2 managers use new reporting systems
b. **Add Quantity (how much)**
   80 percent of level 1 and 2 managers
c. **Add Quality (what kind of change or how good a change)**
   90 percent of users rate new system as better than the old system
d. **Add Time (by when), Cost (amount), and Customer (who)**
   Eighty percent of level 1 and 2 managers use new system by October 1st; and 90 percent of users rate new system better than the old system.

How do you set the right quantitative targets? Choose targets that are sufficient to achieve impact at the next higher level. Setting target Measures is often by negotiating with stakeholders on what is realistic, doable, and warranted. As a first step, you might write in the indicators, but leave blanks for the numbers and dates unless they are readily known. Otherwise, just specify the indicators and set targets after further analysis or consultation. Sometimes, rather

Vague	Better	Best
• Improve Sales	• Improve sales by 30%	• Improve sales of product "X" by 30% in 6 months; with half of increase coming from new customers
• Improve Teamwork	• Reduce team conflicts	• Reduce team conflicts requiring medical care by 40% next month

FIGURE 6.4 Make Measures Clear by Adding Targets

than locking in a single number, it's appropriate to state a rough range.

The targeting process can boil down to negotiated agreement or reliance on past experience. At other times, you may need to define the minimum target levels required to make the necessary ROI, they evaluate the likelihood of reaching those levels. When all else fails, choose a reasonable SWAG (see Glossary for definition).

Figure 6.4 shows some examples of how targeting makes vague Objectives come alive.

How many Measures does each Objective need? Choose the minimum number that clearly demonstrates the progress towards achievement of each Objective. While a single Measure will sometimes suffice, multiple Measures are usually necessary for all but the simplest Objectives.

Tip #4. Choose Independent Measures at Each Level

Because Goal, Purpose, and Outcomes are separate and independent, Objectives, their Measures must be as well. It's logically fallacious to expect Measures at one level to capture performance at another level. Remember, Measures *describe* the Objectives, they do not *cause* them.

Returning to our workshop example in Chapter 3, would you accept "80 percent of participants *learn* concepts" as a valid Measure of the Purpose Objective: "Participants *apply* concepts after workshop?" Just say no. Participant learning is an Outcome in this LogFrame; so Purpose Measures would have to describe the behaviors that constitute "apply."

Keep in mind that the nature of Measures at each level varies.

Goal Measures tend to be broad macro-Measures that include the long-term impact of one project or multiple projects aimed at the same Goal.

Purpose Measures describe those conditions we expect will exist when we are willing to call the project a success. Defining Purpose level Measures can be tricky because Purpose often involves expected changes in the behavior of people or within a system as a result of delivering project Outcomes.

Outcome Measures describe specific tangible results that the project team can make happen and commits to doing so. Describe them as completed results (using the past tense verb form, such as "System developed" or "Training completed"). Doing so makes them easier to visualize in your mind's eye.

Input Measures deal with activity, budget, and schedule. They are described further in Chapter 7.

Remember what Measures are designed to do: Create a shared understanding of what conditions will exist when the Objectives are accomplished.

Measures Sharpen Vague Objectives

The OSRP sealed-source recovery team mentioned in the last chapter employed the LogFrame to build consensus on a strategy to produce their primary deliverable—a comprehensive work plan. Clear Outcome Measures enabled these team members to agree on what the work plan would consist of, and what they were shooting for, even before they knew its specific technical content. Figure 6.5 identifies Success Measures for their work plan.

Make Your Measures Rich and Robust

Like masterfully brewed Kona coffee, the best Measures are rich and robust. They are rich in capturing the essence of the Objective, and robust in providing a way to monitor and manage this project element.

Objectives	Success Measures	Verification
Outcome:	**Outcome Measures:**	
Team prepares a clear, comprehensive, actionable work plan for developing disposal options for sealed-sources.	1. By 4/30, Action Plan completed which specifies a logical process for identifying options, conducting analyses, and selecting the preferred pathway for disposal of sealed-sources.	1. Completed document
	2. The Action Plan identifies key tasks, responsibilities, schedules, Assumptions, and budgets to complete the appropriate analyses.	2. Inspection of plan
	3. The Action Plan is based on the Logical Framework or equivalent planning concepts.	3. Peer review of plan
	4. The Action Plan development process includes involvement of key project stakeholders.	4. Attendance records
	5. The Action Plan formally allows for effective task coordination and communication among team members.	5. Team member feedback
	6. The Action Plan budget and schedule supports the DOE baseline planning process.	6. Budget analyst feedback

FIGURE 6.5 Clarifying the Project Outcome with Measures and Verification

The Oman project Goal was a "stable environment in which social and economic conditions improved throughout the Southern Region." The complexity and multiple dimensions of this Goal required a comprehensive set of Measures and Verifications, as shown in Figure 6.6.

For a fascinating look at a strategy to "Win the Peace" after an insurgency, see the full LogFrame at *www.ManagementPro.com*.

Objectives	Success Measures	Verification	Assumptions

Goal:
Stable environment in which social and economic conditions improve throughout Southern Region/Dhofar.
	Goal Measures:
	1. Literacy rate improves:
	  a. Percentage of persons who can read and write at 3rd grade level increases from _____ % in 1977 to _____ % in 1982.
	2. Health standards improve:
	  a. Percentage of population affected by diarrhea, tuberculosis, trachoma, and other high-incidence illnesses and diseases declines from _____ % in 1977 to _____ % in 1982.
	3. Security situation improves:
	  a. Percentage of population carrying weapons declines from _____ % in 1977 to _____ % in 1982.
	  b. Military incidents and injuries or death resulting from armed conflict declines from _____ % in 1977 to _____ % in 1982.
	  c. Number of enemy "adoo" who have not surrendered declines from 1977 estimate of _____ to a number which is effectively nil by 1982.
	4. Economic well-being improves:
	  a. Average per capita income from productive work activities reaches _____ by 1982.
	  b. Income distributed such that percentage of population at or below "marginal" level as defined by government is less than _____ % in 1982.
	  c. _____ persons employed in livestock, agriculture and fisheries by 1982. _____ persons employed in _____ enterprises which are non-agriculture or fishing by 1982.
		1. Ministry of Education figures and estimates.
		
		2. Ministry of Public Health figures and estimates.
		
		3. Ministry of Defense figures and estimates.
		
		4. OHEW figures and estimates.
			Assumptions to reach Goal:
			1. Providing direct improvements in the health, education and economic status of Dhofaris will result in the support of the government, rejection of insurgent influence and national unification and stability.
			
			2. Maintaining population in the Jebel, Negd and coastal areas and preventing mass migration to Salalah is essential. Providing direct services to those areas is a means of encouraging permanent settlements and the development of communities.

FIGURE 6.6 Clarifying the Goal of Achieving a Stable Environment in Oman

Choose Valid Verifiers

An unusual story from the Oman community development project shows what can happen when you don't have a good means of Verification in place. To provide health care in 15 isolated rural areas, the Omani government set up a "flying doctor service" whereby health aides would helicopter in to remote areas weekly to provide services.

To stem the possible outbreak of a particular disease, they planned to inoculate 95 percent of the population in these remote villages in 12 weeks. They estimated the population to be 6,000 and ordered twice the amount of vaccine necessary to provide a buffer against possible spoilage. Their means of Verification was to count the number of inoculations given. Great verifier, right? Figure 6.7 shows the horizontal logic.

On the day I accompanied the flying doctors, long lines of Omani villagers were already waiting when the choppers arrived. They seemed eager to get their injections, and the early results were impressive. After just four weeks, project records showed some 4,500 people had received inoculations. In the fifth week, this jumped to 5,700; in week six, it passed 6,000. The eighth week, even more people showed up, and the figure climbed to 7,500 people.

Wait! Something was wrong. After ten weeks, their records indicated that they had injected 9,000 people, 150 percent of the estimated population! The managers in charge huddled and concluded that their population estimates must have gone haywire. Only later, after interviewing villagers, did they discover the true problem.

Here's what happened: Less than 20 percent of the population had actually received a shot. But this same 20 percent kept returning

Objectives	Success Measures	Verification
Outcomes 1. Population inoculated against disease	1. 95 % of population of 6,000 people inoculated within 12 weeks of project start	1. Count inoculations given

FIGURE 6.7 Measures and Varification for the Oman Inoculations

week after week on the false belief that if one injection is good for you, lots of them are even better.

Program managers fell into the trap of measuring what's easy to measure (number of inoculations) rather than what was really important (*who* actually received inoculations). With a more valid way to verify, they would have detected the problem earlier. Chalk it up to inadequate education, poor means of Verification, and the lag time in analyzing collected data.

Fortunately, there were no serious long-term health effects to those who received multiple injections. Rest assured that the managers corrected their methodology after discovering their error.

The Goal Measures in Figure 6.6 summarizes how Oman envisioned the stable environment that it sought.

The Importance of Purpose Measures

Purpose Measures are the most important in the hierarchy. Why? Because that's your primary aiming point, the what-should-occur result you expect *after* you deliver what you can. Goal Measures are important too, of course, but they often reflect the result of multiple projects and outside factors, and are, therefore, not impacted by your project alone.

Set Purpose Measures before you set your Outcome Measures. That way you can target and tailor your Outcome Measures at levels sufficient to achieve the Purpose level impact (as indicated by Purpose Measures). The act of defining these establishes the synergy between the Outcomes and Purpose.

Getting From Here to There

Purpose level Measures describe the result of a transformation, from the way things currently are to how we would like them to be. They have a special name—the End of Project Status (EOPS) Measures. EOPS, describes your "walk-away-feeling-proud" indicators, or the conditions that would be in place when you declare the effort a success.

Perhaps your project involves managing soft factors such as attitude and behavior shifts. These hard-to-describe changes can be clarified using "from-to" language. Ren Powers, an accomplished IT project manager, was responsible for an education campaign for employees in a financial service firm whose laptops carried sensitive financial data. Employees sometimes bypassed the recommended

From (The way it is now)	To (How we want it)
• boring and useless	• interesting and helpful
• outdated and old	• future and cutting-edge
• pain in the ass to do	• easy to comply with
• old-fashioned "fuddy duddy"	• innovative
• only benefits me at work	• helps my entire life
• roadblock	• enabler

FIGURE 6.8   From-To Thinking Helps Pinpoint Needed Change

security procedures because they seemed cumbersome and took more time. Her project's Purpose was "Employees understand the need for security and follow defined procedures." Figure 6.8 shows the From-To thinking.

These insights helped her develop a program designed to shift attitudes before attempting to shift behavior. Outcomes included the roll-out of a compelling and entertaining online cartoon featuring a black panther, coupled with "Panthergrams"—monthly newsletters with articles on personal and business security issues. Remember that having a clear sense of Purpose—pinned down with Measures—gives an aiming point for the Outcomes.

She recognized that changing employee attitudes about security procedures was the key to behavior change. Her Purpose Measures were stated using a From-To analysis illustrating necessary employee attitude shifts, where the "To" conditions describe the desired project EOPS. Once their attitudes shifted, their willingness to take security procedures Measures shifted into high gear.

Managing Complex Enterprise-Wide Change

There was trouble at the Fircrest School for the Developmentally Disabled. The school is home to some 800 adults and children who suffer from serious physical and emotional developmental disabilities.

Fircrest is funded both by Washington State and Federal funds, and it is managed by the Washington State Department of Social and Health Services.

A few years ago, several disturbing incidents indicated that residents were being improperly treated and their quality of life was low. There were some unexplained injuries to residents and even one suspicious death. Visiting experts noted overuse of psychoactive medications and restraints. Quality assurance was lacking. Medical and nursing care records were not timely and accurate. Too many nurses were assigned to administrative duties and too few to resident care and treatments.

Following an audit, the school's federal certification was revoked—along with millions of dollars of federal funding. This presented management with a serious problem that needed solving quickly and effectively. Project Manager Katie Cameron used the Logical Framework with her project team to develop a strategy to improve the safety, health, and quality of care in order to regain federal certification.

Their Purpose statement appears in Figure 6.9 and is rich with excellent Measures and Verifications. Note how the Measures pin down what would otherwise be a vague Purpose. There are enough specific and targeted Measures, along with related data sources, to permit an evaluation of the project's impact.

Notice the interplay among the horizontal elements of Objectives, Measures, and Verifications at each level of the LogFrame. This "horizontal thinking" builds a common vision based on measurable Objectives that can be verified. The full Fircrest LogFrame is included in the Appendix to demonstrate best practices usage, while a larger downloadable version is on the website. You'll note that it is jargon free and easy to follow, even for generalists unfamiliar with this type of organization.

The good news: The Fircrest project team successfully implemented their action plan and regained certification. Today, they are one of only three such schools in the nation that continue to meet federal standards.

Special Situations Demand Special Measures

When confronted with stubborn Objectives that are just too difficult to measure directly, consider these three special types of Measures/indicators.

Objectives	Success Measures	Verification
Purpose: People who live at Fircrest are safe and healthy, receive quality care, and their human rights are protected.	**End of Project Status:** 1. A 50% reduction in resident injuries that require nursing or medical care (or other intervention) occurs between 1/1 and 10/31.	1.1 Review and summarize incident reports. 1.2 Review and tabulate injuries from medical notes.
	2. No unusual or suspicious resident deaths occur between 1/1 and 10/31.	2. Review coroner reports
	3. An 80% reduction in restraints and time out use will be achieved between 1/1 and 10/31.	3. Review and summarize restraint and time out records.
	4. A 25% reduction in number of residents being prescribed psychoactive medication occurs between 1/1 and 10/31.	4. Review pharmacy and drug administrative records.
	5. 75% of residents are engaged in paid work activities for three more hours per day by 9/1.	5. Collect, review and summarize resident production records and paycheck information.

FIGURE 6.9 Fircrest's Purpose Statement, Measures, and Verifications

Leading Measures

Look for leading indicators when the key Success Measures won't be available for a long time and you need earlier data to adjust your plan. Leading indicators show up in every context. The index of leading economic indicators accurately predicts economic activity months later. Interest rate changes predict new housing starts. Retail computer sales indicate future microprocessor demands.

The "Big Mac Index" is a leading indicator that has been fun and informal, yet functional for nearly two decades. According to the theory behind this index, when a McDonald's Big Mac hamburger is cheaper in a given country than it is in the United States (expressed in U.S. dollars), then that country's currency may be considered undervalued and usually goes up in a short time to correct the imbalance. Don't knock it—as a leading indicator it has made millions for currency traders who are hip to its value.

The Strategic Project Management workshop LogFrame in Chapter 3 included two Purpose level Measures for "Participants apply concepts after workshop." But these could not be measured until weeks after the workshop was over, which was too late for fine-tune adjustments. How could I, as the instructor, know during the workshop whether application was likely or not? The solution was to add the leading Measure shown in Figure 6.10, which could be determined during the class.

With this Measure in mind, I can occasionally ask, "Tell me how you plan to apply these ideas." Then I can count the bright faces and eagerly raised hands, subtract the quiet-faced hand-hiders, and make a good prediction about future participant application.

More importantly, this leading indicator gave us ample opportunity to modify the workshop pace or emphasis if people weren't getting it. Keeping track at this level (Purpose) versus simply tracking the agenda to maintain the workshop schedule (Input level) permits continually adjusting the workshop direction to best achieve learning Outcomes.

How nimble is your project? Do you have leading indicators of purpose? That way you can spot trouble before it strikes! Are you Purpose-focused?

Projects that benefit most from leading Measures are those emergent or "learning by doing" efforts that involve frequent adjustments and ongoing modification in order to redirect the Outcome strategy during implementation.

Objectives	Success Measures	Verification
Participants apply concepts after workshop.	During workshop, 90% of participants identify at least one way to apply concepts and commit to doing so.	Each person verbally shares their plan.

FIGURE 6.10 Adding a Leading Measure

Proxy Measures

When direct Measures are too difficult, expensive, or unreliable, choose a proxy Measure as a substitute that closely correlates with Measures of interest. While proxies are never as accurate as direct Measures, they are often the best you can do. We use them all the time and they aren't just for tracking projects.

As a young man applying for a summer cowhand job on a Texas cattle ranch, John Huchton encountered a proxy Measure of his qualifications. To start the interview, the wise and grizzled old ranch boss said, "Show me your pocket knife." The boss carefully ran his thumb across John's knife blade and concluded, "It's sharp. Son, you're hired." The boss later explained that a dull blade meant a lazy cowboy—one unprepared to quickly cut a rope tangled around a calf's leg, or slice the head off a threatening rattlesnake.

What proxies might you use for hard-to-measure process dimensions of your project (as distinct from tasks and timeline)? How will you know that people are engaged and committed? How would you measure open communication? Effective coordination? Stakeholder support? Remember, you can't manage what you can't measure.

Unobtrusive Measures

The very act of measurement can distort data accuracy. The overbearing boss who asks his timid secretary how she likes working for him will get the answer he wants, not the truth. Unobtrusive Measures come in handy when attempts to measure more directly would produce unreliable results.

One Measure on the Oman LogFrame concerned how secure villagers felt. How could they make this determination? The chosen unobtrusive proxy Measure was the percentage of the population who carried visible weapons to the village market versus the percentage who did not.

But sometimes an outward observation isn't always focused on what you think is being observed. Southwest Airlines is famous for friendly flight crews. But it's tough to measure a friendly personality during an interview because anyone can fake being nice for an hour or two. So, in the early days, Southwest went unobtrusive. They would fill conference rooms with groups of prospective employees and ask each candidate to make a brief presentation to the group.

As each candidate spoke, Southwest staff, hidden behind one-way mirrors, watched the facial reactions of the candidates listening to presentations. Candidates were judged not on their presentation delivery, but on how they encouraged and supported the other presenters. Audience members who actively listened and gave encouraging facial feedback were perceived to be just the kind of genuinely friendly folks Southwest wanted distributing their peanut snacks.

The Magic of Measures

Adding real-world Verifications and Measures is the crucial step that tethers the grandest of dream Goals to the anchors of reality. Tacking metrics in place energizes the project by increasing confidence in all who read, study, or hear of the project—precisely because those Measures and Verifications have been consciously and formally embedded from the start.

Setting Measures in advance for Goal, Purpose, and Outcome Objectives is essential. If direct Measures don't work, try proxy, unobtrusive, or leading Measures. Remember, if you cannot measure your Objective with some ease and validity, then you don't have an Objective, you have dreamy-eyed fluff.

Key Points Review

1. Having valid Measures in place for all Objectives strengthens confidence in the project design, and reduces later squabbles. Because Goal, Purpose, and Outcomes are separate and independent Objectives, it makes sense that their Measures must be separate and independent as well.

2. Avoid the trap of measuring what's easy rather than what's important. Inputs and Outcomes are most easily measured, but progress towards Purpose and Goal is what really counts.

3. Purpose Measures are the most important because that's your aiming point—the what-should-occur result you expect after you deliver what you can. These EOPS Measures describe the

result of a transformation—from the way things currently are to how we'd like them to be.

4. Make sure your Measures:
   - Are specific in terms of Quantity, Quality, Time, Customer, and Cost.
   - Measure what is important about each Objective.
   - Consist of separate and distinct Measures at each level.
   - Pass the validity test—changes in the status of Measures are attributable to changes in the status of the Objective.
   - Include practical means of Verification.

5. For Objectives that are too tough or expensive to measure, get creative in selecting leading, proxy, or unobtrusive Measures.

6. Think of the Verification column as your project management information and learning system. It forces you to define and concisely summarize how information will be generated, tracked, analyzed, and reported. Look first for already existing and easy-to-use methods and then supplement those as needed.

Application Step #2

Question 2—How Do We Measure Success?

Review the list of Objectives you completed in Step #1 following the previous chapter. Make sure you have a solid statement of Goal, Purpose, and Outcomes.

1. Beginning with Purpose, develop clear Measures using QQT (Quality, Quantity, and Time). Describe each with complete sentences, phrases, or bullet points. At the same time you set Measures, add means of Verification. Measures which can't be verified are worthless.

2. Develop Measures for the Goal, along with means of Verification.

3. Develop Measures for each project Outcome, along with means of Verification.

4. Set them aside for a few days and take a fresh look later. Invite input from others. Continue to improve your Measures; don't prematurely freeze them.

In addition, select a few Measures that track the performance of your project team and management process. These process gears need to turn easily and mesh smoothly to maintain good teamwork.

Question #3—What Other Conditions Must Exist?

Begin challenging your own assumptions. Your assumptions are your windows on the world. Scrub them off every once in awhile, or the light won't come in.

—Alan Alda

Surface and Test Assumptions

Objectives	Success Measures	Verification	**Assumptions**
Goal			
Purpose			
Outcomes			
Inputs			

FIGURE 7.1 The LogFrame Helps Reduce Risk by Managing Assumptions

131

The Whoops Hall of Shame

- When Mars, the maker of M&M candies, was approached by Steven Spielberg's marketing crew, they *assumed* that a movie featuring an alien dropping their candies would be a terrible marketing move. So when *ET—The Extra-Terrestrial* was released, it was Reese's Pieces that became an overnight mega-selling candy—much to M&M's chagrin. *Whoops!*

- When a large family traveled from the Philippines to Canada with their 23-month-old boy in tow, they had barely enough time at the Vancouver airport to catch a connecting flight. The parents and grandparents made a mad dash to get to the gate in time to catch their flight, but along the way they had gotten separated. The family members boarded separately and their seats weren't near each other. Each person *assumed* the little boy was with one of the others. So they didn't immediately discover that they had left their toddler behind—but can you imagine the shock when they did? *Whoops!*

- When NASA's $150 million Orbiter crashed into Mars, analysis showed that the spacecraft builders had worked in the metric system. However, NASA *assumed*, but failed to *verify*, that the builders were using the English measurement system of feet and inches. Thus, the Orbiter's computer contained bogus data and the mission didn't have a chance. *Whoops!*

While these three examples concern flying high in some fashion, dangerous Assumptions hover at all altitudes of business and life. The undefined, unexamined, or invalid Assumptions in these (projects and in countless others) spawned painful *Whoops* consequences.

Think of Assumptions as the external conditions that must exist for our project logic to be valid. They are conditions over which the project team lacks direct control or chooses not to take control.

Faulty Assumptions act as invisible beds of quicksand, waiting to suck good projects and good people under. To be certain, nothing is a sure bet because the world is full of risks that bedevil all human endeavors. While we can never completely eliminate risks, we can reduce them to acceptable levels and prevent nasty surprises down the line.

Assumptions Carry Consequences

Assumptions are often the most critical factor in determining a project's fate out. Every project rests on Assumptions—whether or not they are acknowledged or verified. Every human being naturally makes Assumptions—that's part of the thinking process—but we seldom spotlight them for analysis. The very best project leaders take the time to identify, examine, and validate what they implicitly assume.

The LogFrame matrix is designed to tease out critical Assumptions, which you can either deal with before they become pitfalls or monitor them and have a "Plan B" waiting in the wings. Note that Assumptions outside your sphere of control may be within someone else's control. Sometimes you can coax someone else to make those factors their Objectives. After all, there's no limit to what you can accomplish if you can get someone else to do the work.

Once Assumptions are identified, you can deal with them using methods in this chapter as well as conventional risk assessment and reduction tools. Handling uncertain Assumptions strengthens confidence in the project hypothesis and helps you sleep at night.

The OSRP sealed-source recovery project was highly Assumptions driven; several critical and uncertain political Assumptions show up in their initial LogFrame (available at *www.ManagementPro.com*). For example, project leadership assumed that they would be able find a state interested in being a storage site. They assumed that key decision-makers had the political will to find a permanent solution, rather than defer the problem to future generations. So, in addition to doing the technical analysis of possible disposal sites, the project leader's action plan included "handling the Assumptions column" in an ongoing effort to influence, nudge, and turn uncertain Assumptions into fact.

Consider this possibility: the most important issues you need to manage in your own case may not even show up in the task list of your project plan. But they may, however, lurk in your Assumptions column.

Spotting Trouble Before It Comes

• When a well-known American electronics company first laid out a football-field sized array of television equipment in their Silicon Valley plant intended to later be moved to broadcast the Summer Olympics in Australia, they missed something: Not all countries use the NTSC broadcast format, which is standard in North America. Asia and Europe wanted to watch the summer games, too, but somehow the Americans forgot about the PAL broadcast format used in much of the world. *Whoops, again!*

Not all Assumptions are easily seen. So, how do you surface the most relevant project risks and incorporate them into your LogFrame as Assumptions?

Scan your project's internal and external environment to identify what to keep an eye on. Ask yourself, "What must we Assume?" or "What *are* we Assuming?" in each of these categories:

• Project Team Members
• Stakeholders Interests
• Management Support
• Technical Issues
• Resource Availability

• Related Projects
• Supplier Issues
• Customer Expectations
• Political Climate
• External Factors

If you were assuming that "Bob will be available to give half his time to this project in June," you'd better check with Bob. He did mention something about taking a summer hike along the Appalachian Trail, which could leave boulders in your project path if he plays a critical role.

How the LogFrame Accommodates Assumptions

Think of the Assumptions column as a semi-permeable membrane through which the effects of external factors cross the boundary into your project domain. Recall from Chapter 3 how Assumptions force us to expand the original hypothesis to reflect the more important issues in our logic chain. The original If-Then logic now becomes *If-AND-Then* logic—the essential connecting threads that weave together your strategic hypotheses.

Carefully defining and testing LogFrame Assumptions at each level forces us to think beyond the project scope boundaries and consider what is needed to make the project work. Remember that the intent of working through Assumptions is to spot potential weaknesses in advance—especially the dreaded killer Assumptions—and design the project accordingly.

Three Steps for Managing Assumptions

Turn uncertainty into acceptable risk with this simple but insightful three-step process.

Step 1. Identify Key Assumptions

Get your core team together, or fly solo, and use these kick-off questions to surface underlying Assumptions:

- What conditions must exist, and what factors must be true, for our If-Then logic to be valid?
- How must the world cooperate with us?
- What else must happen for this to succeed?
- What else should we assume?

Brainstorm all the conditions you believe are necessary to go from one LogFrame level to the next. Because different Assumptions operate at each level, do this for each linked level (e.g., Input to Outcome, Outcome to Purpose, and Purpose to Goal).

They may also project precondition Assumptions, such as "Project will be approved and funded," as the initial ante to get the project moving. Note that an additional Assumptions block appears in the lower right-hand box of your LogFrame matrix to capture these.

Express each Assumption as a positive condition that must exist for your If-Then logic to hang together. Make them specific because fuzzy and general Assumptions mask the specific concern behind the

The Museum of Silly Assumptions

The world is full of implicit, unexamined Assumptions where Murphy's Law thrives, such as:

- Management support is etched in stone on this one.
- Everyone is in the loop and on-board for the entire ride.
- Our customers want what we've always delivered.
- The IRS won't audit me two years in a row.
- My brand-name laptop is guaranteed foolproof.
- One more drink won't hurt.
- This approach has always worked since the Stone Age.
- This product is so fabulous it will fly off the shelf.
- No use wasting ink because we all know our plan.
- Europe's economies are tanking, but ours will continue to float.
- We've got plenty of time because no one else will think of this idea.
- They could never outsource *my* job.
- With online start-ups, just getting eyeballs means profits are a sure bet.
- Surely they understand how important this is to the organization.
- If we get behind, it's never too late to catch up.
- We'll be greeted as liberators.
- Sub-prime loans are good for the economy.
- The old tried and true methods always work best.
- The new and modern methods always work best.
- We don't need to examine Assumptions; nothing can go wrong.
- There's nothing we must assume since our plan is clearly mapped out on a gigantic chart.

Assumption. Turn vague Assumptions into well-defined ones by including QQT Measures. The examples in Figure 7.2 show the differences between vague and solid Assumptions.

Vague Assumptions	Better - Stated Assumptions	Best - Stated Assumptions
• Management will support the project.	• The VP's of Finance and Marketing will support the project.	• The VP's of Finance and Marketing will each allocate $100,000 from their budgets by June 30.
• Sufficient resources available.	• System analysts are available to help with the project.	• 6 senior system analysts available to help with the project in June .
• Management turnaround time acceptable.	• Prompt turnaround on deliverables submitted for approval.	• Turnaround on deliverables not more than 5 working days.
• Competitive situation stable.	• Competitor doesn't introduce similar product in the same timeframe.	• Panasonic or Apple doesn't introduce electronic gizmo with similar features at same price point in the next 8 months.

FIGURE 7.2 Expressing Well-Defined Assumptions

Step 2. Analyze and Test Them

Having defined them, now you can test your Assumptions in order to tweak your approach. Chew on questions like these:

- How important is this Assumption to project success or failure?
- How valid or probable is this Assumption? What are the odds that it is valid (or not)? Can we express it as a percentage? How do we know?
- If the Assumptions fail, what is the effect on the project? Does a failed Assumption diminish accomplishment? Delay it? Destroy it?
- What could cause this Assumption not to be valid?" (Note: This one raises specific risk factors.)

Try to assess the *degree of risk* you can expect from these critical Assumptions by using a simple rating system or probability percentages. This first-cut Assumption analysis can offer a jumping-off point for more rigorous risk assessments using conventional risk management techniques.

Even when done informally, the Assumptions discussion will surface easily overlooked issues that deserve team attention.

Decide which Assumptions to highlight in the LogFrame matrix. Don't list the sure-thing high probability Assumptions or the very unlikely and unrealistic ones (i.e., "A wonderful miracle of some sort will happen"). Instead, list those potential deal-breakers that could seriously harm the project and have a reasonable potential for failure.

Root out any totally unrealistic Assumptions, and ignore those that are not critical to the logic or that trivialize the design. While it is true that astrophysicists predict that within two decades an asteroid on a near-earth trajectory has a 1 in 75,000 chance of hitting the earth, the threat is improbable enough that you don't need to list "No asteroids wipe out our building" among your Assumptions.

Step 3. Act on Them

Now comes the fun part. Put each key Assumption under your mental microscope and consider the following:

- Is this a reasonable risk to take?
- To what extent is it amenable to control? Can we manage it? Influence and nudge it? Or only monitor it?
- What are some ways we can influence the Assumption?
- What contingency plans might we put in place just in case the Assumption proves wrong?
- How can we design the project to minimize the impact of, or work around, the Assumption?
- Is this Assumption under someone else's control?
- How could we design the project to make this Assumption moot or irrelevant?

Acting on Assumptions requires making contingency plans and putting preventive solutions in place. For example, if it absolutely, positively must get there overnight, send identical packages by DHL, UPS, and FedEx. If storms are brewing, nail on plywood and get a gasoline-powered pump before the hurricane hits! You get the idea.

Once Assumptions have been evaluated, use them to make informed decisions about project design. But making the effort to *identify* Assumptions is the real rub, isn't it? Assumptions are the water in which projects swim, but the fish, it seems, are the last to learn about their watery environment—and if you're not a fish, you could drown more easily when the tide is high. In other words, people immersed in the daily tasks of doing their job are generally too close to the trees to see the forest. The benefit of this part of the Logical Framework is to bring into the realm of consciousness any and all unconscious Assumptions—which, typically, means most of them.

You can reduce failed Assumptions and the headaches they bring by creating a checklist predictable of items to review as you formulate your plan.

Making Fine Point Distinctions

Though Assumptions have been defined as factors beyond your control, this is not always true. Let's make some fine-point distinctions about what you can do with Assumptions once they are identified. Here are some options for dealing with them.

- *Monitor and respond*—When the issues are way outside your zone of control, the best you can do is keep an eye on them. Interest rates, competitor moves, and the cost of commodities are examples.
- *Influence or nudge*—Though beyond your control, you can sometimes influence conditions underlying the Assumption in the right directions. Example: Keeping key gatekeepers briefed to maintain ongoing support from senior management.
- *Control*—Often you can, in fact, bring an Assumption into your project as an Objective if you choose to, but this takes more resources. Alternately, you can make sure it's covered as an Objective in someone else's project.

Controlling Assumptions means doing one of these two things:

1. *Change the Project Design*—Add Outcomes or Input activities to work around the pesky Assumption.
2. *Add Tasks*—Create a new project or related effort that will counteract or make the Assumption moot.

Finally, you can always choose to:

3. *Do Nothing*—Continue as-is and accept the consequences. The issues may not be under your control, but you choose not to worry about them because the risks don't justify the cost, or the resources just aren't there to manage it anyway.

Assumptions Perform Other Functions

In addition to the distinctions described earlier, Assumptions included in the LogFrame grid may perform other communications functions, such as:

- *Provide reference points for interface projects.* "System design specifications received from Mike by 3/15." Assumptions can identify interfaces and project interdependencies. Remember that one person's Assumption may be another's Objective.
- *Provide diplomatic conversation starters.* "Senior management support is strong" opens the door to discuss who needs to do what, and when.
- *Incorporate other documentation.* Reference other documents and analyses. "Findings of the March Market Forecast remain valid."
- *Highlight related projects or LogFrames.* Program strategies are simply clusters of projects supporting the same Goal. The Purpose-to-Goal link should identify all other projects aimed at the same Goal.
- *State policy/value judgments.* These show up at Purpose and Goal levels, i.e., "It makes sense for us to enter this particular market."
- *Compress logical levels.* Objectives stated in the LogFrame's first column may compress complex hypotheses into simpler ones, relying on the Assumptions column to spell out intermediate links.

(*Note:* Our workshop example in Chapter 3 compressed logical levels by hypothesizing that if participants apply the concepts, then they'll deliver successful projects. But there is a plausible intermediate link: "*If* participants apply concepts, *then* they'll be better project managers; *If* they're better project managers, *then* they'll have successful projects.") The clarifying Assumption would read: "Applying the concepts improves project management skills."

Beef Up Your Team's Confidence

Vetting Assumptions as a team anchors your effort in reality. When finished, you'll have greater confidence in your project design and know what to watch for. By setting up an enterprise-wide radar to scope out incoming and fast-breaking changes, your initiative will be in a strong position to continue to create its future of choice, even when some ugly change slips in under your corporate radar.

As you and your team become adept at Strategic Project Management, you'll be more thoroughly prepared to navigate skillfully and courageously across the sea of change washing over us rather than getting washed out.

Key Points Review

1. Assumptions always exist, whether or not we acknowledge or verify them. Many a project disappointment comes from faulty, ill-formed, undefined or unexamined Assumptions. Make your implicit Assumptions explicit! Get them out of your head and onto paper.

2. Because Assumptions are often the most critical factor in project success, take time to identify, examine, and validate the critical ones upon which your strategy rests.

3. Look for deal-breaking, project-killing Assumptions early, and make sure they are effectively addressed. Assumptions with either very high or low probability should not be in the LogFrame.

4. To be most useful, formulate Assumptions as the desired conditions. Use QQT Measures as appropriate and place them at logical project levels. Make sure you cover all key factors that impact the project.

5. Determine if any of your Assumptions are the focus of another team's project. Communicate and collaborate with them in order to minimize the negative impact their plans could have on your project (and vice versa).

6. Have back-up plans ready to roll for anticipatable problems.

Application Step #3

Question 3—What Other Conditions Must Exist?

Squeeze out known and knowable project bugs by examining your Assumptions using this process:

1. *Identify* all key Assumptions in your project, especially the mission-critical (a.k.a. 'killer') ones.

2. *Analyze* their probability and the consequences of their impact, along with the various means and costs of possible deflection or amelioration by your team.

3. *Take action* to manage what you can. Before faulty Assumptions cause trouble, beef up defenses to prepare for their arrival, and communicate effectively with other stakeholders as warranted.

Refer back to pages 135 to 139 for the detailed how-to information of these three steps.

8

Question #4—How Do We Get There?

Planning is bringing the future into the present so that you can do something about it now.

—Alan Lakein

Identify Action Steps

Objectives	Success Measures	Verification	Assumptions
Goal			
Purpose			
Outcomes			
Inputs			

FIGURE 8.1 The LogFrame Helps Organize Activities, Budgets, and Schedules

The Ancient Project that Saved the World

Do you wish you could have been there long ago when God instructed Noah to build an ark? Maybe the message came via a memo carved in stone or typed on God's personal stationery.

> I have decided to make it rain real hard for 40 days and 40 nights. Noah, I want you to build an ark big enough to hold a pair of all the animals on earth (and people) so you can survive the flood. After the flood, you can restore life on earth and ensure the long-term survival of human and animal life.
>
> Get everything necessary ready before the big rains start in six months. Build a seaworthy ark, bring a pair of each type of animal and people aboard, along with necessary supplies. Here's an advance copy of *Strategic Project Management Made Simple*. Read about and use the Logical Framework for your project plan. Don't feel pressured just because the future of civilization depends on your project management skills. Good luck.

Whew! Definitely a career-defining opportunity—if he could pull it off! Noah realized he needed some high-powered Strategic Project Management concepts and started reading his new book. He flipped to the section about chunking.

Chunking 101

"Chunking" is the art and science of creative grouping. Chunking means breaking down something BIG (problem, strategy, Goal, etc.) into smaller, more accessible "chunks" (phases, components, Outcomes, categories, aspects, etc.). The word chunk doubles as a *verb* as well as a *noun*. The verb expresses the thinking process, while the noun describes the resulting categories. For some projects, the most logical chunks will be obvious, while others will leave you furrowing your brow and wondering where to begin.

FIGURE 8.2 **Sloppy Chunking Leads to Problems**
King Features Syndicate. Reprinted by permission.

Smart chunking avoids the problems expressed in the Bizarro cartoon shown in Figure 8.2. The bin categories are not sufficiently discrete to enable someone to decide what goes in which container. Can you decide where a blue, bumpy toy elephant belongs? Do you have a clue where a cue ball goes? There are both gaps and overlaps in the bin labels. Worst of all, the categories don't relate to the higher Objectives motivating the project.

Sloppy chunking can jam up your system from the start and make your effort sputter. Smart chunking helps you to:

- Identify logical phases for a multi-phase project.
- Clarify how the diverse program and project elements relate to one another (as shown in the Objective Trees in Chapter 3).
- Define the cluster of project LogFrames that support a larger program or corporate Goal.
- Select the set of proposed Outcomes to achieve a project Purpose.
- Choose the set of Inputs needed to produce each Outcome.

The most common first-order chunking logic is by phases, but secondary chunking can take place within each phase. Use whatever chunking criteria make most sense in achieving your higher Objectives.

Decisions about project chunking begin emerging during Question #1 when you consider whether your LogFrame plan will cover the whole project or just one part or phase.

Noah Chunked Wisely

Noah wisely chunked his project into three phases—(1) Pre-Flood, (2) Flood, and (3) Post-Flood. Each phase shared a common over-arching Goal, with phase-specific Purposes and a unique set of Outcomes for each.

Because he was a Strategic Project Manager (among the first ever), he began by creating three scrolls with a LogFrame for each phase.

Starting with the Pre-Flood phase, he gathered his team and tackled Question #1—What Are We Trying to Accomplish and Why? Their vertical logic may have looked like this:

Goal	Ensure long-term survival of human and animal life on earth.
Purpose	Survive the flood
Outcomes	1. Ark built 2. Ark loaded with necessary supplies 3. Animals and people collected and loaded

Noah was tempted to jump to bar charts, but his naval architect spouse Noelle reminded him to answer Questions #2 and #3 before addressing schedule, which happens during Question #4.

So they tackled Question #2—How Do We Measure Success? They began by identifying Measures and Verifications for the Purpose "Survive the flood."

Purpose	Purpose Measures	Verification
Survive the flood.	1. Ark lands with 100% of animals and humans who boarded still alive, healthy and fertile.	1.1 Review passenger manifest 1.2 Conduct health tests

Note how defining requirements at higher levels sets parameters for what is necessary at the next lower level. In this case, the Purpose Measures of health and fertility remind us that the "Animals collected" (Outcome #3) must be healthy, breedable, and willing pairs. Without being clear about the need to breed, his animal collection team could easily have considered "a pair of each animal" to mean two of each species without regarding gender, thus thwarting survival for that species. (Maybe that's how we lost the unicorns.)

Always progress top-down from Goal and Purpose Measures before setting Outcome Measures. That way you can set the Outcomes Measures at the magnitude needed to reach higher level Objectives.

After Noah's team answered the first three questions, their LogFrame looked like the one shown in Figure 8.3.

Organizing Inputs: Nitty Gritty Project Planning

By now you can appreciate that the LogFrame Input row accommodates tasks along with schedules, responsibility charts, and resource budgets. A wisely chunked activity list is the starting point for all three of these management tools.

The LogFrame Inputs are meant to offer a high level summary, not a comprehensive action plan. Consider Inputs as the jumping off point for more detailed planning, using Work Breakdown Structures (WBS), networks, and my old friend the Gantt chart. Putting too much detail into the matrix defeats the LogFrame's value as a summary document that can concisely communicate the project design to

	Objectives	Success Measures	Verification	Assumptions
Then ↰	**Goal:** Ensure the long-term survival of human and animal life on earth.	**Measures of Goal Achievement:** 1.1 All species propagate within their next gestation cycle and continue to multiply. 1.2 After 100 years, total # of animals is > # before the flood.	1.1 Birth rates. 1.2 Census count after 100 years.	**Assumptions to reach Goal:** 1. No environmental catastrophes (e.g., tidal wave). 2. Plant life returns after flood. 3. Animals reproduce.
If ↰ **Then** ↰	**Purpose:** Survive the flood.	**Purpose Measures:** 1. Ark lands with 100% of animals and humans who boarded still alive, healthy and fertile.	1.1 Review passenger manifest. 1.2 Conduct health tests.	**Assumptions to achieve Purpose:** 1. Rainfall stops in 40 days; water subsides in 20 days. 2. Severe storms do not damage ark. 3. Food and supplies sufficient. 4. Operations and maintenance systems on ark do their job.
If	**Outcomes:** 1. Ark built. 2. Ark loaded with necessary supplies. 3. Animals and people collected and loaded.	**Outcome Measures:** 1. By week 20, seaworthy ark is built according to design. Ark capable of holding one pair of all the animals on earth. 2. Ark is loaded with supplies & equipment. Supplies include X lbs. of food per animal per day; medical and maintenance equipment, seeds, etc. 3. At least 1 healthy breeding pair of each species are aboard ark by week 22.	1. Physical inspection and float tests. 2. Compare against supply equipment list. 3. Health tests for all animals on checklist.	**Assumptions to produce Outcomes:** 1. Rain will not start before six months. 2. Good weather for construction. 3. All animals on board are on checklist.

FIGURE 8.3   **Logical Framework for Noah's Ark Project (after Answering the First Three Questions)**

stakeholders not interested in the details. You can keep Inputs general and illustrative, or paste a reasonably accurate summary of your detailed work plan generated from the other planning tools back into your LogFrame's Input row, or cite more detailed plans.

Noah's Noisy Planning Session

A noisy discussion broke out among Noah's team about the relationship between Inputs and Outcomes. Take, for example, "Build ark." Is this an Input or an Outcome? It could be both. As grammatically stated, it's clearly an Input activity. But if you are responsible to deliver a completed ark, then it becomes an Outcome and should be restated in past-tense, fully completed language, as in "Ark built".

Let's trace the logic, starting with this If-Then relationship:

Outcome   1. Ark built
↑
Inputs   1. Build ark

The relationship "If we built ark, then the ark is built" is true, but not very useful. Utility comes when you then explode or break out the activity of "Build ark" into its component parts, like this:

Outcome   1. Ark built
   ↑
Inputs   1.1 Design ark
              1.2 Hire labor
              1.3 Cut lumber
              1.4 Construct ark

Keep your Inputs at roughly the same magnitude. If the chunks are still too large, you can elevate the Inputs into Sub-Outcomes using past tense verbs. If you "slide Objectives up a level," that creates space for more detailed Inputs such as in this example:

Outcome   1. Ark built
   ↑
Sub-Outcomes   1.1 Ark designed
                   1.2 Labor hired
                   1.3 Lumber cut
   ↑   1.4 Ark constructed

Inputs   1.1.1 Hire architect
                   1.1.2 Develop specifications
                   1.1.3 Etc.

When elevating Inputs to Sub-Outcomes, add, delete, or modify your sub-Outcomes as needed so you don't have a confusing mix as in the Bizarro cartoon. You can then identify three to five new Inputs for each Sub-Outcome, which provide finer-grain chunks suitable for building out the action plan.

If this reminds you of work breakdown structures, it's no accident. That's exactly what this process is. And if you are eagerly waiting to crank up your project management software—*Let 'er rip!* You can now lay out a coherent action plan with confidence that you are aiming at the right set of well-tuned Outcomes. Software plays an essential role in project management—but only after sound strategies are in place.

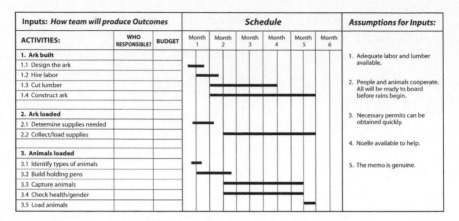

FIGURE 8.4   Noah's Ark Project Inputs

At this point, Noah's team descended into a dark tunnel and began sketching a giant grid on the wall with hunks of charcoal (black tape had not yet been invented). Some of his crew held up torches to provide the glimpses of light needed to develop their bar chart, capturing the steps until roll out of this life-saving, breakthrough transportation technology. You can see the result of Noah's Input planning in Figure 8.4.

Clarify Resource Requirements

The LogFrame structure invites innovation and flexibility in planning resources. In any undertaking, the three major resources of interest are time, people, and assets (money and the things money can buy—equipment, materials, and so on).

Start with a solid activity list. For each activity, identify the type of resources and estimate the cost each requires to produce the stated Outcomes. With reasonably good estimates at this level, you will end up with a defensible budget that shows what it will take to deliver your defined Outcomes. The more precision you demonstrate, the better. Smart manager can partially inoculate their project against potential budget cuts by being able to trace back the impact of cuts on the project Outcomes.

Choose the resource categories and formats that are most relevant in planning your project. Noah organized his resource budget

Inputs:	Resource Budget					Assumptions for Inputs:
	A. Materials/supplies needed	B. Cost	C. Manpower needed	D. Cost	E. Total Cost	
Action Steps:						
1.1 Design the ark	Blueprint materials	--	Architect, 2 weeks	--	--	1. Adequate labor and lumber available.
1.2 Hire labor		--	25 strong men	--	--	
1.3 Cut lumber	Saws, trees	--	50 man-days	--	--	
1.4 Construct ark (hull, deck, interior details):	Nails, saws, jigs, lumber	--	260 man-days	--	--	2. People and animals cooperate. All will be ready to board before rains begin.
hull		--		--	--	
deck		--		--	--	
interior details		--		--	--	
2.1 Determine supplies needed		--	2 man-days	--	--	3. Noelle available to help.
2.2 Collect/load supplies	Food, medicine, equip	--	10 man-days	--	--	
3.1 Identify types of animals		--	Zoologist	--	--	4. Necessary permits can be obtained quickly.
3.2 Build holding pens	Nails, saws, jigs, lumber	--	10 man-days	--	--	
3.3 Capture animals	Mating bait and calls	--	Trappers, 20 days	--	--	
3.4 Check health/gender	Vet kits	--	Vet, 20 days	--	--	5. The memo is genuine.
3.5 Load animals		--	10 man-days	--	--	
Total Cost B + D =		B	+	D	E = Total Cost	

FIGURE 8.5　Noah's Ark Resource Budget Details

by first identifying the materials and supplies needed for each activity, then estimating the manpower requirements, and finally turning these into financial figures. How he did this is shown in Figure 8.5.

Make Responsibilities Clear to All

The Saga of the Confused Project Team

Four people named Everybody, Somebody, Anybody, and Nobody worked together. An important Outcome needed managing, and Everybody was sure that Somebody would do it. Anybody could have done it, but Nobody actually did it. Somebody got angry, because it was really Everybody's job. Everybody thought Anybody could do it, but Nobody realized that Somebody wouldn't. As it turned out, Everybody blamed Somebody when Nobody did what Anybody could have done!

—Author Unknown

Sound familiar? Blame, wasted effort, and sour feelings occur when something important drops through the cracks due to poor communication or faulty coordination. Sorting out roles and

Linear Responsibility Chart General Format

Inputs	Responsibilties						Responsibility Code
Action Steps:	Name	Name	Name	Name	Name	Name	R = Responsible to do P = Participates C = May be Consulted I = Must be Informed A = Approves

FIGURE 8.6   The Linear Responsibility Chart Shows Actions and Actors

responsibilities is tricky when tasks involve multiple people, as they usually do. Fortunately, there's a simple tool to assist us: The Linear Responsibility Chart, as shown in Figure 8.6.

The Linear Responsibility Chart identifies project "actions" (tasks or activities) and "actors" (organizations/individuals) in a matrix that shows:

- All persons or organizations involved in the project (along the horizontal line).
- All tasks or activities (along the vertical line).
- The nature of the involvement of all persons in the project task (by code in the matrix).

Use this simple letter code in the cells of the chart itself to identify responsibilities of each player:

R: **R**esponsible to do (but may **D**elegate)
P: **P**articipates
C: May be **C**onsulted
A: **A**pproves
I: Must be **I**nformed

How to Construct a Responsibility Chart

Ideally, gather together your key players in front of a large whiteboard or blackboard to discuss the project and create your Responsibility

Chart (preceded by a LogFrame). Alternatively, one or two people can develop and circulate the chart (stamped "Draft") to others for review. Either way, follow these steps:

1. Clarify the Outcome or task of interest.
2. Draw a large matrix (on a blackboard, whiteboard, spreadsheet, or oversized paper).
3. List all the activities vertically.
4. List key actors horizontally (leave some blank columns).
5. Discuss each activity and define roles (indicate with a letter code).

Team discussion concerning task roles frequently leads to a redefinition or finer-grained breakout of tasks. For example, "Hire architect" may break out into "Write specifications," "Identify possible architects," "Conduct interviews," "Make selection," and so on.

While you can have more than one person Participate (P), Approve (A), Consult (C), or be Informed (I), only one person gets to wear the Responsibility hat (R). That person can delegate, of course (and the people delegated to would be labeled with a "P"). But one unbreakable rule is that every action only has one "R." Having multiple R's for a single task diffuses accountability and invites multi-directional finger-pointing. You can easily turn Responsibility Charts into conventional job descriptions by reading each column vertically and putting that information into standard narrative format.

Figures 8.7 and 8.8 show examples of two Responsibility Charts: Figure 8.7 identifies the responsibilities that Noah and his team agreed upon.

The chart shown in Figure 8.8 comes from the Caribbean Agriculture Research and Development Institute (CARDI), a 13-nation consortium of small island nations that pool their limited technical resources to tackle problems of common interest.

This one illustrates how responsibility charts can cut across multiple organizations. Major actors included in this example include both internal and external parties who played a role in creating their annual research and development (R&D) plans. External actors include the national Ministries of Agriculture from participating countries, while internal actors are the leaders of CARDI functional groups involved in R & D planning. Note how responsibility shifts by activity, and that some require dual levels of approval.

Noah's Ark Responsibility Chart

Inputs:	Responsibilities								
Action Steps:	God	Noah	Noelle	Ham	Shemp	Moe	Sue	Workers	Animals
1.1 Design the ark	A	P	R	P	-	-	-	-	-
1.2 Hire labor	-	R	-	-	-	-	-	P	-
1.3 Cut lumber	-	-	I	R	-	-	-	P	-
1.4 Construct ark	I	R	A	P	-	-	-	P	-
hull	-	-	-	-	-	-	-	-	-
deck	-	-	-	-	-	-	-	-	-
interior details	-	-	-	-	-	-	-	-	-
2.1 Determine supplies needed	C	A	-	-	-	-	R	-	-
2.2 Collect/load supplies	-	I	-	-	-	-	R	P	-
3.1 Identify types of animals	A	I	-	R	-	P	-	-	C
3.2 Build holding pens	-	-	-	P	R	-	-	P	-
3.3 Capture animals	-	-	-	-	P	R	-	P	P
3.4 Check health/gender	-	-	-	R	P	P	P	-	P
3.5 Load animals	I	A	P	R	-	-	-	P	P

FIGURE 8.7 Noah's Ark Responsibility Chart Pins Down Roles

CARDI Responsibility Chart

Outcome: **CARDI R&D Plan Developed**	Code:
CARDI = Caribbean Agriculture Research & Development Institute	**R** = Responsible to do **I** = Must be informed **P** = Participates in doing **A** = Approves **C** = May be consulted

Activities	CARDI INTERNAL					EXTERNAL		
	Board of Gov.	Exec Dir.	R & D Dir.	Budget Dir.	Research Teams	Jamaica Govt.	Barbados Govt.	Belize Govt.
1. Evaluate Prior Year Results		I	R		P	C	C	C
2. Clarify Research Objectives		A	R	P	P	C	C	C
3. Set R&D Priorities	I	R	P	P	P	C	C	C
4. Establish Budget Levels	R	P	P	P	P			
5. Prepare Preliminary Project Proposals		I	A	C	R	P	P	P
6. Review and Rank All Proposals		A	R	C	P			
7. Choose Proposals to Fund		A	R	P	I	C	C	C
8. Prepare Final Plan/Budget	A2	A1	R	P	C			
9. Publish and Communicate Plan	I	R	P	P	P	I	I	I

FIGURE 8.8 CARDI Responsibility Chart Clarifies Internal and External Roles

Applying Schmidt's Law of Planning Density

It may not be written in stone, but you would be wise to consider *Schmidt's Law of Planning Density*, which is as follows:

Schmidt's Law of Planning Density recommends that you plan the upcoming phase/chunk at the level of detail you need to manage it effectively, and simultaneously create less detailed preliminary plans for future phases.

For simplicity, let's assume that you have a one-year project with four phases of three months each and have created a detailed Phase One plan. *Schmidt's Law of Planning Density* suggests that the subsequent Phases Two, Three, and Four should have roughly $\frac{1}{2}$, $\frac{1}{3}$, and $\frac{1}{4}$ the level of detail as Phase One. If, for example, Phase One is a three-month effort with 25 action items, your preliminary plans for the next three phases would have roughly 12, 8, and 4 action items, respectively. A graphic depiction of this concept is shown in Figure 8.9.

Preliminary plans for future phases will have much less granularity and specificity than for your current phase, but include enough detail to spot long-lead items and future issues with present action implications.

Each phase will have its own LogFrame with phase-specific Purposes and Outcomes, but all phases will share a common, over-arching Goal. You can create future phase preliminary plans as separate LogFrames. You could also include future phase planning into your current phase LogFrame as an Outcome described as "Preliminary Plans for Later Phases Developed."

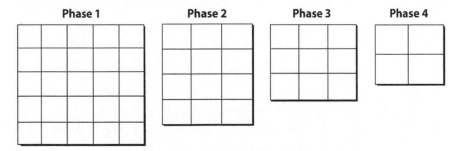

FIGURE 8.9 Schmidt's Law of Planning Density

Well-established phases-gate methodologies exist in many industries (e.g., pharmaceutical development, construction, software development, etc.) When standard phase names and chunks already exist (e.g., Design, Build, Test, Operate, and Maintain) use these.

But what about open-ended, non-routine or ad-hoc projects? While ready-made phase names do not exist, you can still characterize and name each phase so you have bounded execution chunks. For example, the sealed-source project team labeled an early phase "Analyze Alternatives" for doing extensive paper studies concerning the characteristics of 15 potential sites.

When you face large issues and don't know where to start, call Phase One "Problem Definition" or even "Figure Out What the Heck This Is All About." Your Phase One LogFrame Purpose might be "Problem sufficiently well understood to define a preliminary path forward." The Outcomes might include things as Stakeholders consultation completed, additional information gathered, options formulated and so on. Realize that your chunking logic will likely change in subsequent project phases (and possibly within a single phase).

Strategic chunking is more essential than you might think. Teams can stay stuck and stagnate (or drown) because they failed to chunk their project meaningfully. Naming your chunks appropriately can lead you and your team along the path more smoothly—no matter how many twists and turns may greet you.

Straight Line versus Curved and Twisty Paths

Let's contrast straight line with curved and twisty path projects. With straight-line projects, you can usually plot a clear path to the end when you start, and use your initial plan and manage, more or less, as a blueprint that won't change very much. When painting your bedroom, for example, after you choose the colors, you buy the paint, then brush, spray, or roll it on. The unknowns are reasonably few and bounded (i.e., Did I buy enough paint?) and less sensitive to environmental factors outside the project. Changes in the price of paint pigment from Peru won't affect your plans to paint your pad in pale pink.

But in curved path projects, you can only see a limited distance ahead. Think of traversing a mountain road with lots of twists and switchbacks. You know the destination and general direction is northwest, but you can't see around the corners. You must round the bend and see the lay of the land before you scope out the next phase of the journey. Because emergent projects are curved path, chunking and phase-naming are particularly valuable to structure your project into successive phases, guided by a LogFrame for each.

Selective Zooming

At times you'll need to zoom in on a project component for more visibility. For example, here's an excerpt showing Outcome #3 from the Fircrest School LogFrame found in the Appendix. Note the appropriate density of the Input activities, which are descriptive but not overwhelming. The Inputs could then be fleshed out further as needed, but this gave enough description that the team knew the major aspects were covered.

Note that some of the tasks for Outcome #2 are large enough to justify their own LogFrame. Activity 2.2—"Design System"—is clearly a project in itself (see Figure 8.10). While this is condensed to an

| Input Activities | Responsibility | Resources | | Schedule |
		$	People Resources (man-weeks)	
2.1 Assign staff	Superintendent			~~~
2.2 Design System	Expert	$25K	4	~~~
2.3 Purchase Computers	Bus. Manager	$10K	1	~~~
2.4 Create Prototype	QA Team	—	3	~~~
2.5 Collect QA Data	QA Team	—	3	~~~
2.6 Distribute QA Data	QA Team	—	1	~~~
	Total	$35K	12 man-weeks	

FIGURE 8.10 Inputs for Fircrest Project Outcome #2

Input on this Master LogFrame, the expert in charge created a spin-off LogFrame for system design.

Format Variations and Innovations

Because the LogFrame's systems thinking underpinnings are generic and flexible, so is the grid format itself. Be innovative and customize the LogFrame to your needs and add your own categories.

One such hybrid format, shown in Figure 8.11, inserts two new columns at the Input level to capture the information needed and its source. Rather than displaying a full Linear Responsibility Chart, this same Input level variation simply identifies who is responsible and lumps all other actors into an "Others involved" category next to the "R."

Some users add a fifth row beneath Inputs to describe general resource requirements when LogFrames are used for early stage feasibility studies and it's premature to cost out Inputs. Other users simplify by combining the Measures and Verification column.

This system offers you the ability to loosely couple together several LogFrames as "linked clusters," which work together towards a common Goal. The ability to bundle multiple LogFrames around themes that cut across separate organizational units can be very potent because the system flexes to match the team configuration.

You have carte blanche to tinker with the LogFrame. Remember, it's a tool that should amplify your thinking and serve your needs, rather than constrict you like an outgrown pair of pants.

Input Activities	Primary Responsibility	Others Involved	Complete By When	Resources Required	Information Needed	Information Source
1.1						
1.2						
1.3						
etc.						

FIGURE 8.11   Innovative Format for Input Planning

Defining the Next Action Step

Do you know anyone who occasionally procrastinates on key tasks because they seem too big (that you don't even know where to start); so simple (that you feel you could put it off); or too fuzzy (that you aren't sure what needs to be done)? Do you sometimes want to move ahead, but aren't sure about your next step? Your mind can play tricks and bombard you with reasons to not take action.

A professional associate and master of exquisite execution, David Allen, taught me how to solve that problem. He shares this next tip in his must-read book *Getting Things Done*, as paraphrased here:

"Define the next action step" is a success principle that has proven itself enormously valuable. For example, confronting a task like "Improve marketing plan" can lead to getting overwhelmed or stuck because you can clearly see several tasks within the task. So, it starts to look huge every time you try to get going on it.

What is the solution? Define the next discrete, doable step that you can take. What is it? "Review the present plan?" "Locate the present plan under other stuff on your desk?" "Retrieve the plan from the circular file?" Then, define the next action step, i.e., "Read old plan." What then? "Highlight good parts in yellow." And then, oh, "Find yellow highlighter!" (Side Note: This last step suggests that a "get organized" project is required soon in order to get your steps truly in sync.)

By breaking your big task into discrete packets at this level of granularity, you effectively defuse your fear by showing yourself that the big scary task is actually a series of small, simple tasks. You don't need to go atomic on your "What do I do next?" breakdown. Just take it to the level where you can envision yourself doing those necessary, important, mostly ordinary tasks that effective humans do to get things done. Some of the most productive next steps might be to:

- Meet with other people
- Call someone on the phone
- Send an e-mail
- Locate a document on your computer
- Do online to research about some question
- Make a decision
- Create a new electronic file and brainstorm some ideas

To make your actions most productive, ask yourself whether or not there is still some prior step to be done in preparation for the meeting, phone call, or e-mail such as getting some missing information. That is your real next step. Take it now, and take your next step after that, and then the next, and soon you'll be river dancing yourself, and your team, into a flow of true project productivity. There's a psychological lift from getting into this "flow state" because breaking seemingly insurmountable tasks into sure-thing next steps builds inner strength and momentum.

Key Points Review

1. Chunk smart to avoid categorical pitfalls that can roadblock your project from the start. Get the chunks right, and you are on the way. Be explicit and name your chunks, then LogFrame at least the first one.

2. In any undertaking, the three major resources of interest are time, people, and assets. A wisely chunked activity list is the starting point for the schedules, responsibility charts, and resource budgets.

3. Make your LogFrame a high-level summary rather than a detailed action plan. LogFrame Inputs can be illustrative and not definitive. They are simply the starting points for more detailed planning using other task management tools. The LogFrame structure affords you great flexibility.

4. Developing a project Responsibility Chart provides a way to sort out potential coordination difficulties in advance. Turn these into job descriptions by putting the contents into standard narrative format.

5. *Schmidt's Law of Planning Density* recommends that you plan the upcoming phase/chunk at the level of detail you need to manage it effectively, and simultaneously create less detailed preliminary plans for subsequent phases. Like the law of gravity, *Schmidt's Law* is more than a law; it's also a good idea.

6. "Define the next action step" that is discrete and doable is a success principle that has proven itself enormously valuable. Break down tasks into the very next action you need to take.

Application Step #4:

Question 4—How do we get there?

At this point you can use software or continue with old-fashioned technology—pencils!

1. Confirm the Outcomes. Affirm that they are your current best guess as to the necessary and sufficient set needed to reach the Purpose.
2. List key activities for each Outcome, chunked out at roughly the same level of detail. Limit your activities to four to seven per Outcome, so you don't get overwhelmed.
3. Identify tasks sequences by examining predecessor or successor events. Determine what the next step would be after each step as you ask yourself if there's anything else that needs to be done before, after, or in between. Develop a Gantt chart or similar task schedule. (Keep in mind that although this process may be tedious, be thankful you're not working with rolls of black tape.)
4. Identify resources needed for each task.
5. Clarify responsibilities using the Responsibility Chart.

If you've been doing the Application Steps at the end of Chapters 5, 6, 7, and 8 to your project, you have now fleshed out a first draft LogFrame. In the Appendix, you'll find a self-administering quality checklist that you can use to determine how well your project design hangs together. Use this to spot and correct weaknesses. After cleaning up your design, stamp it *draft* and circulate it to a few key players for some live feedback.

This chapter concludes the section about the LogFrame Approach proper. Return to this section again and again for more insights on using it for current and for all future projects, both personal and professional.

Part Three

Putting The Concepts Into Action

Prior chapters guided you in creating a first-draft project plan by plugging the answers to the Four Critical Strategic Questions into the LogFrame structure. The final three chapters in this section cover other essential issues for getting the results you seek.

- *Chapter 9* examines how to keep your project plans current and relevant by managing the ongoing strategic action cycle.
- *Chapter 10* explores ways to manage stakeholder dynamics and use Emotional Intelligence to energize your efforts.
- *Chapter 11* illustrates over one dozen typical high-payoff applications, and offers tips to keep in mind as you put these concepts into action.

9

Managing the Strategic Action Cycle

You have to be fast on your feet
or else a strategy is useless.

—Lou Gerstner, IBM

Taking a "Cycle-Logical" Approach

In Chapter 1, I cited "one-shot planning" as one of the six dangerous planning mistakes. The chapter at hand offers thoughtful ways to overcome that mistake.

All living systems have the ability to learn from, and adapt to, their environment. Projects are living systems as well and the most useful project plans are "living documents" that evolve as unfolding internal or external circumstances force a shift in approach.

Keeping your plans timely and relevant is an excellent *proxy measure* of how well you are handling the project's management process.

You do so by building feedback loops into your project plans and deliberately manage the *strategic action cycle*.

Taking an adaptive "cycle-logical" approach allows you to make intelligent responses to obstacles and opportunities that the project encounters *after* it starts and is under way.

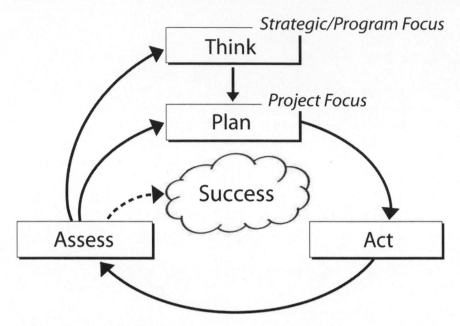

Figure 9.1   Strategic Action Cycle

This same philosophy is behind other management systems which include feedback loops (e.g., the Shewhart Cycle of Plan-Do-Check-Act).

Building any useful management model begins by considering the functions it needs to perform and then putting concepts together in a meaningful way. In our case, this model must integrate strategic/program planning with project management.

To derive an appropriate model, let's start with the concepts of Think-Plan-Act, the rallying cry of the Association for Strategic Planning.

We'll expand that model by adding *Assess* to get "Think—Plan—Act—Assess" (TPA²). Figure 9.1 shows the strategic action cycle in visual form.

The cycle begins with "Think," the big picture strategic/program focus which follows the process from Chapter 4, or an equivalent strategic planning process.

Results of strategic thinking identify projects to be managed with the Plan-Act-Assess cycle.

Project plans created with LogFrames provide a solid foundation for action (execution/implementation) and Assessment.

The Assess block can complete the loop in three ways. If assessment shows that success has been achieved—as defined by project Purpose—the project can be considered complete.

More frequently, Assessment results in project replanning and making fresh plans which stimulate and restimulate the cycle.

In more volatile environments or highly iterative projects, an Assessment may involve substantially rethinking the larger strategic approach. Such assessments mean "you have another think coming."

The more volatile your environment, the more important to fine-tune your original hypothesis over time, improve your LogFrame plan and process, and document the evolution of design changes. With each cycle, each aspect of the LogFrame must be reconsidered—with special attention to which Assumptions remain valid and which new ones may emerge.

A well done LogFrame sets the stage for all three types of Assessment.

Three Types of Assessment

The Assessment step grounds your project in reality by looking at the environment and adjusting based on real-world feedback.

Consider how these three vital but different Assessment functions—Monitoring, Review, and Evaluation—should be part of your project.

Project *Monitoring* is an ongoing process of tracking budget and schedule against deliverables and making tactical adjustments. It presumes the Logical Framework is the best design and focuses team attention on translating Inputs into Outcomes.

Project *Review* is an occasional process that asks managers to step back from the day-to-day work and reassess their approach. It challenges the project design and invites changes in the LogFrame, with emphasis on the Outcome to Purpose link.

Project *Evaluation* examines impact and cost effectiveness. Project evaluations are often timed as the end of one phase nears and another is about to begin, or after the project is over. evaluation examines Purpose to Goal linkages.

Obviously, not everything about the project can or should be constantly assessed, unless you're in an exceptionally fluid situation.

In all three types, Assessment examines the casual linkages as well as critical Assumptions. Changes in the status of Assumptions always introduce issues to react and respond to.

Sharpening Information Needs

Assessment requires sifting through and making sense of information related to accomplishment of Measures at each level. In well thought-out LogFrames, the Verification column identifies where you'll get the necessary information concerning key Measures.

Project managers must consider how best to get the needed information throughout the project. Relevant information is the basis for real-time Monitoring and collects baseline information for the other two functions.

Communicating well starts by defining the nature of the information that project team members, executives, and other stakeholders will need. Consider these questions:

- Who needs to know what and why?
- What is "must-have" versus "nice-to-have" information? What is the benefit/cost of additional data?
- What information will automatically be provided by existing organizational systems, and what must be home-brewed (at a cost)?
- Who will be the responsible for collecting and processing what information?
- How will we set up an effective archiving and retrieval system?

Don't rely only on reports and other system-generated information to keep your finger on the project pulse. A reliable project MIS not only includes databases, computers, and formal status reports, but actively embraces the informal and human information processes.

Formal systems provide an incomplete picture because they miss the soft stuff. Keep in mind meaningful key process indicators, such as project team effectiveness, productivity of meetings, as well as levels of trust and open communications. A brief and candid hallway conversation often yields richer information than may be provided in formal project Briefings.

Type One Assessment: Project Monitoring

To illustrate the three levels of Assessment, let's call on our Workshop example from Chapter 3, as shown in the LogFrame on page 45 and summarized below:

Goal   Deliver successful projects.

↑

Purpose   Participants apply what they learned following the workshop.

↑

Outcomes   Participants learn key concepts and tools during the workshop.

Monitoring primarily examines progress in turning Inputs into Outcomes. The dynamics of most projects require multiple means of monitoring, which aim to put together a reasonable picture of what's happening by actively communicating with task managers, reading reports, juggling e-mail, touching base with key stakeholders and doing appropriate analysis. Earned Value Analysis (EVA) is a commonly used monitoring tool in larger projects to relate Input consumption with Outcome production.

Meaningful monitoring requires first establishing major milestones to measure against. If you were to drive from San Francisco's Golden Gate all the way to New York's Battery Park, you could search frantically for every milepost, telephone pole, and center-line dash along the way, which serve as evidence of forward motion toward your New York Goal. Or, you could accept Salt Lake City, St. Louis, Columbus, and Pittsburgh as reasonable milestones on your journey. Set your focus on significant milestones and be judicious in selecting those primary project checkpoints.

How frequently and fine-grain should you monitor?

The late project management expert Arnie Ruskin suggested the term "inch-pebbles" to track more closely than "milestones." If your project requires even more fine-grained tracking, consider using "centimeter sand grains."

What justifies being called a major milestone in LogFrame terms? By definition, Outcome completion is always one. The start

---

Schmidt's Law of Milestone Frequency

Schmidt's Law of Milestone Frequency provides some basic guidelines for how many to include in your own project. As a general rule of thumb, a one-month project might have one or two milestones per week. A six-month project usually needs somewhere around 12 to 15 milestone points, or one every two weeks or so. On longer duration projects, avoid going more than three weeks between milestones, or otherwise people may lose focus.

---

or completion of critical activities, Assumptions verification, and management process activities such as mid-project reviews may also constitute milestones. Choose what matters most.

In our Workshop example, monitoring progress toward our desired Outcome "Concepts Learned" is based on observation of individual learning activities during the workshop itself to see how well people seem to "get it." Heads-up instructors continually make fine-tune adjustments to stay on target by changing their teaching approach, perhaps by offering more examples or asking for questions.

Trip-Wire Events as Milestone Reminder

Consider inserting early "trip-wire" points ahead of a milestone's due date to provide an early status check and a gentle prod to action. This recognizes the natural human tendency to procrastinate.

I still recall with horror some dreaded college term papers that were assigned two months in advance, but I would wait until a few nights before due date to start working on it, maybe even pulling all-nighters to finish. The papers passed, but clearly weren't my best work. My favorite college professor taught me a valuable project management lesson by requiring that we submit a thorough outline three weeks before the term paper due date. This forced an earlier start, which resulted in a better final product. Can you identify with "term-paper syndrome"? Would the trip-wire concept be useful in your projects to spot potential problems early?

Don't Ask This Question

We've all encountered people who don't deliver on time as promised. Reduce these nasty surprises by asking better questions ahead of time to get an accurate picture of where things stand. The most common (and worst) question project managers ask when determining status, is, *"How's it going on this task?"* Bad question. You are likely to get vague answers. Here are better quality questions that generate dialogue and encourage candor:

- Are you having any difficulties that would keep you from meeting targets?
- Are you getting the support you need from others?
- Is there anything else I should know about this?
- What do you need from me?

Type Two Assessment: Project Status Review

Sit in on most any project meetings and you'll hear discussion of issues, problems and actions, mostly at the Input to Outcome level. That's fine—but what's your mechanism for occasionally rethinking the whole project?

On occasion, rise above the day-to-day focus and ebb-and-flow of your project to review where things are, because Murphy's Law can strike at any time.

Project monitoring asks "Are we *on* track?"; project reviews ask "Are we on the *right* track?"

A well-done LogFrame provides an action plan as well as a baseline for subsequent review and improvement. Periodic project reviews should challenge the design in order to strengthen it; which can be a potent mid-stream tool for redirecting any project. Use the LogFrame to challenge your strategy by posing questions such as:

- Is our Purpose still valid? What's our progress toward Purpose?
- Is our Purpose likely to be achieved with this plan? Will this Purpose get us to the Goal?
- What is the status of Assumptions?

- Are these the right Outcomes? Are we producing them effectively?
- Should new Outcomes or Assumptions be added? Existing ones dropped?
- How should we revise our key strategic hypotheses (Outcome to Purpose to Goal) to produce better results?

Review sparks replanning. A shifting mix of Outcomes is to be expected and encouraged. Some Outcomes will be completed and others can be deleted while new ones may need to be added.

Project reviews are an ideal time to examine the current state of stakeholder involvement and support.

Changes in the status of a key Assumption can sabotage your project, as well as open new options. When the OSRP sealed-source project began, it had been thought impossible to bury radioactive waste in the Waste Isolation Pilot Project (WIPP), which was a suitable New Mexico site that had been designated only for military waste, not civilian waste. So the task force had started conducting detailed studies to characterize 15 other potential sites.

But the events of September 11, 2001 changed everything. At a post-9/11 project review, the project team sensed a change in the political environment that made it possible to overcome the bureaucratic obstacles to burying the waste in the WIPP. Suddenly, the originally planned Outcomes of completed site characterizations were not needed and could be dropped.

Market dynamics may be blowing the schooner of corporate progress across a lake of opportunity, but well-timed project reviews might reveal that you'll soon be off-course unless you steer lightly back toward your Goal.

Type Three Assessment: Project Evaluation

While common in international development, evaluation in the corporate world remains underused and underappreciated as a management function. When done well, it provides a high ROI and yields critical lessons learned that may benefit future projects.

Project evaluations (sometimes called "post-mortems") occur after the project is complete. As noted earlier, project completion and project success are two very different concepts. Your project may be finished when Outcomes have been delivered, but it is not really successful until Purpose has been reached. We built it, but did they come? Workshop participants learned concepts, but did they apply them?

Remember that evaluation is, in itself, a project that takes time and resources. Before committing to evaluation, make sure the intent is positive so that it's an exploration rather than an inquisition. Evaluations might examine questions like these:

- To what extent were Outcomes produced and Purpose achieved?
- What was the impact on Goal?
- What went right, and why? What went wrong, and why? Were we to do this over again, what would we do differently?
- What Assumptions may have been invalid?
- What did we learn that was worth learning?
- How can these insights be captured, shared and integrated organization-wide?
- How do we codify our learning and apply the lessons to future efforts (pamphlets, case studies, knowledge banks, web-pages, and so on)?

The LogFrame Approach to Project and Program Evaluation

The LogFrame was created with evaluation in mind. First, note that in a well-done LogFrame we have set up a basic evaluation framework with the Purpose and Goal level Measures and Verification. We can evaluate *project* success at the Purpose level; and *program* success at the Goal level. As we trace through the workshop example of Chapter 3, consider how you might apply a similar evaluation planning process to your own project. Recall the basic workshop LogFrame from that chapter on page 57.

Our workshop project could be evaluated at multiple LogFrame levels. The first level is the project Outcome level: Concepts learned. We would check extent of learning against our predefined Outcome Measures, using the shown means of Verification: in-class exercises and formal tests. In most projects, Outcome production is relatively easy to measure. If we can't, it's because we left them too vague (which was planning mistake number one).

But the real payoff occurs at Purpose and Goal. To determine "Concepts applied," our first evaluation occurs six weeks after the workshop, with a second, more extensive evaluation six months later.

Our key Purpose Measure is that 60 percent of people begin applying the concepts within six weeks after the workshop. Unless there is prior experience to show this level is reasonable, this is an estimate. Remember, for open-ended, R&D, and process-type projects, QQT Measures are not stated targets to reach, but merely indicative of what might be possible.

Achieving 40 percent might be enough to justify the workshop. In fact, just one person applying these concepts might have a tremendous impact—if it were applied to the right project. But, on the other hand, let's say that the actual result was a disappointing 10 percent. What went wrong?

The first place we look to determine causes of failure is *Assumptions*. Here we have two key ones:

1. *Participants have opportunity to apply concepts (nature of their job is suitable)*. Let's say we found out that only half the participants had a project that was suitable for applying these concepts. Already our 60 percent target would be way too high; 30 percent might have been a more realistic maximum.

2. *Participants' boss and/or organizational environment support and encourage use of the concepts*. This one examines the on-the-job fit and the degree of receptivity. Was there active support and encouragement? Or was there resistance because of the "Not Invented Here" syndrome?

The means of evaluating these key Assumptions might include surveying the boss as well. This inclusive step would give more clues as to how to adjust future projects of this type.

Let's say that the evaluation results showed that there was not much boss encouragement, and the reason was lack of understanding and appreciation by the executives overseeing the project managers. This might identify the need for a "boss briefing," or an advocacy document to inform them of the LogFrame value and benefits. (On our website, you'll find a free special report written for this purpose.)

One could also conduct a Goal level evaluation of project results and the effectiveness of the project/program management system. This would involve a much wider scope than just training workshops.

Evaluation Data and Methods

While designing projects using LogFrames, you simultaneously establish the basis for later evaluation.

The Fircrest School project, previously discussed (see the full LogFrame in the Appendix), provides an outstanding example of how this tool helps to identify data needed for evaluation at the time of project design. The Purpose Measures spelled out in advance the necessary data, while the Verification column showed how it should be gathered. Together, Measures and Verifications should identify what data you might need to collect on a regular basis from day one, or at least establish a baseline to work from.

Periodic evaluation can yield money-saving insights, but only if the relevant data exists. Your project team may not know exactly what data is needed or have collection mechanisms at the beginning of their project. In this case, explicitly create an Outcome devoted to learning what is required, so that evaluative data can, and will, be collected along the way. If some of the means identified in the Verification column do not currently exist, they may need to be created under an Outcome called "Verification Mechanisms Developed."

Just Do It

After the project is complete, there will be all kinds of reasons not to evaluate (people are too weary, too drained, or are moving on to other things). Guard against this by building an evaluation milestone into the project plan, so clear expectations are there from the beginning. On occasion, you'll encounter unplanned events that attach a cachet of negativity to the project. You reached your Goals, but just as everything was about to come to an unmitigated success, one of your delivery trucks ran over Narfy the Dog, casting a pall of angst over those in your organization who were fond of old Narfy. Step up and defuse these unfortunate finale-killers as quickly as possible.

Don't treat setbacks or embarrassments as something beneath the capacity of your organization to deal with effectively. The accidents that happen along the way need smoothing over, so smooth whatever hiccup occurs in a quick, humane, and compassionate manner.

During the Tylenol scare, when saboteurs had laced on-the-shelf bottles with poison, Johnson & Johnson rapidly responded without attempting a cover-up. They were widely praised for reassuring the public, and their stock price rose because they handled it so well. This may well have been a milestone they didn't want to occur in their company history, but they turned it into a positive impression.

Celebrating Success

Take time to acknowledge on-time performance when your team does reach their milestone targets. Remember, you're working with fellow humans who could really appreciate an "Atta-girl" or "Atta-boy" for making their milestones on time. Sure, they're getting paid, but if you give public kudos and recognition when they hit the mark, they'll give their best to hit their other targets, too.

My philosophy is simple: Celebrate success early and often. Every worthwhile project has pushed people through frustration, disappointments, and setbacks. But with commitment and encouragement, good people rise to new heights of accomplishment. Along the way, simple recognition—like bringing a big box of bagels to project meetings—leaves a good taste behind. When the end arrives, recognize and reward participants. Team efforts should be heralded openly, publicly, and joyfully. Can you create a ceremony or ritual that signals and celebrates the end?

More elaborate rewards, such as promotions, study sabbaticals, vacations, cash bonuses, or awards presentations may also be appropriate at the project celebration. Make it worth the candle for all participants, but especially for anyone who might be perceived as "the little guy" so that your organization is seen as fair and just in rewarding effort, particularly on-target effort that benefits the whole organization. Make it special enough to be interesting. Invite some organization big shots, and team members' guests. Go beyond mere mechanics and make yours *a Project-Ender to Remember!*

LogFrame Limitations and Best Practices

For all its obvious benefits, the LogFrame is no cure-all or magic management solvent that dissolves each and every problem. Indeed, if such a super-solvent could be invented, what material could be used to make a container to hold it?

No matter how clearly understood and skillfully applied, no approach can guarantee you will design foolproof programs or projects. While this tool is an organizing *frame* for *work*, you still have to *do* the work to *make* it work.

Molly Hageboeck is a LogFrame pioneer and evaluation expert who has conducted numerous evaluations, both as a consultant and as a USAID employee. Her research and that of others has identified common LogFrame usage errors and limitations that could affect the health of your project, such as:

- *Suffering from LogFrame tunnel vision*—Presuming that it provides a comprehensive view. At best, it's a snapshot in time. The LogFrame is a valuable map, but the map is not the territory.
- *Confusing LogFrame Outcomes and Purpose*—Choosing Purpose Measures which are actually a restatement of Outcomes.
- *Jamming the Goal*—Bundling too many separate or linked Objectives into one level.
- *Doing the LogFrame in isolation*—Excluding key players whose role is important.
- *"Box filling"*—Adding context to fill each LogFrame cell without following the guidelines for best practice.
- *Playing "Gotcha"*—Using the LogFrame as a club to punish (as in "You missed this target—*Gotcha!*")

Best Practice Tips

Prevention is the best medicine. Use the following best practice tips to prevent or cure these limiting ailments when they flare up or fester.

- *Treat the matrix as a summary.* Keep it clear and concise; supplement with other documents.
- *Make sure everyone on the team has working understanding* of the LogFrame (at a minimum, knowing the four questions).
- *Ensure that the right people are involved.* Invite key stakeholders to participate in project planning. (One team member can sketch out initial ideas, then shares them with the team to elaborate and collaborate.)

- *Stress the importance of the process of planning* as much as the plan that comes out of the planning process. Supplement liberally with other supporting tools.
- *Do not force detailed targeting* of Measures too early during the planning stages. Identify the indicators, but don't prematurely lock in to numbers.
- *Iterate to make it great.* Consider the first Logframe to be a rough draft that will require revision and reworking, perhaps through many cycles.
- *Build in specific milestones* on the calendar at which you refine and revise the matrix in the light of new information.
- *Monitor and manage changing Assumptions* over time.

When used properly, the benefits of using the LogFrame Approach as your planning foundation far outweigh any limitations. The multiple thinking perspectives blend the project ingredients into a strategic recipe so that it can bake at the right temperature for the right duration. Use it when the heat is on—without getting scorched.

Key Points Review

1. Be cycle-logical and manage successive iterations of the Think-Plan-Act-Assess learning cycle. To stay sufficiently nimble over time, build in evaluation and replanning events as milestones.
2. Monitoring, review and evaluation are linked assessment processes with very different functions. Monitoring asks, "Are we on track?" Review asks, "Are we on the *right* track?" And evaluation asks, "Did this track get us where we want to be?"
3. At the outset, break your effort into logical chunks and phases. Name each phase and create a LogFrame for each. Update your LogFrame each time you review or evaluate, with probable rechunking of the Outcomes.
4. Remember to acknowledge forward progress and celebrate small victories along the path to project success.

10

Managing the People Dynamics

If we don't worry about who gets the credit,
just think how much we can accomplish.

—Ronald Reagan

The Heart and Soul of Projects

We sometimes equate project management with the visible planning artifacts—timelines, budgets, and reports. But the heart and soul of every project concerns people—their relationships, skills, and ability to work as a team. Shrewd project managers focus their attention from day one on understanding the human dynamics of every step, and even anticipate probable human interactions as the project unfolds.

Putting people first boosts your probability of success. Consider this key premise: *How you develop a project plan and who you involve is as important as the actual plan itself.* People who perceive themselves as co-creators of a vision are more positively involved and committed. The challenge lies in getting that critical buy-in and maintaining stay-in.

Engaging Your Key Stakeholders

Paul Newman, playing an aging pool hustler in the movie *The Color of Money*, revealed his secret of success to his protégé, played by Tom Cruise: "I'm a student of human moves." Becoming a master student of human moves by applying psychology is critical for any successful project leader. Understanding people's interests, nurturing relationships, and building a supportive coalition is as crucial as managing tasks, budget, and schedule.

Do your initial stakeholder analysis early and update it often as the project evolves with emphasis on two often overlapping groups: Stakeholders and team members. Begin by identifying the spectrum of possible stakeholders whom the project affects, involves, or concerns. Probe with the following questions:

1. Who are we doing this for? (customers or end-users)
2. Who really wants to see this happen? (champions)
3. Who might be opposed? (blockers)
4. Who else is affected? (indirect beneficiaries and/or victims)
5. Whose support or assistance do we need to execute the project? (implementers)
6. What resources do we need, and who controls them? (gatekeepers and enablers)
7. Who is paying for this? (sponsors)

Analyze Stakeholder Interests

Stakeholder analysis yields the most accurate insights when done by the core team, with input from project sponsors and champions. Using a large whiteboard, sketch a simple matrix and list the major players vertically. Then identify, as best you can, their major interests and issues concerning the effort. (See Figure 10.1)

Next, identify the degree of support you *need* from each stakeholder, and the degree of support you *predict* you will have. Then you can decide how best to involve them in the initial planning and in subsequent stages.

Look for gaps between the support you need and the support you predict you'll have. If a stakeholder's support is crucial, or

Stakeholder	Interests & Issues	Degree of Support Needed			Degree of Support Predicted		
		Crucial	Somewhat	Not Needed	Strong	Neutral	Opposed

FIGURE 10.1 Stakeholder Analysis Matrix

somewhat important, and you predict neutral support or outright opposition, figure out what you might do to get their backing. Some options include:

- *Enroll them*—Get them enthused about the vision.
- *Convince them*—Use reasoned discourse.
- *Accommodate them*—Incorporate their interests in your solution.
- *Trade them*—Commit to owing them one in the future.
- *Pressure them*—Use legitimate power to reduce resistance.
- *Love them*—Use your personality to smother them in good will.

If these approaches don't work, your remaining options are to:

- *Moot them*—Make them irrelevant by insulating the project from their non-support.
- *Ignore them*—Acknowledge their concerns, but press ahead anyway.

A stakeholder analysis for small projects can be handled with tools as simple as a pencil, some paper, and a few moments of time. Big projects may need many days of intense, thought-provoking sessions, during which several people are phoning, e-mailing, meeting, and listening to all those who hold a stake (one way or another) in the project.

Consider this stakeholder analysis example from the Asian Gypsy Moth project, which formed to combat a major pest invasion that

Stakeholder	Interests & Issues	Degree of Support Needed			Degree of Support Predicted		
		Crucial	Some-what	Not Needed	Strong	Neutral	Opposed
1. Governor's Office	Minimize active public opposition.	X			X		
2. Legislators	Represent constituent interests. Visible, active oversight.	X				X	
3. Dept. of Health	Ensure safety and health.		X			X	
4. Agriculture Industry	Minimize costs to farmers.	X			X		
5. WSDA Personnel Dept.	Hire necessary staff.	X				X	
6. Ecologists	Restore healthy interaction webs. Minimize "collateral" damage to non-target species.		X		X		
7. Butterfly collectors	Minimize "collateral" damage to non-target species.		X				X
8. General Public	Be safe.	X					X
9. Media	Inform the public.	X				X	
10. Moths	Survive!			X			X

FIGURE 10.2   Stakeholders Analysis of the Asian Gypsy Moth Project

threatened to destroy the forests of the Pacific Northwest, as described in Chapter 2 and shown in Figure 10.2.

The Governor was fully supportive, along with the timber and agriculture industry. Ecologists, eco-activists, and environmentalists, who could potentially have stopped the project, were generally united in their desire to rid the beautiful Northwest of a truly dangerous pest using proven natural predators rather than damaging insecticides.

But several troubling gaps appeared in the stakeholder chart. Note that legislator support (stakeholder #2) was crucial, but initially predicted as neutral because the lawmakers did not yet understand the project Objectives and the urgency. This pinpointed a need to brief them personally and win their active support. Big gaps between needed and predicted support also showed up with the general public.

The general public's support (stakeholder #8) was vital since low-flying helicopters would soon be buzzing their neighborhoods and spraying a mysterious mist. Special efforts were required to educate the public. Media cooperation was essential to get a fair warning out to the citizens about the seriousness of the problem, while not triggering a panic. Butterfly collectors, a politically influential group, initially opposed the effort, but they lent support after the project team added funds to restock the butterfly population.

This analysis revealed that only one set of stakeholders was strongly opposed to the effort: The moths themselves. Fortunately, their support was not needed.

Building Your Own Dream Team

When the 1980 U.S. Olympic Hockey Team beat the Russians, the whole world was shocked. How could a bunch of amateur college players whip a seasoned professional Russian team? If you saw the movie *Miracle*, you'll remember that dramatic moment when the twenty U.S. hockey players gelled to become a team, not just a collection of individuals.

Harmonizing the efforts and energies of the team is so much more than courtesy or politically correct maneuvering. Hold in your mind the image of a six-cylinder engine firing on all cylinders but badly out of timing. Misaligned cylinders use their strength against each other, and the leftover energy is barely enough to move the car. Setting the timing, gapping the plugs, and ensuring a close fit on the valves is analogous to harmonizing a project team. With some conscious attention, the various components can be honed and fitted to work with each other to build forward momentum, instead of against each other or simply at random.

A valuable secondary benefit accrues when the LogFrame is used together as a team. The LogFrame quickly highlights issues and stimulates dialogue among all players, which helps members discover and eliminate ignorant spots and facilitates inter-player cooperation. The bottom line: Better projects and committed teams.

Start with Your Core Team

Core team members are your backbone of trusted team members needed to get the ball rolling and keep it rolling. They are usually not the high rollers or champions, but the prime doers. Who are they in your case? Are they committed? Do they bring the right resources—technical, interpersonal, and emotional—needed to help produce spectacular results? You don't need to identify every team member at once, but you'd better find a few sparkplugs early on. Here are some questions to ask, as you ponder the composition of your team:

1. What technical skills do we need to get the job done, and who has them?
2. What other skills or perspectives do we need, and who has them?
3. Who would it be smart to include for political reasons?
4. Whose involvement would give the project greater credibility and visibility?
5. Who gives us access to information and other resources?
6. For each potential person, what's their track record as a team player?

You may be assigned people or you may have to beat the bushes to recruit team members. Either way, make sure you understand the critical concept presented in the next section.

Yes, It's All About Me!

Let's face it: We all seek to fill our psychological needs. Everyone is extremely busy, and your target part-time team members may already be overextended. They may not be thrilled at being recruited, so you must appeal to individual human needs by answering the primary question swirling in each of their minds: *What's In It For Me? (WIIFM)*.

What can serving on your project offer each participant? Figure out people's hot buttons and communicate how your project can fulfill their desire to:

- Work on challenging problems
- Be recognized and visible
- Learn, grow, and gain new skills

- Apply their core expertise
- Experience variety and stimulation
- Accomplish something important
- Get tangible rewards (e.g., bonuses)
- Work with new people in different parts of the organization
- Have fun

While we're on the subject, be sure to figure out your own personal WIIFM. Motivating yourself is even more essential than motivating others, especially when your project runs for a long while. No one stays energized and focused all the time, so occasionally remind yourself of the many payoffs in it for you and recognize that projects are marathons more often than sprints.

Size Matters

How large should the core team be? That all depends on the project's size and complexity. Avoid making it so large that it becomes cumbersome, or so small that it fails to include diverse perspectives. My experience suggests that the ideal size is between five to seven persons (plus or minus two). This group size is optimum for active and balanced give-and-take discussions.

When a core team has between 9 and 15 people, it becomes more of a committee than a team, and the expression "nothing ever gets done in a committee" often proves true. If you are forced to include a large number of people, take extra care that the group is extremely well-structured, or it can become a well-meaning but unruly and unproductive mob. The larger the number, the more important it is to engage a neutral external facilitator to conduct the initial meetings so you start on solid footing.

Team dynamics must gel. You are not just recruiting good individuals, but good individuals who will function well as a team. Shaquille O'Neal and Kobe Bryant were both exceptional basketball players individually, but they fouled up and fouled out when playing together for The Lakers. Good team play beats gifted individual stars every time.

Seven people with key operational roles made up the core Asian Gypsy Moth team. Over the project's first two months, the project team grew to nearly 300 people as field teams were deployed. But like a human pyramid of cheerleaders stacked five persons high, the stability of the project structure depended on the core team providing a strong and solid base.

Your best efforts may produce a team, but not the team you really want to work with. You can't always get the right people. In the final analysis, if you've exhausted all other selection and recruiting tactics, and you've done as much persuasive enrolling as possible, then accept the people on your team and realize that there's plenty of opportunity to make it a success. Accept them for who they are and who they are not and then busy yourself equipping them with the necessary tools and common language to execute the project.

You can complain about the availability or non-availability of "the right people" until your window of opportunity has long since slammed shut, or you can turn your people into the right people. Put your faith in those you have. Transform the people you have into the people you need.

When You Serve on the Core Team

When you are asked to be part of a project team, you owe it to yourself to take a few moments and think through your own role in the grand scheme of the project. Questions that can help you sort out your commitment include:

- Why do they want me?
- What role would I like to have?
- What might this role develop into?
- What's in it for me?
- What do I have to give up to be involved in this?

Be sure your conscience is clear so you can commit with all you've got. A halting, on-again/off-again approach—being neither slow nor fast—usually ends up half-fast and does everyone involved a disservice. Be able to commit completely to bring all of your talents to the table, to bear down on the project, as if you personally owned it. You *do* own it!

When you and other team members move with swift certitude, conviction, and clarity of Purpose, your project will become an unstoppable force.

Creating Shared Norms for High Performance

The need for shared norms and guiding principles (or rules of the game) may be obvious to you. But other team members, support staff, or secondary enablers may not think it's that necessary. Therefore, take steps to discuss this early in the process. Team chemistry can make or break a project; so it's worth your time and effort to build the right expectations from day one.

The OSRP sealed-source team developed norms that promoted operational efficiency. These included:

- When we disagree, we attack the issue and not the person.
- We respect, honor, and support each other.
- We acknowledge good ideas and creative contributions from all.
- We all do our job and deliver products on time.
- We begin each meeting by defining expectations and Outcomes, and by reviewing decisions and action items.
- We self-monitor to make sure we are all contributing value.

Norms must be deliberately shaped. If left to chance, inefficient practices and dysfunctional behavior can quickly become acceptable standards.

On this project, Frank was a technically superb but long-winded task force member who frequently talked about experiences and situations totally outside the team meetings' agendas. But the other team players deferred to and respected his seniority and expertise, so they were reluctant to interrupt his meandering monologues.

The team leader approached Frank privately and acknowledged his valuable input while pointing out that the extraneous conversation was annoying and counterproductive. "Could you help me break this habit?" Frank asked, and the team leader assured him of his help.

At the next project meeting, the team leader explained that, as a team leader, he sometimes talked too long, So if he (or others on team) were getting too talkative, they had permission to set "these" into action. He then handed out a set of wind-up mechanical chattering teeth to each team member! With help from the clattering of incessant incisors, Frank quickly learned to cut short his off-topic spoken strolls, and did so with a chuckle.

Grow Your Own Norms

No single list of best-practice norms works in every context. Take the list above as a starting point and add to it. Better yet, start from scratch and grow your own, based on an open discussion of principles that have made past projects successful.

When Hewlett-Packard project leader Joe Cronin kicks off new project teams, he shares some of the flub-ups from his early career days, and thus develops rapport with the group. He also asks each person to describe their most successful and satisfying projects, and then has the group distill an agreed upon set of best-practice principles to apply to the project at hand.

Getting all team members focused on what makes for good teamwork leads to the definition of good teamwork, the practice of good teamwork, and the benefits of good teamwork. Norm-setting is a great way to enhance professional respect, and promote *esprit de corps* among what would otherwise be polite strangers.

People thrive on challenges, overcoming obstacles, winning against the odds, and doing an exceptionally good job. Call your team to the harmony of excellence, and enjoy the tabernacle choir sounds of their harmonized efforts.

Making Meetings March in Formation

Meetings can become a time-sucking swamp for all because it's so easy to get sidetracked or spend excess time on minor issues. One team burdened by excessively long discussions of technical issues adopted the following protocols to close an issue and move on. They agreed that when things got bogged down, the project manager could end discussion on a topic with any one of these statements:

- *"I've got it."* Enough! We understand the issues; now let's move on to the next item.
- *"We'll revisit it later."* Table it for now, but decide when to revisit it.
- *"We need more information."* Assign someone to write up the issue or do research.
- *"Let's summarize."* Summarize the agreement or decision we made and proceed.
- *"Our next steps are . . ."* Agree on an action and by-when date for someone on the team.

The most important protocol to keep meetings on track is to clarify expected meeting Objectives at the start. Apply our Question #1 to the meeting itself to affirm what's most important to accomplish and why during the meeting. Another productive protocol to build accountability is by having all persons recap their action responsibilities and due dates at the meeting's end and review these at future meetings.

Sharpening Your Emotional Intelligence

Bring to mind the most outstanding project managers you have ever known. Chances are that they have strong Emotional Intelligence (EI) skills, in addition to their technical and project management skills. EI simply means being strategic and intentional in using your emotions—and those of others—to achieve project objectives.

EI matters because project management requires that you achieve results through others. This means being able to build trust, handle conflict, give and take criticism constructively, deal with people who don't deliver, generate team commitment, and keep yourself and others motivated over the long haul. Skillfully handling situations like this means tapping into an innate capacity that we all have—our Emotional Intelligence—but few fully develop.

EI is not about suppressing or denying your emotions, it's about recognizing the signals they give you, learning from them, and then being willing to manage and control them. When you are disappointed, for example, it does no good to deny that feeling. It is valuable to understand the message behind the disappointment, which is the sense of being let down.

Emotional Intelligence gives you the edge in projects and in life. Sharpening your EI means developing yourself in four major domains:

1. *High self-awareness.* This is the ability to tune into yourself, self-monitor in real time, see the impact of your behavior, and fine-tune your approach to get the results you want. High self-awareness begins with listening to how you talk to yourself. By becoming more mindful about how your inner dialogues shape your feelings, actions, and reactions, you can work to change any self-defeating thought patterns.

2. *Mood Management.* Learn to manage your moods and choose the most productive ones to be effective now. Recognize that it's

not the event that causes you to feel good or bad; rather, it's how you appraise the event that determines your emotional reaction. When emotions such as anger and anxiety come up, what counts is how skillfully and swiftly you can move out of those debilitating states to more productive ones. Practice paying attention to the specific statements you make to yourself when you are emotionally aggravated or distressed. Remind yourself to talk to yourself in ways that help you manage your emotions instead of letting your emotions manage you.

3. *Self-motivation.* The best leaders can jump-start themselves into action, and stay focused on what's most important now. Self-motivation keeps you energized, minimizes emotional swings, and help you bounce back quickly from setbacks. Spark your motivation by constructing instructional self-statements to remind you that you have the knowledge, skills, and drive to get a particular task done. Create positive pep-talks to give to yourself, such as, "I can do this marketing plan. I've fully researched all the issues. No one understands the marketplace as I do. No matter what, I will prepare an absolutely outstanding plan."

   Inoculate yourself against future difficulties by writing instructional self-statements in advance. What are some potentially difficult situations you might face when dealing with customers, clients, and team members? What instructional self-statements could you create now that would help you sail smoothly through future storms?

4. *Interpersonal expertise.* This is the ability to handle the inevitable conflicts, disagreements, and criticisms that crop up in all projects. Strong interpersonal expertise lets you respond effectively to team members and stakeholders, no matter how negative their emotional states might be. Strong interpersonal expertise equips you to help other people deal with their emotions, resolve their conflicts, and stay productive.

Techniques for Increasing Your Emotional Intelligence

Successful project managers are able to attract people and create a positive atmosphere. In our forthcoming book, tentatively titled *Emotional Intelligence for Project Managers*, Dr. Hendrie Weisinger (author of

Emotional Intelligence at Work) and I identify ten techniques to do so. One of the simplest and most fun is to generate humor.

From a scientific point of view, laughing releases endorphins—hormones and enzymes that make you feel good—as well as help you relax, and even heal.

Using humor effectively requires being able to sense when humor is appropriate, because the intent of humor is not to embarrass or humiliate people but to make them laugh and dispel tension. Ask yourself if the joke you plan to tell could offend somebody. If the answer is yes, or maybe, you had better choose another joke.

To work more humor into your projects, start the ritual of beginning team meetings with a joke or two. Open the next meeting with jokes of your own. Then ask for volunteers to come to the next meeting with their own. There are still plenty of jokes around that will generate hearty laughter without offending others. The World Wide Web is a rich source. Do a Google search for terms like "project management humor" or "management jokes." The very best form of humor is self-deprecating humor, where you make yourself the butt of the joke.

Can you see how Emotional Intelligence and the Logical Framework mesh? The linkage shows up as Assumptions regarding team chemistry.

When coaching a team in crafting their project LogFrame, I'll sometimes suggest adding the following Assumption: "The project team will perform in an emotionally intelligent manner." This catalyzes the team conversation about what EI means in their context, and the behaviors it will take to make that Assumption valid.

Projects function best when the manager and team are emotionally intelligent. The emotionally *un*intelligent manager who, for example, criticizes team members so harshly that he damages their spirits, will have a tough time getting them to go the extra mile when it's needed. Set the bar high by increasing your EI and everyone will feel the difference, which allows the team to perform at their peak.

Develop a Start-Up LogFrame

Experienced project managers understand that team selection and team formation are crucial parts of any successful project. Whether team members have been recruited, selected, or appointed, the way that the initial team comes together and gels (or doesn't) will

Objectives	*Success Measures*
Goal: Successful Project	1. Project meets identified Objectives on-time and within budget. 2. Team enjoys the experience: learns, grows, and feels satisfied. 3. All key stakeholders are pleased.
Purpose: Team gets smooth, quick start.	Within _____ days of formation, team develops and agrees on approach in Start-up LogFrame, then accepts their task responsibilities and is active in implementing them.
Outcomes: 1. Project Team formed and functioning	1.1 Key team members identified and recruited by _____. 1.2 Team formed and holds initial meeting by _____. 1.3 Team modifies and develops this or similar Pre-Project LogFrame by _____.
2. Stakeholder analysis completed	2.1 Key players and their interests identified by _____. 2.2 Decisions made about who to include in developing the project LogFrame and how to involve other stakeholders.
3. Initial project LogFrame developed	3.1 By _____, team constructs first cut LogFrame for the project. 3.2 LogFrame includes Objectives, Measures, Assumptions, and Tasks, and meets quality standards for a good LogFrame (see checklist in Appendix).
4. Supporting tools and processes developed	4. Team creates WBS, Gantt charts, and/or Responsibility Charts as needed by _____.
5. Execution and monitoring system in place	5. Team decides on how they will monitor progress, report to others, adjust plans, etc.
6. (Other Outcomes as needed)	

FIGURE 10.3 Sample Start-Up LogFrame

have a significant impact on their performance throughout the life of the project.

Once the team has come together and been adequately informed of the parameters of their mission (should they choose to accept it), one outstanding way to get them focused and moving ahead is to have them prepare a LogFrame of the larger project system. A start-up LogFrame is broader than your project-focused LogFrame (where the project-focused LogFrame appears as one of several Outcomes on the start-up matrix). This broader LogFrame typically addresses wider issues involved in early start-up.

Developing a start-up LogFrame will also familiarize the team with the LogFrame model, encouraging them to use it on the project in different ways. This action, best done soon after the team is formed, can transform the team into a high-caliber crew with all the requisite attitudes, skill sets, and knowledge to accomplish its most ambitious Goals.

Figure 10.3 shows a sample start-up LogFrame that includes typical start-up Outcomes. Adjust and adapt it to your project. Consider if there are better ways to express your own start-up Goal and Purpose? Review the Outcomes list. Identify what other Outcomes your project needs (e.g., benefit/cost or rate of returns analysis)? Note that Assumptions are not shown in this example, but your team should definitely include them in your start-up LogFrame as well.

Use this generic template to jump-start the process of building your team and your project plans together. You'll be delighted at the time it saves in getting a smooth and effective start — which carries over throughout the remainder of the project.

Key Points Review

1. The heart and soul of every project concerns people—their relationships, skills, and ability to work as a team. Remember the WIIFM principle, and create wins for all.
2. Powerful team-building occurs when teams use the LogFrame. The LogFrame process guides the conversation in a way that efficiently surfaces issues and helps create agreement (or, equally useful, it quickly pinpoints areas of disagreement). Developing a

start-up LogFrame helps the team avoid tunnel vision, sharpen success factors, and get thing moving swiftly.

3. Size up your stakeholders, their interests, and the degree of support predicated and required. If there is a gap, you have work to do. To bring them on board, involve them in plan creation because people who perceive themselves as co-creators of a vision are more positively involved and committed.

4. The *process* of planning is more crucial than the planning documents that emerge at the other end. The collaborative use of the LogFrame helps you simultaneously build and shape a strong team while they work together to create an actionable plan.

5. Riding the project rollercoaster without getting queasy requires sharpening your Emotional Intelligence. Learn to use your emotions—and that of others—as a powerful and productive project resource. As your career evolves, sharpen your skills in four major domains: (1) High self-awareness, (2) Mood management, (3) Self-motivation, and (4) Interpersonal expertise.

6. Being emotionally intelligent matters because project management requires that you achieve results through others. Good EI skills help you to build trust, handle conflict, give and take criticism constructively, deal with people who don't deliver, generate team commitment, and keep yourself and others motivated over the long haul. Team chemistry can make or break a project. Work to create productive shared norms for how the team will perform together. It's funny how well humor works.

11

Applying These Ideas In Your World

*Man with open mouth must wait long time
for roast duck to fly in.*

—Chinese proverb

Exploring a Dozen Dynamic Directions

You've now seen how Strategic Project Management equips you to evolve your project from messy beginnings to a polished plan. Now, what will you do with what you have learned? The potential applications are virtually limitless. Ken Howell, a Sony Electronics champion of this method says, "Show me something that this *doesn't* apply to."

Begin with the issues currently on your plate. Scan your internal environment; look for "hot-button" topics and start there. Be opportunistic and apply it bountifully.

If you read this book with a specific current or upcoming project in mind, you may be eager to get started. Do it! Get your team together. Follow the Application Steps at the ends of Chapters 5 through 8 and you'll end up with an insightful plan.

Because the underlying systems thinking concepts are so flexible, the LogFrame Approach can guide you in many different directions. The Appendix includes brief client case studies accompanied by project LogFrames for the first seven of these one dozen high-payoff, dynamic applications that my clients have put to work. More possibilities may come to mind as you read these.

1. *Develop or Update the Strategic Plan.* This thinking method supports a broader strategic planning process that is critical to any organization. Regardless of the context in which you operate, at least on an annual basis, it is wise to review and redefine your portfolio of strategic projects. Prioritize them and create LogFrame plans for the most essential ones. The case study in the Appendix shows how the Safety and Security Division of Lawrence Livermore National Laboratory did just that.

2. *Strengthen Teams Across Work Functions.* The LogFrame helps bring together a new, diverse team and reduce the stovepipe or silo problem. The four simple questions and logical matrix provide a common vocabulary and structure to work smoothly across organizational boundaries. This case study shows how ARINC, an Annapolis systems engineering company, used this tool to unite executive level task forces.

3. *Reinvent Your Department.* From time to time, take a fresh look at where you are and where you need to go, and then develop strategies to get there. When performance lags or your mission changes, this becomes a necessity. In this case study, the Facilities Maintenance Unit at the Los Alamos National Laboratory aimed for nothing less than a total transformation to meet growing customer demands.

4. *Develop Information Technology Solutions and Algorithms.* The LogFrame offers a general purpose analytic tool that helps structure algorithms of every sort and integrates technology solutions into core processes. Our case study example, from the U.S. Department of Energy, illustrates the design of an anomaly tracking system supporting the annual certification of nuclear stockpile reliability.

5. *Design and Launch Marketing or Sales Initiatives.* Flesh out initiatives that support strategic sales and marketing plans. This case study describes how an Asian international joint venture

planned to expand sales of a cancer-treating medical supplement in the provincial areas of Thailand.

6. *Focus On People*. Bringing a major project to an end requires not only wrapping up the documentation but helping team members transition to new situations. Forward-thinking leaders at the Washington State Department of Transportation organized this close-out for a major bridge project in a way that met all federal and state contract requirements and helped all project staff secure new positions.

7. *Improve Critical Processes*. Identify and harvest the low-hanging fruit, where a modest process improvement effort yields big returns. The LogFrame can be put to work to analyze and redesign any process or organization that needs an overhaul unit, as the Appendix LogFrame from our Chapter 4 GIS case study shows.

8. *Develop Recommendations and Make Decisions*. Use this tool to be systematic and transparent about how to set decision criteria, identify alternatives, collect information, conduct analyses, and make decision recommendations.

9. *Handle Emergent Issues*. Got a hot potato? This approach works well on non-standard projects that arise suddenly and demand quick solution roadmaps. Bake your project potato with proven recipes by defining your problem or issue, converting it into Objectives, and structuring the solution hypothesis. Get cooking!

10. *Unstick Stuck Stuff*. Take a fresh look at stalled projects, programs, and strategies; identify and evaluate alternatives; and redirect your efforts along promising directions. Use LogFrames at any project phase to plan and execute current and future phases. Break loose from stale thinking by brainstorming fresh Purpose statements and see what new possibilities emerge.

11. *Structure Project Evaluations*. The LogFrame can be used to organize evaluations of ongoing projects in the portfolio as well as completed projects. The LogFrame Purpose will describe the evaluation intent, while the Outcomes will identify the various analytic and information chunks you need to make informed decisions.

12. *Organize Learning and Development*. This tool works well to sharpen learning and development programs of all types. Purpose describes desired behavior change; Goal highlights the expected benefits; and Outcomes define the learning delivery

system. Progressive teams use this tool to identify and develop the competencies required now and in the future. What new skills or cross-training does your team need?

Try as I might, whittling the possibilities down to an even dozen was difficult. Here are two bonus applications beyond this dynamic dozen.

13. *Take a High Level First-Cut.* Planning a research program to find intelligent life on Mars? Purchasing a remote island and starting your own country? Use the LogFrame as a front-end tool for high-level scoping of super-sized projects.

14. *Adjunct for Outside-the-Box Projects.* If your organization has a formal project development system, this approach offers a practical adjunct. For example, Procter & Gamble has a superb new product development system, but their system is not suited to handle initiatives such as developing excellent teamwork, fostering a culture of excellence, or shifting corporate directions. The LogFrame offers a fresh perspective for just about anything that doesn't fit your organization's standard project management methodology.

Terry's Tips for Doing the Project RAP (Rapid Action Planning)

The best way to harness the minds and hearts of key people and design a great project is through a well-structured "RAP" (Rapid Action Planning) workshop. In these focused planning workshops, the core team (plus other major stakeholders) carves out a plan of attack using the LogFrame to guide the conversation and document the results. This gets you going on the right track, even if some details are still hazy. RAP events follow custom-designed agendas that fit the project context, and are often professionally facilitated.

How long does this take? It all depends. A small or medium project might take half-a-day to two days to sketch out sufficiently, and even large initiatives can be 80 percent planned after two or three days of continuous or intermittent planning. Large projects do not necessarily require longer initial planning time because core segments can usually be broken off and begun while planning continues in an ongoing parallel effort.

But don't short-change your upfront planning or you'll pay for it later. Remember NASA Rule #15 and Remers Rule of 10. You can save a lot of time, money and headaches by doing the initial planning right.

The quick formula for a successful team RAP session is summarized here with these five tips.

Tip #1. Invite the Key Players

Who are your core team members? These are the people you absolutely want there. You can also invite your high-level champions for the entire session, or just to kick it off by sharing their expectations at the session start. They can also join in at the end of the session to review the draft design, offer comments, and learn what is expected from them.

Make sure that everyone on the team has read this book and is familiar with these tools beforehand, or be prepared to spend some time educating them yourself. Having a common framework and planning language will harmonize your team and accelerate forward progress.

Tip #2. Use a Skilled Process Facilitator

The key word in process facilitator is *process*. A skilled facilitator makes all the difference in the world. You know from personal experience how difficult it is to be a competent project manager. Well, it's even more difficult to be a competent project manager and a good facilitator at the same time. While exceptions exist, people who try to fill both roles usually end up doing both poorly.

For major projects, bring in a neutral, but skilled facilitator who is outside the project system to guide the RAP sessions. This could be an external consultant or an internal facilitator (check with Human Resources). Seasoned facilitators do not feel threatened if they are required to ask hard questions, point out gaps, or bring a rambling discussion back on track. Their expertise at moving meetings forward productively makes them a smart investment.

Of course, you may not have the option of using an external facilitator, so I've included some guidelines for flying solo later in the chapter.

Tip #3. Set up the Room for Productive Results

Meeting room setups dramatically affect the quality of your process and results. Your group will generate a lot of information, which you want to rapidly capture and plug in when and where it's needed.

Consider how to arrange the room for maximum interaction and idea capture. Keep information visible to all during the process. Have a flip-chart pad (or several), plenty of marking pens, and masking tape to paste up pages on the walls. Post key ideas where all can see, add to, and own their ideas.

The best results occur when everyone can see their ideas being plugged into a large LogFrame grid. For this reason, work from a large whiteboard or blackboard on which you sketch a LogFrame grid. (See the Appendix resource section for a large laminated, reusable LogFrame grid that's ideal for team use.) Another option is to link a computer to an LCD projector and display the LogFrame grid as a work in progress.

Make a large LogFrame visible to all invites collaborative teamwork. The least effective way is to write responses on a pad of paper where only one person can see them. Also, avoid having only one person keep notes of the LogFrame on a personal notebook or computer while everyone else sits around a table. The energy of putting the LogFrame together as a team visibly multiplies enthusiasm and builds shared commitment.

When team members are dispersed remotely and face-to-face meetings aren't practical, find ways to work collaboratively using on-line technology.

Tip #4. Follow the Strategic Questions and LogFrame Structure

The Four Critical Strategic Questions offer a user-friendly, jargon-free way to get the group started. Go deeper with the detailed trigger questions found in Chapter 4 to coax out the issues and fine-tune the project design.

As the discussion proceeds, listen very carefully. Without necessarily using the LogFrame terminology, people will describe Objectives, Measures, and Assumptions. Your task is to plug their ideas into the LogFrame structure and populate the grid.

Periodically test for consensus, beginning with the vertical logic (Goal, Purpose, and Outcomes). Once this is in place, you may proceed to Measures, then Assumptions. This is iterative planning that will benefit from adjustments and refinements as the RAP session proceeds.

Tip #5. Capture the Results

At the start, have the team decide how they will record the information they generate. Draft somebody with a laptop to capture and circulate the end results. Better yet, assign one or more people the task of writing up the final results. Having two sets of eyes working on any document ensures greater accuracy and more thorough information capture.

Lots of other ideas will come up too that are not immediately germane. Note this on a "bin list" posted on the wall. Don't allow your effort to become sidetracked or derailed by getting off the topic.

You can also capture flip-chart sheets and work products pasted to the wall with a high-resolution digital camera, and transcribe them later.

Facilitating by Yourself

Like an orchestra conductor, when you facilitate, you do not play an instrument. Rather, you wield the baton and bring the individual musicians' best skills into harmony to produce satisfying music.

There may be times when you'll have more technical expertise than the group members, but do not be overly directive in steering them toward any single approach. Let them own it too. Your role is to build from the ideas of the whole group, not supply all of the right answers. If you want to make substantive comments, call timeout and let the group know you are stepping out of your process facilitation role for a moment to make your subject matter comment, and then return to that role.

Experience shows that a good design, developed and supported by the team, has a much better chance of success than a perfect design developed by a project manager (or external consultant) with only minor team involvement.

The Four Critical Strategic Questions are your primary tool for steering the group. Ask lots of related questions and work their answers into the LogFrame cells. You will often need to read between the lines to interpret and supportively restate their responses before plugging them into the matrix.

Skilled facilitators often use flip-charts to capture raw ideas and move selected information into a LogFrame grid as the evolving discussion makes it apparent where all the information fits. This technique allows you to incorporate all of the good ideas while diplomatically ignoring those that do not fit.

Team comments will often reveal a clear project approach, but you may need to sharpen their thinking.

- Suggest different phraseology. For example, you may say, "By the phrase 'Make it work better,' do you mean 'Improve system operations?'"
- Point out and test project linkages. You can increase confidence in the strategic hypothesis by showing how things fit together using LogFrame logic.
- Integrate comments made by various members. For example, "John said the project Objective is to 'Deploy the new product,' and Bill said the Objective is to 'Increase market share.' Does it make sense that, if you deploy the new product, you will increase sales, which will increase market share?"

Think not only outside the bar chart but outside the LogFrame itself. While the LogFrame provides focus, don't let it limit you. Allow and encourage broader discussion about the environment, project context, and critical factors for success.

Taking Strategic Action Now

Now, Are You Strategic?
If my Assumptions are correct, you are!

If you've read this book mindfully, you're well on your way. And, if you've applied the concepts and tools by following the Application Tips (or plan to do so soon), you're even further down the path.

The upfront investment of time and energy you make in mastering these concepts will pay handsome dividends again and again in delivering successful projects while saving time, money, and frustration. Keep the book handy, reread it often, and consult the references in the Appendix.

Remember that developing the LogFrame is a *process*, which is more important than the resulting project plan that documents your rigorous thinking process. The finished products offer a *Means of Verification* that you've tackled the right questions and followed a quality planning process where all involved should truly understand *why* they are doing the project, as well as the *how, who, what* and *when*.

Putting a brief LogFrame document in the hands of key stakeholders and executive team members will keep everyone focused and on-path. The ultimate value from using The LogFrame approach, however, is that it changes how you and your team think, plan, act, and assess in order to turn your project ideas into spectacular successes.

I strongly encourage you to commit to doing at least one LogFrame—on any topic—within the next week. Research shows that retention of newly learned skills increases dramatically when practiced soon after initial exposure. Maximize the payoff from your investment in reading this book by applying the information quickly, while it is still fresh in your mind.

Keep your first LogFrame simple. Avoid trying to make it great or perfect—instead, just get the first version done. Review it with the self-scoring checklist in the Appendix. Then, make it better step by step.

By mastering these ideas, you'll upgrade your effectiveness and reap long-term benefits, no matter what field you're in. I'd love to hear about how you are using this approach to gain the strategic edge in your work and life.

My ultimate aim in writing this book was to give you the ideas and inspiration you need to be more effective. As I mentioned at the end of the Introduction, Strategic Project Management helps you think smarter, move faster, and accomplish ambitious Objectives more quickly. People who can do that are a rare breed—and now, you are one of them.

APPENDIX
Reference Tools and Resources

Blank Logical Framework Grid

Objectives	Success Measures	Verification	Assumptions
Goal:	Goal Measures:		Assumptions to reach Goal:
Purpose:	Purpose Measures:		Assumptions to achieve Purpose:
Outcomes:	Outcome Measures:		Assumptions to produce Outcomes:

Inputs: *Activities and Resources*	Responsible	Resources	Schedule (in weeks, months, etc.)																			Assumptions for Inputs:
1. Outcome #1																						
1.1																						
1.2																						
1.3																						
2. Outcome #2																						
2.1																						
2.2																						
2.3																						
3. Outcome #3																						
3.1																						
3.2																						
3.3																						
4. Outcome #4																						
4.1																						
4.2																						
4.3																						
5. Outcome #5																						
5.1																						
5.2																						
5.3																						
6. Outcome #6																						
6.1																						
6.2																						
6.3																						

207

Logical Framework Quality Checklist

Review how well each element of your LogFrame meets these criteria
(*? = Maybe*).

Goal Check

___Yes ___No ___?   1. Supports or describes an important strategic objective.

___Yes ___No ___?   2. Stated clearly in measurable terms.

___Yes ___No ___?   3. Not the project name, a restatement, or summary of the Purpose/Outcomes.

Purpose Check

___Yes ___No ___?   4. LogFrame has a single Purpose, clearly stated.

___Yes ___No ___?   5. Describes change in behavior, performance, or conditions expected.

___Yes ___No ___?   6. Describes impact expected from Outcomes; doesn't summarize them.

___Yes ___No ___?   7. A level above the implementation team's direct control.

___Yes ___No ___?   8. Purpose plus Assumptions are both *necessary and sufficient* to reach the Goal.

Outcomes Check

___Yes ___No ___?   9. Outcomes clearly describe what the team can deliver or make happen.

___Yes ___No ___?   10. The Outcomes are logically chunked. No overlaps/gaps.

___Yes ___No ___?   11. All Outcomes necessary to achieve Purpose are included (none missing).

___Yes ___No ___?   12. Each Outcome is necessary to achieve Purpose (no non-essentials).

___Yes ___No ___?   13. Collectively, this set of Outcomes will achieve Purpose.

___Yes ___No ___?   14. Outcomes plus Assumptions are both *necessary and sufficient* to achieve Purpose.

Activities Check

___Yes ___No ___?   15. The key activities for each Outcome have been listed.

___Yes ___No ___?   16. Activities are chunked at roughly the same level of detail.

___Yes ___No ___?   17. Together, the activities can produce the Outcomes.

Measures Check

___Yes ___No ___?   18. Specific in terms of quantity, quality, and time.

___Yes ___No ___?   19. Measures what is important about each Objective.

___Yes ___No ___?   20. Each Measure has a practical means of verification.

___Yes ___No ___?   21. Changes in status of Measures attributable to achievement of Objective.

Assumptions Check

___Yes ___No ___?   22. Formulated as desirable, positive conditions that must exist for valid *If-then* logic.

___Yes ___No ___?   23. Placed at the level of Objective they affect.

___Yes ___No ___?   24. Clearly stated and include Measures as appropriate.

___Yes ___No ___?   25. Cover all key outside factors that impact the project.

General Check

___Yes ___No ___?   26. Acronyms and abbreviations have been spelled out.

___Yes ___No ___?   27. The logic among Inputs, Outcomes, Purpose, and Goal is sound.

___Yes ___No ___?   28. Developed by key players, or will be reviewed by them.

___Yes ___No ___?   29. Permits development of linked tools (WBS, Gantt, etc.).

Logical Framework Application Case Studies

The following case studies illustrate a variety of client applications of the LogFrame. Many of these may serve as basic templates that you can modify and use to fit your projects.

Organization Turnaround and Best Practice Example
(Fircrest School for the Developmentally Disabled)

Fircrest School for the Developmentally Disabled is a residential home for some 800 adults and children who suffer from serious mental, physical, and emotional developmental disabilities. Fircrest is funded by both the State of Washington and the federal government, and is managed by the Washington State Department of Social and Health Services.

Several disturbing incidents indicated that residents were not being properly treated and their quality of life was low. There were some unexplained injuries to residents and even one suspicious death. Visiting experts noted an overuse of psychoactive medications and restraints. Quality assurance was lacking. Medical and nursing care records were not timely and accurate. Too many nurses were assigned to administrative duties and too few to resident care and treatments.

Following an audit, federal certification was revoked, along with millions of dollars of federal funding. This presented Fircrest management with a serious problem that needed solving quickly and in the right way. Project manager Katie Cameron used the Logical Framework with her project team to develop a strategy to regain federal certification.

This example reflects a best practice use of LogFrame concepts. In particular, it includes good Measures and Verifications at all levels along with a clear and well-organized work plan (Input level).

Logical Framework for
Improving Social Service Delivery (Fircrest School for the Developmentally Disabled)

Objectives	Success Measures	Verification	Assumptions
Goal: Federal certification standards are achieved and maintained at Fircrest School.	**Goal Measures:** 1. Sometime after October 31, all ICF/MR regulatory surveys will be completed with no findings of conditional level deficiencies. 2. Fircrest continues to operate at high standards of health, safety, quality care and human rights.	1. Written decision from survey team with no conditional level findings. 2. Follow-up annual surveys with no negative findings.	**Assumptions to reach Goal:** 1. DSHS Secretary does not make agreement with government that Fircrest is unaware of. 2. No unanticipated Federal government (Dept. of Justice) litigation actions. 3. State Attorney General will have plan in place to file appeal by 8/3.
Purpose: People who live at Fircrest are safe, healthy, receive quality care and their human rights are protected.	**Purpose Measures:** 1. A 50% reduction in resident injury that requires nursing, medical care or intervention occurs between 1/1 and 10/31. 2. No unusual or suspicious resident deaths occur between 1/1 and 10/31. 3. An 80% reduction in restraints and time out use will be achieved between 1/1 and 10/31. 4. A 25% reduction in number of residents being prescribed psychoactive medication occurs between 1/1 and 10/31. 5. 75% of residents are engaged in paid work activities for three or more hours per day by 9/1.	1.1 Review and summarize incident reports. 1.2 Review/tabulate injuries from medical notes. 2. Review coroner reports. 3. Review and summarize restraint and time out records. 4. Review pharmacy/drug administration records. 5. Collect, review and summarize resident production records and paycheck information.	**Assumptions to achieve Purpose:** 1. Resident injuries are all reported on incident reports and progress notes. 2. Coroner conducts autopsies on all deaths. 3. Staff fill out restraint/time out records. 4. Production records are kept with sufficient detail.

Objectives	Success Measures	Verification	Assumptions
Outcomes:	**Outcome Measures:**		**Assumptions to produce Outcomes:**
1. New resident rehabilitation program system is implemented.	1.1 By July 1, 95% of resident (awake) hours will be organized and managed by new treatment programs.	1.1 Observe each hour of program at each training site.	1. Staff are adequately trained and aware of new program expectations.
2. Quality Assurance system is implemented to maintain rehabilitation program changes.	2.1 At least 10 FTEs are assigned to conduct QA activities.	2.1 Check personnel records.	2. Union agreement can be reached.
	2.2 QA checklist with target program indicators is implemented in all training locations.	2.2 Checklist published.	
	2.3 QA data is used by program teams to modify/ revise/correct faulty programs.	2.3 Survey all program teams for use of data.	3. Chosen leading indicators are accurate reflections of good programs from the perspective of the survey team members.
3. Facility reorganized with staff redeployed.	3.1 By June 1, 100% of affected staffing change will be completed. Staff better deployed to support resident care and treatment.	3.1 Check personnel records.	4. Forms and records changes selected will result in "real" rather than "perceived" time savings for targeted personnel.
4. Human rights protection is implemented.	4.1 100% of resident behavior programs and 100% of prescribed psychoactive medications have consent from legal representative by 9/1.	4.1 Records reviewed.	
	4.2 By September 1, 80% of resident-initiated grievances will be recognized/responded to by at least one protection committee member within 48 hours.	4.2 Minutes reviewed.	5. Maintenance man-hours and funding available.
	4.3 An ombudsman is available for residents and families by June 15.	4.3 Appointments announced.	
5. Medical and nursing care records are streamlined to free up more MD and nurse treatment hours.	5.1 By June 15, new medical record forms are in 100% of resident charts and are being completed accurately.	5.1 Sample 25% of records.	6. Budget authorized.
	5.2 By September 1, at least 85% of nurses and MDs will increase treatment hours by 20%.	5.2 Nurses and MDs will conduct one week of self-survey/work-time study.	
6. Physical plant "beautification" and modifications to support new programs are completed.	6.1 1000 square feet of a new day program space is created by June 1.	6.1 Tour and measure space.	
	6.2 New living room furniture and furnishings will be in place in 28 houses by August 1.	6.2 Tour all homes.	
	6.3 All campus lawns are cut to "acceptable "level and maintained on weekly basis, beginning May 1.	6.3 Spot check weekly.	

213

Inputs: How team will produce Outcomes			Schedule (in months)												Assumptions for Inputs:
Action Steps	Responsible	$	J	F	M	A	M	J	J	A	S	O	N	D	
1. NEW RESIDENT REHABILITATION PROGRAMS		$60K													1. QA System/data can be computerized
1.1 Retain technical experts	Director		▌												2. Computer staff have expertise to design adequate system
1.2 Develop schedule	Expert			▌											
1.3 Retrain staff	Expert							▌							3. Union agreement reached
1.4 Write new resident programs	Staff														4. Sufficient volunteers and non-staff committee members can be appointed
1.5 Implement and modify new programs as needed	Staff												▌		
2. QUALITY ASSURANCE SYSTEM		$25K													
2.1 Assign staff	Superintndnt			▌											
2.2 Design system	Expert			▌											
2.3 Purchase computers	Bus. Mgr.														
2.4 Create prototype	QA Team														
2.5 Collect QA data	QA Team														
2.6 Distribute QA data	QA Team												▌		
3. REORGANIZATION															
3.1 New/changed roles and responsibilities determined	Expert														
3.2 Roles matched to job classes	Personnel				▌										
3.3 Resources for new roles determined	Superintndnt				▌										
3.4 Negotiate with unions	Superintndnt														
3.5 Notify affected staff	Personnel														
3.6 Staff practice new roles	Staff														
4. HUMAN RIGHTS SYSTEM															
4.1 Write policy/procedure	Expert			▌											
4.2 Establish new committees	Superintndnt														
4.3 Appoint committee members	Superintndnt												▌		
4.4 Analyze QA data	Chair														
4.5 Review with Superintendent	Chair					▌									
5. MEDICAL RECORDS		$3K													
5.1 Identify target records	Expert						▌								
5.2 Draft new forms and chart contents	Records						▌								
5.3 Change forms/reprint new forms	Records										▌				
5.4 Retrain staff	Staff														
5.5 Purge and revise charts	Staff														
6. PHYSICAL PLANT MODIFICATIONS		$500K													
6.1 Design new program space	Staff			▌											
6.2 Determine furniture requirements	Staff			▌											
6.3 Purchase materials and furnishings	Bus. Mgr.						▌								
6.4 Remodel/construct	Plant Mgr.									▌					
6.5 Install new furnishings	Plant Mgr.									▌					
6.6 Grounds maintenance scheduled implemented	Plant Mgr.												▌		
	$ Total	**$588K**													

Develop or Update Strategic Plan
(Lawrence Livermore National Laboratory—LLNL)

This case study shows how the LLNL Safety and Security Division (SSD) defined their strategic thrusts and turned each into LogFrame execution plans.

The services provided by this organization became even more important after 9/11. The organization's responsibilities ranged widely from physical security (guns, gates, and badges) to computer security to protection of vital nuclear assets on site. Division leadership recognized the need to upgrade their strategic plans in order to increase operational effectiveness.

To give you a feel for how an outside process consultant can catalyze an organization's strategic planning efforts, read about what happened when I was invited to facilitate SSD's planning sessions. My consulting support consisted of a one-day preparation session with eight top leaders, a two-day training session with 30 senior leaders and supervisors, and a one-day follow-up session with all participants.

On the morning of the preparation session, I met with their key leaders to understand the context of and constraints on the effort. In the afternoon, an 18-person management team brainstormed possible strategic Objectives by pulling from related strategic plans. The list of some 40 Objectives was refined into logical categories, which were later re-chunked into four LogFrame Strategies.

These four selected strategies form a useful acronym (CLIM), which stands for:

1. *C*ommunicate Effectively
2. *L*ead & Develop People
3. *I*mprove Processes
4. *M*anage Strategically

At a two-day, off-site session a week later, I trained a 30-person leadership team. They then organized themselves into four project teams that would develop Logical Frameworks for each strategy. They left the session with solid draft plans, and the CLIM acronym helped managers communicate the general strategy with their teams after the workshop. A one-day follow-up was held a month later to review progress and fine-tune their plans.

SSD has since moved forward on all four strategies at a pace that has allowed them to make steady progress, but not overwhelm the people who still had their other operational roles and responsibilities.

One of their LogFrames, *Communicate Effectively*, is included here.

Logical Framework for Communicate Effectively

Objectives	Success Measures	Verification	Assumptions
Goal: Effective departmental communication.	**Goal Measures:** 1. UC Contract, DOE, institutional performance measures are met.	1. Finding free this year.	**Assumptions to reach Goal:** 1. Information is credible and has value.
Purpose: Disseminate information effectively both externally and internally.	**Purpose Measures:** 1. Quality of communications improved, people feel better informed.	1. Customer survey.	**Assumptions to achieve Purpose:** 1. Employees embrace organizational values.
Outcomes: 1. Employee and customer information needs are established. 2. Expected methods of communication are identified and used. 3. Forums of communication are established and utilized. 4. Communication GAP Analysis conducted.	**Outcome Measures:** 1. Conduct baseline survey and evaluate results by March 31. 2. Expected communication methods are developed and implemented by April 30. 3. Forums are developed and documented via communication plan by May 31. 4. A survey to identify strengths and weaknesses is conducted by June 15.	1. Survey findings. 2. Communication plan. 3. Communication plan. 4. Completed document.	**Assumptions to produce Outcomes:** 1. Resources will be available to implement improvements (people, money). 2. Culture supports continuous improvement philosophy. 3. The "Daily Grind" will not override attempts to "make it better." 4. No unanticipated external factors will intervene to stunt improvement.

Inputs: How teams will produce Outcomes

Action Steps	Responsibilities	Resources	Schedule (in weeks, months, etc.)							Assumptions for Inputs:
1. INFORMATION NEEDS · Establish team · Define structure of focus group · ID focus group participation · Develop employee/customer survey · Review survey and analyze data										
2. COMMUNICATION METHODS · Identify current methods of communication · Define expected methods										
3. FORUMS ESTABLISHED · Consider alternatives · Choose appropriate ones										
4. GAP ANALYSIS · Identify organizations to benchmark · Poll customers and employees · Analyze data · Develop and implement solutions										

Reinvent Your Department
(Los Alamos National Laboratory—LANL)

The Facilities Maintenance Unit (FMU) at the Los Alamos National Laboratory (LANL) aimed at nothing less than total transformation because customer demands were increasing and they were falling far behind.

The role of a FMU in any organization is seldom glamorous but always vital. The FMU at LANL keeps the electrical, mechanical, HVAC, and other systems operating so that scientists can carry out their work in support of national security.

This Lab FMU served 8 very old facilities dispersed over a 30-square-mile radius. The level of maintenance required exceeded staff capacity. As the backlog of work orders climbed, conflicts increased and morale declined.

The FMU Director recognized that a major transformation was necessary, not just minor improvements. Assisted by outside consultants, his team collaboratively developed a vision, mission, values, and code of conduct. All staff participated in the process through a series of brief workshops over a two-month period.

With those elements in place, it was time to shape the master improvement strategy, summarized by the included LogFrame. Outcomes such as "Roles clearly defined" and "Priorities sharpened" are part of any improvement strategy and were vital to achieving clarity. Later, sub-teams were formed to create additional LogFrames for key projects.

The FMU LogFrame is interesting because of the specificity of its Purpose level Success Measures. The Outcomes offer a set of ideas about possible improvement elements that can transform your own organization's future.

Logical Framework for
Facilities Maintenance Unit (FMU) Transformation

Objectives	Success Measures	Verification	Assumptions
Goal: Improve facility infrastructure and services at the Lab.	**Goal Measures:** 1. Conditions improve as measured by standard criteria in documents x, y and z.	1. Annual Facility Assessments.	**Assumptions to reach Goal:** 1. Resources available to perform annual assessments. 2. Data maintained/reported.
Purpose: Transform Facilities Maintenance Unit (FMU) into a highly responsive, effective, and efficient facility management organization.	**Purpose Measures:** 1. By October 31, annual customer satisfaction rate is consistently >90%. 2. Work order response time decreases from current average of ___ days to average of <30 days by ___. 3. Work order backlog of ___ is reduced to <200 and maintained <200. 4. Work order age is reduced to <60 days and maintained <60. 5. Monthly and annual PM compliance rate reaches and is maintained at 100%. 6. Employee satisfaction reaches and remains above 90% and 90% of employees give team environment high rating. 7. 95% of all projects are completed on schedule, within approved budget, and with change orders totaling less than 10% of approved budget.	1. Survey results. 2. Weekly work order reports. 3. Weekly work order reports. 4. Weekly work order reports. 5. Monthly PM schedule compliance reports. 6. Annual employee survey. 7. Monitor project.	**Assumptions to achieve Purpose:** 1. No unforeseen calamities. 2. Maintenance staff is committed to program. 3. Good communication among staff.
Outcomes: 1. Analysis of strengths and weaknesses of facility management unit completed. 2. Roles and responsibilities within the organization clarified. 3. Key strategies, objectives, and priorities identified. 4. Facility condition assessments for all major facilities completed and updated annually. 5. Objective priority system established for work orders and projects. 6. Plan for improving cooperation and team work among employees developed and implemented. 7. Formal processes established to effectively support improved operations.	**Outcome Measures:** 1. Completed analysis performed by March 1 with customers and employees involved. 2. Meeting with employees where roles and responsibilities are explained, understood, and accepted by April 1. 3. By June 1, management team has agreed. 4. All major facilities have completed condition assessment by June 1. 5. Completed priority system document completed by July 11. 6. Plan developed and endorsed by employees; employees satisfaction reaches and remains above 90% by July 15. 7. 100% of team-identified formal process needs have been met by August 1.	1. Written analysis. 2. Meeting minutes. 3. Sign-off on document. 4. Finished Asessments on file. 5. Document on file. 6. Plan on file. 7. Quarterly Inspections on file.	**Assumptions to produce Outcomes:** 1. Maintenance staff is capable and willing to do this. 2. Group meetings held monthly.

Strengthen Teamwork Across Functions
(ARINC Director Action Group Task Force)

ARINC, an Annapolis systems engineering company, is best known for managing aircraft communications over the Atlantic Ocean as well as for their airport status display systems.

ARINC used the LogFrame with executive task forces. They adopted this tool as an innovative way to help groom director-level staff members and ready them to become VPs. Promising executives were selected from across the company and put into a Director Action Group (DAG). DAGs were assigned a business initiative sponsored by the president of the company and given six weeks to deliver. The LogFrame helped them get a rapid start and facilitated discussion across the various functional perspectives represented in each group.

This case study LogFrame aims at establishing an overseas infrastructure to strengthen their business in Europe.

Logical Framework for
Building Infrastructure for Global Growth through Acquisition

Objectives	Success Measures	Verification	Assumptions
Goal: ARINC has an infrastructure that facilitates global growth in multiple market segments.	**Goal Measures:** 1. Revenue and EBIT grows by 15–20% within two years in at least two identified international markets 2. Five Year Plans contain significant revenue and EBIT from international sources. 3. ARINC expands into a new global location within three years.	1. Financial reports show actual growth over fiscal years. 2. Backlog and bookings figures for future/current business associated with new products/services. 3. ARINC establishes a viable business entity within another region.	**Assumptions to reach Goal:** 1. ARINC will have the capital funding that may be required to support growth.
Purpose: Executive Management has sufficient information to implement an effective international business operations infrastructure.	**Purpose Measures:** 1. Within 6 months of briefing, at least 50% of recommendations have been adopted in at least three of the sub-categories. 2. Within 1 year, 75% of corporate business units have adopted at least 80% of recommendations in each sub-category. 3. Two new product/service offerings identified that are specific to a unique international market.	1. Review corporate business policies. 2. Review policies. 3. Review plans.	**Assumptions to achieve Purpose:** 1. Corporate management is receptive to change in their international operations. 2. In order to meet corporate growth goals, ARINC needs to expand into global markets. 3. Core products and services can be adapted to different market segments.
Outcomes: 1. Summary report on company selection criteria for 8 potential acquisition companies completed. 2. Benchmark study of 5 companies (including ARINC) completed. 3. Comparative analysis of 5 companies performed. 4. Alternative structural analyses completed. 5. Presentation completed and Executive Management is briefed.	**Outcome Measures:** 1. Sponsor concurs with both criteria and with 80% of companies identified by June 11. 2. 75% of required data collected for each company by July 1. Template is compiled for each selected company by July 4. 3. 90% of DAG members and sponsor review completed studies by July 10. 4a. Responses are categorized and assembled in matrix form. 4b. Value judgment and expertise applied to comparative data to develop analyses that are relevant and/or will benefit ARINC. 5. All six sub-categories contain comparative data relevant to ARINC.	1. Successful sponsor meeting. 2. Completed templates are reviewed and approved by the DAG group and sponsor. 3. Matrix and comparative analyses are finalized for review with sponsor at July DAG meeting. 4. Feedback from executive staff during presentation. 5. Completed briefing.	**Assumptions to produce Outcomes:** 1. Outside company respondents are credible. 2. Data are accurate. 3. Eight companies provide a representative and comprehensive platform to conduct review. 4. Responses can be obtained on schedule. 5. Enough similarities exist between companies to conduct a valid comparative analysis.

Develop Information Technology Process Solutions and Algorithms
(U.S. Department of Energy)

Nuclear weapons remain an essential component in the national security strategy of the United States. Each year the U.S. Department of Energy (DOE) Secretary must certify to the President that the stockpile is reliable. A team from the DOE developed a new anomaly tracking system to support the Energy Secretary's need to provide this certification.

Since 1992, various international treaties have prevented the occasional live testing of a nuclear weapon from the arsenal to make sure that all of them would still function if needed. To maintain these weapons as a potent deterrent, reliable nuclear weapons assessment methods (other than detonation above or below ground) must be used.

Ensuring nuclear stockpile reliability involves lab tests, computer simulations, and analyses of all types. Surveillance of nuclear assets is critical, and the system to do so is complex. Occasionally, an anomaly shows up that needs investigating and resolution.

This LogFrame was developed by a team responsible for developing and managing an anomaly tracking system. Speeding up anomaly disposition allowed for more timely decisions, which supports the overall Goal of certifying stockpile reliability.

Logical Framework for
Reducing Cycle Time for Anomaly Detection

Objectives	Success Measures	Verification	Assumptions
Super Goal: Ensure stockpile reliability.	**Super Goal Measures:** Stockpile fitness report reflects more up-to-date information in regards to Anomaly disposition.	Compare current and past reports.	**Assumptions to reach Super Goal:**
Goal: Reduce cycle time from Anomaly detection through closeout.	**Goal Measures:** 1. X% of ATs closed w/in established limits by _____. 2. Y% of ATs dispensed within established limits by _____.	1. Review dates from start to finish and compare to metrics identified in process.	**Assumptions to reach Goal:** 1. AT process performs as designed.
Purpose: Release and implement new "Anomaly Tracking" (AT) process.	**Purpose Measures:** 1. X months after process release, lifecycle will be reduced from _____ to _____ days. 2. By _____, lifecycle will be reduced to _____ days.	1. Compare data with baseline data from value stream report.	**Assumptions to achieve Purpose:** 1. Complex is on-board. 2. Management support continues.
Outcomes: 1. New Anomaly Tracking (AT) process released. 2. PMO created and staffed. 3. PMO launched. 4. AT Process Training Program developed and taught.	**Outcome Measures:** 1. Reviewed, signed and released to WFS. 2.1 Org. chart released to 2950 website by _____. Describes roles of project manager, tech lead and Anomaly chair; including reporting and test results. 2.2 Dept. roster includes PMO updated to reflect new employees. 3. PMO begins to facilitate Anomaly tracking meetings and effectively manage the AT process. 4.1 Release training to TEDS and add to course curriculum for appropriate organizations by _____. 4.2 X% of SEEs receive training by _____. 4.3 Y% of system/component engineers trained by _____.	1. WFS # assigned and visually located. 2.1 Visually inspect 2950 website. 2.2 Verify additional staff are included in dept. roster. 3. Review meeting minutes, track budget costs and scorecards. 4. Visually inspect TEDS curriculum catalog of courses.	**Assumptions to produce Outcomes:** 1. Management champions committed to process. 2. Staff available and management approves budget and process approved. 3. Staff want to be trained; management supports training; and corporate training will help implement training.

Inputs: *How team will produce Outcomes*	1. Who's Responsible	2. Other Persons Involved	3. Complete by Date	4. Resources Required	5. Information Needed	6. Information Needed	7. Comment
Activities:							
1. New Anomaly Tracking (AT) Process Released.							
1.1 Develop a standard for reporting requirements for dismissing an anomaly.							
1.2 Develop and implement anomaly review board w/defined roles.							
1.3 Develop a preliminary investigation process/criteria w/timelines capability to report and escalate.							
1.4 Define and implement standard requirements for opening documents.							
1.5 Define content and threshold of Project Plan (include risk management and movement of hardware).							
2. PMO Created and Staffed.							
2.1 Identify PMO requirements.							
2.2 Define roles and responsibilities of key staff.							
2.3 Announce organization.							
3. PMO Launched.							
4. AT Process-Training Program Developed and Released.							

Design and Launch Sales or Marketing Initiatives
(Avemar Cancer Treatment in Thailand)

This case study describes how an international consortium planned to expand sales of a cancer-fighting nutrient to provincial areas in Thailand.

Virtually every organization needs to expand sales, increase customers, or open new distribution channels. BioMedicare, Inc. is a joint venture company with Hungarian, Korean, and Thai partners. The Thai partners are the sole distributor in Thailand. Their focus is on distributing Avemar, a medical nutrient proven effective in fighting cancer. The company also funds substantial clinical research in various medical schools and hospitals around the world.

After establishing strong sales operations in Thailand's capital city of Bangkok, and in other large cities, they needed to expand sales into provincial areas. This required a well-trained sales force and a program for educating doctors. This LogFrame shows their plan for rolling out the product to rural provinces.

Logical Framework for
Expanding Sales of Avemar Cancer Treatment in Thailand

Objectives	Success Measures	Verification	Assumptions
Goal: To promote quality of life by Avemar to cancer patients nationwide.	**Goal Measures:** 1. Prescribed numbers nationwide increased by 20% in current year. 2. Product achieves 15% market share in 3 years.	1. Market Report and Analysis Market Report 2. Sales Report	***Assumptions to reach Goal:*** 1. No economic crisis. 2. No breakthrough medical method of curing cancer. 3. Quality of product to meet proven medical benefits contribute as promised.
Purpose: To achieve greater number of satisfied customers nationwide.	**Purpose Measures:** 1. Within next year, 100% sales increase in target provincial areas; 5% increase in existing areas. 2. Customer satisfaction increased from 80% to 95% satisfaction.	1. Sales Report 2. Customer Survey	***Assumptions to achieve Purpose:*** 1. No serious blame on the product in public. 2. Existing oncologist accounts still believe in and continue to prescribe our product. 3. Customers appreciate new support and service.
Outcomes: 1. Promotional materials developed and published. 2. Prospects introduced in target provincial areas. 3. Sales revenue from existing accounts maintained. 4. Sales force strengthened. 5. Customer support programs introduced.	**Outcome Measures:** 1. Includes information brochures, materials for both doctors and patients. 2. Minimum of 500 doctors are newly introduced to product and its benefits through personal contact from Reps. 3. 5% sales deviation from existing accounts. 4. By Jan 31, new salespeople hired and trained by experts. Training covers product's detail and selling technique. 5. Programs include medical advice, online and toll-free ordering.	1. Visual Review 2. KPI Report 3. Sales Report 4. Customer Survey 5. Assessment and Test results	***Assumptions to produce Outcomes:*** 1. Clinical data are proven and available to public. 2. Information and data on prospects are available and accurate. 3. Sales reps do their job. 4. Adequate number of sales reps. 5. Training material and facility are in place.

Inputs: How team will produce Outcomes

Action Steps	Responsible	Resources (BHT)	1	2	3	4	5	6	7	8	9	10	11	12
1. Promotional materials developed and published														
1.1 Print 2nd edition handbook.	Jumpol	50,000		*										
1.2 Develop new brochure.	Nathapol	20,000		*										
1.3 Create new discount coupon.	Nathapol	5,000	*											
2. Prospects in target provincial areas introduced														
2.1 Identify and select prospects in general hospital.	Tony		*											
2.2 Meet prospects and introduce product effectiveness,	Sales rep.			*	*	*	*	*	*	*	*	*	*	*
2.3 Deliver handbook and brochure.	Sales rep.	100,000		*	*	*	*	*	*	*	*	*	*	*
2.4 Arrange monthly meeting by a seminar with prospects.	Dr. Kumpo & Dr. Banjob	1,000,000	*	*	*	*	*	*	*	*	*	*	*	*
3. Sales revenue from existing accounts maintained														
3.1 Increase time table and frequency of visit.	Sales rep		*	*	*	*	*	*	*	*	*	*	*	*
3.2 Remind about product effectiveness and update news or latest improvement.	Sales rep		*	*	*	*	*	*	*	*	*	*	*	*
4. Sales force strengthened														
4.1 Recruit five new sales reps to be responsible for target area.	Nuna	1,500,000 1st year	*											
4.2 Train sales reps on product knowledge, selling technique, etc.	Dr. Nayada and Tony		*											
5. Customer support programs made														
5.1 Medical supportive calls.	Dr. Nayada		*	*	*	*	*	*	*	*	*	*	*	*
5.2 Install toll-free number.	Nathapol	30,000	*											
5.3 Install online ordering.	Nathapol	10,000			*									
5.4 Offer rebate discount coupon.	Sales rep	2% of sales												*
	Total	x baht												

Month

Assumptions for Inputs:

1. Editing is completed by Jan 15.
2. Well-identified prospects.
3. Sales reps understand product.
4. Management approves budget by Dec. 31.
5. Sales reps have ability to reach prospects or customer in person.
6. Dr. Nayada devotes necessary time.
7. Sales reps are trainable and willing to sell the product.
8. Dr. Kumpol and Dr. Banjob available at every seminar.
9. Online ordering is working and secured.

Close Out Projects with a People Focus
(Washington Department of Transportation)

Project closure requires not only wrapping up the documentation at project end but also helping team members transition to new positions. This project plan from the Washington State Department of Transportation (WSDOT) was developed three years ahead of the planned completion of a major bridge construction project.

The Hood Canal Bridge Project Team was established to administer the construction of this major project in Washington State. The employees served in project positions, which means that they would go back to other positions within the organization when work is completed. Project leadership made a commitment to find positions for both state and consultant employees that would benefit their careers. They would also be closing several work sites, including vacating office space and disposing of equipment and vehicles at different times as the work at each site wraps up. There is also extensive documentation to complete for both the state and federally funded work.

"Finish Strong" is a project plan to take care of the people by lining up good positions for 60 employees spread over several sites after this project finishes. Even though scheduled completion was three years away, using a LogFrame early helped to identify tastes necessary to ensure smooth execution.

Logical Framework for
Hood Canal Bridge Project Closure "Finish Strong"

Objectives	Success Measures	Verification	Assumptions
Goal: Effectively care for our Team employees and physical assets through the project closure process.	**Goal Measures:** 1. Employees stay with the project until reassigned per the employee database. 2. No cost for assets we are finished using.	1. Per the employee database. 2. Per the finance report.	**Assumptions to reach Goal:** 1. Employees accept the closure plan. 2. Employees participate in the plan. 3. Accessible assets available elsewhere in state govt.
Purpose: Successfully close out the project in accordance with state and federal regulations to the benefit of our employees.	**Purpose Measures:** 1. Region approval of all documentation. 2. FHWA approval of all documentation. 3. 75% of all employees in career-enhancing positions per the employee database.	1. Region approval letter received. 2. FHWA approval letter received. 3. Match reassignment results to employee database.	**Assumptions to achieve Purpose:** 1. Region staff available to process packages in a timely manner. 2. FHWA reviews the submittals in a timely manner. 3. Employees communicate changing career goals. 4. Acceptable positions available when needed.
Outcomes: 1. Complete all documentation required for project closure.	**Outcome Measures:** 1a. All packages completed on time per project documentation checklist. 1b. All documents properly achieved on time or properly distributed on-time per documentation schedule. 1c. All documents properly distributed on time per the documentation schedule.	1a. Project documentation schedule. 1b. Documentation checklist.	**Assumptions to produce Outcomes:** 1a. Project employees remain with the team until planned transition date. 1b. Any changes in documentation requirements are communicated to the project office.
2. Reassign all project staff in a manner that supports project delivery.	2a. Workforce budget meets baseline in accordance with the finance plan timelines. 2b. Changes in employee status occur within 30 days of workforce planning tool date.	2a. Finance Report. 2b. Employee Database. 2c. Workforce planning tool.	2a. Project employees remain with the team until planned transition. 2b. Employees contribute to database setup. 2c. Employees communicate desired changes to database in a timely manner.
3. Decommission facilities and equipment.	3a. No costs incurred for office space 30 days after it is vacated. 3b. No costs incurred for unused equipment 30 days after it is no longer needed on the project.	3a. Finance Report. 3b. Finance Report.	3a. Real Estate Service has staff and funding available to manage property disposal. 3b. Regional stores have staff and funding to work disposal issues.
4. Communicate the plan to employees and region managers through project closure.	4a. Closure plan update newsletter sent out quarterly.	4a. Newsletter sent on schedule.	4a. Project staff available.

Inputs: *How team will produce Outcomes*

Action Steps:	Responsible	Resources	Schedule (in weeks, months, etc.)	Assumptions for Inputs:
1. Complete all documentation required for project closure.				
1.1 Determine Federal requirement for documentation	Danks			
1.2 Build documentation database	Danks			
1.3 Compile documents required	Danks			
1.4 Complete document packages for Regions	Danks			
1.5 Complete document packages for FHWA	Danks			
1.6 Transmit document packages	Danks			
2. Reassign all project staff in a manner that supports project delivery.				
2.1 Develop questionnaire	Ireland/Cutler			
2.1.1 Consult HR	Ireland/Cutler			
2.1.2 Draft questions	Ireland/Cutler			
2.1.3 Review questions with managers	Ireland/Cutler			
2.1.4 Finalize questionnaire	Ireland/Cutler			
2.2 Present questionnaire to all staff	Soderquist			
2.3 Develop Employee database	Melchior			
2.4 Populate employee database based on questionnaire information	Melchior			
2.5 Consult with Region Managers on future employee opportunities	Ireland/Moon			
2.6 Consult with Parametrix on future employee opportunities	Cutler			
2.7 Match opportunities to employee career goals	Melchior			
2.8 Meet with employees to discuss results	Soderquist			
2.9 Develop training plans as required	Manager			
2.10 Monitor database for employee changes	Manager			
3. Decommission Facilities and Equipment.				
3.1 Vacate facilities				
3.1.1 Generate summary project schedule for facilities and equipment use	Danks			
3.1.2 Overlay facilities onto summary schedule	Danks			

230

Team Conduct of Operations
(Los Alamos National Laboratory—Geographic Information Service)

As described in Chapter 4, the Los Alamos National Laboratory's Geographic Information Service (GIS) conducted a unit level strategic plan, and identified eight necessary improvement initiatives.

The LogFrames that follows presents the plan for Team Conduct of Operations. The Team Improvement LogFrame can be found on our web site.

Logical Framework for
GIS Team Conduct of Operations

Objectives	Success Measures	Verification	Assumptions
Goal: GIS-related activities are conducted in a manner that demonstrates to customers a high level of excellence.	**Goal Measures:** 1. X% of customers satisfied with high quality, quick turn-around deliverables.	1. Customer survey.	**Assumptions to reach Goal:** 1. Different GIS functions and staff will collaborate on setting the standard.
Purpose: Products/Services are consistent, cost-effective, high quality, and delivered with increased productivity.	**Purpose Measures:** 1. Services meet agreed quality specs. 2. 100% of team members using procedures by 3/1. 3. 100% of projects using procedures by 3/1. 4. Improve work productivity by 30% by 12/1.	1. Check. 2. Conduct annual audit. 3. Management walk-arounds. 4. Compare annual productivity changes.	**Assumptions to achieve Purpose:** 1. Staff cross-trained and versatile. 2. GIS staff willing to put effort into achieving conducts of operations program. 3. Management has 100% of valid metrics necessary to justify budget. 4. Formality of operations increases productivity. 5. Workload can be prioritized to allow for development of processes/procedures.
Outcomes: 1. Processes/procedures to be included are selected. 2. Have agreed-upon standards and regulations. 3. Process and procedures are written. 4. Alternative models/test practices reviewed. 5. Team metrics identified. 6. Tools/procedures are selected. 7. Team members are trained in procedures.	**Outcome Measures:** 1. List of agreed-upon procedures completed by 10/17. 2. Best Management standard and guidelines identified and adopted by 11/20. 3.1 Develop Quality Assurance Procedures (QAP) by 6/1. 3.2 Develop procedure template by 10/4. 3.3 Procedures completed and approved by management by 3/1. 4. Business models reviewed, applicable one selected and adopted by 12/19. 5. Metrics defined and in place by 4/1. 6. Tools/procedures reviewed, modified if necessary, and adopted by 3/1. 7. Team-procedure training conducted and documented by 4/1.	1. Completed list. 2. Adopted standards and guidelines. 3.1 Completed QAP. 3.2 Completed template. 3.2.1 Completed procedures. 3.3 Procedures completed and approved by management. 4. Selection of business model completed. 5. Metrics completed. 6. Tools/procedures in place. 7. Training reviewed for completeness.	**Assumptions to produce Outcomes:** 1. GIS staff wants Conduct of Operations to exist. 2. Improved staff communication and coordination occurs. 3. Best management practice standards and guidelines are available in all areas. 4. Division funds activities. 5. Procedures will be updated as processes change.

Inputs: *How team will produce Outcomes*	Responsible	Resources	Schedule (in months)												Assumptions for Inputs:
Action Steps:			Oct	Nov	Dec	Jan	Feb	Mar	Apr	May	Jun	Jul	Aug	Sep	
1. Processes/ procedures to be included are selected.															
1.1 List/identify processes.				│											
1.2 Review processes for effectiveness.				│											
1.3 Select process for Conduct of Operations.			│												
2. Have agreed-upon standards and regulations.															
2.1 Review standards and regulations.				│											
2.2 Select standards and regulations.				│											
3. Processes/procedures are written.															
3.1 Develop QAP.										│					
3.2 Develop procedure template.			│												
3.21 Write procedures.							│								
3.3 Team reviews procedures.							│								
3.4 Management reviews and completes procedures.						│									
4. Alternative models/test practices reviewed.															
Etc.															

Ongoing Support and Services

www.ManagementPro.com

We've designed our corporate website to help you apply the concepts in *Strategic Project Management Made Simple*. It offers practical information in an easy-to-use format. Visit us often for the latest workshop schedules, new articles, free special reports, and timely tips.

On-Site Rapid Action Planning (RAP) Workshops

Train your entire team in best practices as you simultaneously build shared commitment and jump-start project execution. These customized planning workshops guide your team in doing the upfront strategic thinking necessary to rapidly develop LogFrame plans and confidently begin implementation.

Public Seminars and UCLA Extension Technical Management Program

Join Terry Schmidt and other thought-leaders at the esteemed UCLA Extension Technical Management Program for one week of intensive learning every March and September. Learn best practices and network with technical and management professionals at the nation's premiere educational program for mid-career professionals. Get the latest information at the program's website: *www.uclaextension.edu/tmp*

Go to *www.HainesCenter.com* for a global calendar of quality seminars available from our strategic partners.

Executive Briefings, Custom Seminars, and Keynotes

Invite our experts to deliver a custom briefing to your executive team on a variety of timely strategic management topics. Go beyond the buzzwords and gain insights geared to your specific issues. These events range from half-day to two-day seminars and are tailored to your needs. Our keynote speeches entertain as well as educate audiences of all types. Check the website for our most value-adding topics.

Articles and Special Reports

On our website, you'll find plenty of free and informative articles and Special Reports. Our most popular include:

- *"Turn Strategy Into Action: The Logical Framework Approach to Managing Strategic Change"*
- *"Reinventing Strategic Planning"*
- *"Plan to Plan: Building a Strong Foundation for Successful Planning and Change"*
- *"Scanning the Changing Environment"*
- *"The ABC's of Strategic Management"*
- *"Becoming a Strategic Thinker on a Daily Basis"*

Others are continually being added.

LogFrame Project Designs

Access our growing collection of LogFrame project designs. You'll find interesting examples from research and development, information technology, marketing, process improvement, and strategic planning. These examples can give you ideas that may refine your project design.

Take It From Terry™ Monthly Report

Each informative issue includes expert articles, self-mastery tips, book reviews, and healthy doses of humor. You'll also find LogFrames for interesting projects. Get your free subscription. We also hate spam, and never rent, share, or trade your email address.

Terry's Toolbox™ (Blog)

Sometimes the best tips are short, sweet and to the point. Check on *www.TerrysToolbox.com* for new insights on a wide array of topics that matter in business and in life. Join the conversation.

Virtual Project Design Coaching

Our team provides long-distance support to you in designing solid projects. After an initial conversation, you create a first draft LogFrame using our electronic template, submit it, and we will sharpen your design through email and phone conversations. If you prefer, we do a first cut. It's an economical way to get expert consulting and create plans that work.

Logical Framework Application Support Tools

The best dynamics occur when teams huddle around a large wall-mounted matrix so everyone can see and discuss the issues as they flesh out the design. You can sketch a LogFrame on a whiteboard, or use our reusable laminated LogFrame. These LogFrame grids allow several people to gather around and actively collaborate. Available in multiple sizes, they are color-coded to match the strategic questions. (Use with non-permanent, wet erasable pens such as Vis-a-Vis.)

Our company store offers a variety of learning aids, LogFrame grids, electronic templates, wall posters, and other support tools at *www.ManagementPro.com.*

Glossary and Usage of Terms

Activities   The action steps or tasks to be undertaken, and resources necessary to produce Outcomes.

Assumptions   External factors that influence project success over which the project manager lacks direct control. Assumptions can be monitored, influenced, and sometimes managed.

Baseline data   Data describing the conditions when a project is started. Provides a basis to assess the nature and extent of change caused by the project.

Bottom-up   In LogFrame terms, beginning at the Input level and using *If-Then* thinking to link to Outcomes, Purpose, and Goal. Bottom-up thinking can test the causal logic of a strategy and validate top-down planning.

Chunking   The logical grouping of information into "chunks" according to appropriate criteria.

Chunking logic   Criteria chosen for organizing project elements, which may include phase, function, discipline, and so on. Be clear about your logic.

Coupling   Situations in which one element of a project affects or depends upon an element from another project. Coupling (or dependencies) can be acknowledged by making Assumptions in the LogFrames.

Disaggregation   Breaking down a large or complex Objective into smaller components—chunking down.

End of project status (EOPS)   The set of success Measures that signals achievement of the project Purpose, and thus the success of the project. Identify and gain agreement on these Measures in advance.

Evaluation   An orderly examination of progress at each level of Objective using evidence. Examines the validity of hypotheses, and identifies redesign and replanning actions. Evaluation examines Outcome-Purpose and Purpose-Goal linkages, while monitoring examines the Input-Outcome linkage.

Execution   The process and systems for moving plans into action and achieving project Objectives.

Flow diagram   A graphic tool depicting the operation of a system as a network of activities. Shows origins, directions, and sequences of decisions and events.

Gantt chart   Also called a bar chart, this graphic tool helps schedule and monitor project tasks and activities. Gantt charts display key activities vertically and estimate activity duration against a horizontal time scale.

Goal   The higher level, broader strategic, or program Objective immediately above project Purpose. Goal specifies the "Then" statement for which the project Purpose (plus Purpose-level Assumptions) provides a plausible "If."

Horizontal logic   A term that expresses the combination of Objectives, Success Measures, and Means of Verification at each level.

Hypothesis   An educated guess; a predictive statement about a causal relationship involving uncertainty. The predicted and intended means-end relationship between each level in the Logical Framework constitutes a set of linked, If-Then hypotheses.

If-Then thinking   A way to express cause-effect, means-ends relationships as a series of If-Then links.

Indicators   Part of Success Measures. Indicators are targeted by a description of quantity, quality (performance), and time as well as by cost and client/customer.

Inputs   Activities and resources (time, money, and people) needed to produce each Outcome.

Leading indicators   Success Measures that are observable now, which also predict the future status of Objectives.

Linked hypotheses   A series of predictive If-Then statements about project relationships, which show up in the Objectives column of the LogFrame.

Logical clusters   A bundle of activities and Outcomes based on a real or imagined similarity of implementation. Cluster themes can be drawn from across different projects, programs, or organizational elements to provide synergy, operating economies, or other implementation benefits

Logical Framework   A set of interlocking concepts organized into a 4×4 matrix, which helps to logically design sound projects.

Management contract   An agreement that the Project Manager will deliver Outcomes given the required Inputs (and valid Assumptions) aimed at achieving Purpose.

Manageable interest   Defines the responsibility of the Project Manager, which is to deliver Outcomes that will achieve Purpose aimed at delivering the agreed upon Goal. The Project Manager commits to produce Outcomes by effectively managing the activities, given appropriate levels of resources. It is within his/her manageable interest to modify activities and do whatever else is necessary to produce Outcomes.

Master activity list   A thorough list of all the key activities required to produce project Outcomes. It serves as a basis for creating three core management tools—resource budget, schedules, and agreement charts.

Matrix for the Logical Framework   A 4×4 matrix that displays the interrelationships of the design and evaluation components of a project. The matrix is divided into four *rows* (for Goal, Purpose, Outcomes, and Inputs) and four *columns* (for Objectives, Success Measures, Verification, and Assumptions).

Means of Verification   The source and means of obtaining data that will be used to verify an indicator or Measure (e.g., market share as determined by the marketing department).

Monitoring The management function of following the progress and overseeing the operations of a project. Monitoring focuses on the Input-to-Outcome linkage of the Logical Framework in contrast to evaluation, which focuses on Outcome-to-Purpose and Purpose-to-Goal linkages.

Network A graphic representation of the logical sequence of activities and events required to reach a specified Objective.

Objective A desired project result or intention. Can be an Outcome, Purpose, Goal, Super Goal, or Vision.

Objectives Tree A visual tool using If-Then logic to clarify relationships among Objectives in complex environments.

Outcomes The specifically intended results believed necessary and sufficient to achieve Purpose. Outcomes can be expected to result from good management of Input activities.

Outputs A term used in some public sector LogFrames to express what we call Outcomes.

Program A "strategy" consisting of groups of projects all contributing to the same Goal. A *program* is managed to achieve a Goal, just as a *project* is managed to achieve a Purpose.

Project Classic definition: An organized system of interrelated activities and processes established to achieve specified Objectives on time and without budget. Schmidt definition: Engines of Change.

Project cycle A systems perspective of a project that considers the three distinct phases of a project (design, implementation, and evaluation) as an integrated system.

Project design A summary of what the project is expected to achieve (Goal and Purpose), what it must deliver to achieve Purpose (Outcomes), and how it will deliver Outcomes (Inputs). The key elements of a project design may be summarized in the Logical Framework format.

Project Implementation Management System (PIMS) A set of interrelated management tools and techniques for managing the project cycle that are based on a common set of management principles and a common language.

Project Manager   The individual who holds himself or herself personally accountable for project success by accepting responsibility for producing the agreed-upon Outcomes with given Inputs.

Purpose   What is hoped to be achieved by undertaking the project; the real motivation. Purpose describes the anticipated change in behavior or system conditions expected when the required Outcomes are produced.

RAP (Rapid Action Planning) session   Focused workshops which build key products with a core team quickly, while establishing good team norms.

Reporting   Providing relevant project information to appropriate people for timely decision making. Includes both formal and informal communications, such as reports, meeting notes, or personal discussions.

Scientific method   Procedures for pursuing knowledge through formulating a hypothesis and testing its validity through experimentation.

Strategic hypothesis   Represents a prediction that *if* the expected results at one level of the LogFrame hierarchy are achieved, and *if* the Assumptions at that level are valid, *then* the expected results at the next higher level will be achieved.

Strategy   An organized set of initiation programs and projects undertaken in order to achieve the organization's vision.

Success Measures   Measures that have quantity, quality, and time targets (and sometimes, customer and cost). Stated in terms such that an informed skeptic and a proponent of the project would agree on what progress has or has not been made. Measures established during the design phase of a project provide the basis for subsequent monitoring and evaluation.

SWAG   Acronym for the term "Scientifically Wild-Assed Guess," an approach for targeting Measures when there is little valid or prior experience. Considered more scientific than a simple WAG. Not to be confused with the less accurate guestimating technique known as PFA (Plucked from Air).

System   A set of interrelated elements which work together to reach the overall Objectives. Systems are sometimes described as a strategy or throughput process for producing Outcomes from given Inputs.

Top-down thinking   Planning that proceeds from the general to the particular, or from the broad to the detailed. In the LogFrame, this begins with Goal and Purpose, then proceeds to Outcomes and Inputs.

Vertical logic   A way to summarize the If-Then linkages among Objectives.

Work breakdown structure   Tool for disaggregating a system or Objective into component parts. Each Outcome is broken down into smaller components. The process continues to develop logical work packages that can be costed, scheduled, assigned, and implemented.

Zig-Zag logic   A term which expresses the vertical logic of linked Objectives plus Assumptions.

About the Author

Terry Schmidt is an internationally known management consultant who helps organizations become more strategic, productive, and profitable. He has three decades of experience as an executive, educator, project coach, and strategist in assisting corporations, governments, and research institutions in 34 countries worldwide.

Terry is the founder and president of ManagementPro.com, a Seattle-based company that helps organizations achieve their objectives with better approaches, faster implementation, and greater certainty. He is affiliated with the Haines Centre for Strategic Management, a global alliance of master consultants in more than 20 countries.

A dynamic thought leader and hands-on consultant, Terry has helped hundreds of organizations successfully turn strategy into action. His North American clients include eBay, Boeing, Sony Electronics, Walt Disney Imagineering, DirecTV, Blizzard Entertainment, Northrop-Grumman, Microsoft, Cargill, the Los Angeles County Assessor's Office, Transamerica Insurance, *The Los Angeles Times*, PATH, the Caribbean Agriculture Research and Development Institute, AEGON USA, Los Alamos National Laboratory, Lawrence Livermore National Laboratory, and Sandia National Laboratory. He has consulted with virtually every federal agency and Washington State government department. His international clients include Thai Airways, Nokia Mobile Phones, and the Bank of Thailand.

Terry conducts seminars and keynotes all over the world. He is a certified Project Management Professional (PMP) and teaches Strategic Project Management to adult professionals at UCLA's esteemed Technical Management Program, where he is rated in the top 10 percent of all program faculty. A passionate instructor, he also conducts Strategic Project Management seminars for the University of Wisconsin's Professional Development Program. In addition, he teaches team-building and emotional intelligence for project teams at the MIT Professional Institute. Terry is on the faculty of the Institute for Management Studies and the Executive Forum.

Terry is active in the Association for Strategic Planning, and served on the national task force which developed standards for certifying professional strategic planners.

The author of seven management books, Terry earned his BS in Aerospace Engineering from the University of Washington and his MBA from Harvard University. His career accomplishments are cited in *Who's Who in International Training and Development* (3rd ed.), *Who's Who in Finance and Industry* (23rd ed.), and *Who's Who in the World* (6th ed.).

He is past president and current board member of the Harvard Business School Club of Puget Sound.

Index